Roger L. Emerson

'THE PEOPLE ABOVE'

'. . . they had a wonderful jargon, which nobody could understand, but which had a strange effect in *benumbing* and *stupifying* all their hearers. They talked perpetually of PEOPLE ABOVE, THE GREAT FOLKS, of THE PEOPLE IN POWER; and now and then would whisper *Peg* herself, that, if she kept her temper, THE PEOPLE ABOVE might possibly make her a present of a hood, or a tippet, or a new petticoat at a proper time: and though she did not know who the Devil these PEOPLE ABOVE were, she was perpetually *gulled* with this sort of talk. Those who pretend to understand these matters say, that the *PEOPLE ABOVE* were such as had the naming of *John Bull's* servants; and that they contrived new offices, and a variety of perquisites and veils, on purpose to allure people who were willing to sell their souls to Hell, and cheat their own father and mother.'

Adam Ferguson, *The History of the Proceedings in the Case of Margaret, Commonly called Peg, only lawful Sister to John Bull, Esq.* (London, 1761), pp. 89-90.

'THE PEOPLE ABOVE'

Politics and Administration
in Mid-Eighteenth-Century Scotland

ALEXANDER MURDOCH

JOHN DONALD PUBLISHERS LTD
EDINBURGH

ISBN 0 85976 053 7

Printed in Great Britain by Bell & Bain Ltd., Glasgow

Preface

WHY mid-eighteenth-century Scottish politics?

I chose to attempt such a study because I could find nothing to read on the subject when I first thought of studying Scottish politics after the Act of Union. The standard histories mentioned someone called a manager, specifically the second and third Dukes of Argyll, who had supreme authority over the distribution of government places in Scotland and thereby ensured that Scottish Members of Parliament supported the government of the day. They were later succeeded by the Earl of Bute, and still later by Henry Dundas, who presided over the Tory reaction in Scotland at the time of the French Revolution. 'After the Union of 1707,' wrote T. C. Smout in the most widely available general history of Scotland in this period, 'Scottish Parliamentary life as reflected in the careers of Scottish members at Westminster became for a long time so moribund as to be scarcely relevant any longer to a general history of Scottish society.'[1]

There were some studies available. Dr. Patrick Riley had published a good monograph, *The English Ministers and Scotland, 1707-1727*, but it concentrated on the adjustments made in Scottish government immediately after the Treaty of Union, and nothing like it was extant for the rest of the eighteenth century. There was a splendid essay on patronage by John Simpson ('Who Steered the Gravy Train?'), Dr. William Ferguson's magisterial thesis (still unpublished) on the Scottish electoral system, biographies and constituency essays by Lady Haden Guest and John Simpson in the *History of Parliament* volumes, and a few biographies of Henry Dundas. Administration, however, as Dr. Riley had studied it, was neglected. My first thoughts were of a study of Archibald Campbell, Earl of Ilay, later third Duke of Argyll, principal Scottish lieutenant of Sir Robert Walpole during the latter's long period of political supremacy between 1721 and 1742; but these thoughts were abandoned when I discovered that Mr. Richard Scott was already well advanced in a research project on the Walpole years. I then decided to complement Dr. Riley's book and Mr. Scott's research by studying the end of the third Duke of Argyll's career, after the rebellion of 1745, and the efforts to replace him after his death in 1761. Thus the work incorporated in this book as Chapters 2 to 5 is meant as a continuation of Riley and Scott's work, leaving room for yet another monograph on the years of Henry Dundas's domination of Scottish government. My work was undertaken in the conviction that this kind of detailed research was necessary to arrive at a more genuine assessment of the evolution of the Union settlement of 1707, and to arrive at an assessment of what that evolution has meant for Scotland.

The limitations of this book have to be made clear at the start. It is limited to the tiny electoral nation of Scotland, the political elite who owned the land, had made the Union, and sent their representatives to Westminster. They cannot be viewed in a vacuum, as John Simpson so rightly pointed out,[2] but their lack of numbers does not reduce their significance; for they both reflected and ruled the distinctive Scottish society beneath them. The subsequent abandonment of their Scottishness did much to produce the ethereal quality of Scottish nationality in modern times. I have studied them in the belief that one must understand the apex of society as well as its grass-roots, that while most of the criticisms levelled at elitist history are quite justified, there is no virtue in mirroring its defects by attempting to exclude the elite from the study of society in the past.

Thus this book has grown while it has been written. It contains a detailed monograph on a very short period of Scottish political history; but implicit in this material is the question of how a distinctive proto-national elite served its interests when it lacked the machinery of a state. This study reaches out, however inadequately, to try to touch the political consciousness of that elite as reflected in the politicians who served its interests. In this sense it is concerned with the relationship of Scotland and England as abstract entities. A third concern, more ambitious than the first but less complex than the second, is to outline the means by which Scottish society was governed in the eighteenth century, to demonstrate the *ad hoc* post-Union system which political scientists today would label intermediate government.

A last point falls within the compass of a preface. I am often asked why an American should take so intense an interest in Scottish history. Part of the reason is apparent in my name, though all too many Scottish-Americans are satisfied with the tartan kitsch that is served up to impress them with their heritage; but in addition to a desire to penetrate the myths perpetuated among the descendents of those who were forced to leave, there is an ambition to contribute to the wider question of national identity in Europe. This is not to make inflated claims about the importance of this book; only an attempt to remind the reader of its wider context.

Alexander Murdoch.

Acknowledgements

THIS book has been so long in the making, and I have received so much help from so many people, that now that I can make my acknowledgements I hardly know where to begin, far less where to end. My work would never have been possible without the support, both moral and financial, of my grandmother and my parents. I will always be grateful to all three of them. I have also been fortunate in finding good advice. Nick Phillipson has been a constant fund of encouragement, Harry Dickinson has always been ready to give me the benefit of his acute criticism, and John Simpson has always been willing to listen to me try to articulate just exactly what I thought I was doing. Richard Scott and John Shaw, fellow workers in the same field, have helped as well, as have Professor Maurice Larkin and Professor John Brewer. Perhaps I owe most to Rick Sher, who has taken time from his own work to act as my adviser on so many matters, particularly in my first year of research.

Those kind enough to speak to me or answer written enquiries when I first undertook this project include Rosalind Mitchison, P. W. J. Riley, Mary Cosh, Eric Cregeen, William Ferguson, and Ken Logue. Miss Catherine Armet, archivist at Mount Stuart, was particularly helpful during my visit there. I am very grateful to the Marquess of Bute, the Duke of Atholl, Mrs. Dundas-Bekker, the Earl of Seafield, Lord Polwarth, Mrs. D. L. Pringle, the Hon. G. E. Maitland-Carew, the Duke of Buccleuch, the Trustees of the Bedford Estates, Mr. J. T. T. Fletcher of Saltoun, the Trustees of the National Library of Scotland, the Curators of the Signet Library, South Glamorgan Libraries (Cardiff), the Marquess of Zetland, the North Yorkshire County Record Office, the Huntington Library, the William L. Clements Library, the Trustees of the British Library, and the Keeper of the Records of Scotland for permission to use unpublished material in the preparation of this study. The staff of the National Library of Scotland make research a pleasure.

The research on which this book is based could never have been carried out as happily as it was if I had not met Mairi Stewart. I have gained much from conversations with the following friends in many ways, both academic and non-academic: Ian Maclean, Lyn Worrell, Terry Rodgers, Ronnie Turnbull, Vera Macdonald, Carol Craig, Stuart Wallace and Andy Aitken. Beverley Spear patiently prepared the typescript under rather trying conditions. I am also indebted to Mr. and Mrs. I. R. Grant. Above all else, this book has taken the form it has in response to the city of Edinburgh and the people who live there. I hope it might represent some kind of repayment for all the learning I have done here.

Edinburgh, 1980.

Contents

Tables

A Note on Proper Names, Dates and Quotations

EIGHTEENTH-CENTURY Britain was not overly concerned with consistency in spelling. I have chosen one form for each name and stuck by it, usually choosing that which is currently accepted. Thus while James Stuart Mackenzie signed his will 'Stewart Mackenzie' I follow the practice of the reference books and continue to refer to him as 'Stuart Mackenzie'. The only exception to this is Archibald Campbell's first title of Ilay. It was thus universally spelled at the time and I have found it impossible to differ.

Spelling and punctuation of quotations have been modernised except in instances where I have felt that it would change the sense of the quotation. Dates before 1754 are given in Old Style, but with 1 January as the beginning of the year. Quotations of passages in cipher are given in upper case letters (see 'a note on ciphers' in the section on the Saltoun papers in the bibliography). I have used Scots, Scotch and Scottish interchangeably because there are more important distinctions to make than these semantic ones.

I have persisted in using extensive notes, printed at the back of the book, safely out of the general reader's way, because they are the means of making an historian accountable to his readers. It should also be noted that in cases where I have made a tentative point, particularly in the very detailed work incorporated in Chapters 2 to 5, the footnote lists the evidence which has led me to that tentative judgement, not evidence which proves it.

The author as indexer, it should be noted, has contented himself with an elementary subject and person index.

1

The Government of Scotland, 1707-1784

Introduction

THE Treaty of Union of 1707 remains a unique constitutional settlement in that there was no conquest and no surrender; nor was there a federation. Instead, two separate nations were to submerge themselves in a new political entity under the monarch they had formerly shared. The first and third articles of the treaty are quite specific: 'THAT the Two Kingdoms of Scotland and England, shall . . . forever after, be United into One Kingdom by the name of GREAT BRITAIN: . . . THAT the United Kingdom of Great Britain be Represented by one and the same Parliament to be stiled the Parliament of Great Britain.'[1]

The reality behind the constitutional niceties, of course, was decidedly different. Apart from the revolutionary hiccup of 1637-51, Scotland had been governed from London ever since her King had gone south to take the English throne in 1603. A monarch resident in London, presiding over a large and prosperous kingdom of some importance in the European world, very soon lost what interest he might have had in his poor possession to the north. It is true that there were always Scotsmen present at court in London, and that there were royal visits in 1617, 1633, and 1641; but Scotland had become a backwater of very minor importance to her own Kings. The very infrequency of their visits tells its own tale. When Charles II was crowned King of Scotland at Scone in 1650 he was a desperate refugee from England. The residence in Scotland of the future James VII for most of the period 1678-1682 was entirely due to the sensitive political situation in England. With the monarch almost permanently absent, Scottish affairs were normally the province of the King's Privy Council at Edinburgh, acting under sporadic instructions from their Royal Master at London.

This situation was altered by the revolution of 1688 in England, and the settlement of 1690 which followed in Scotland. These political developments placed definite limits on the power of the monarchy, allowing the parliaments of England and Scotland much more initiative than they had enjoyed previously. This shift in the centre of political gravity upset the balance of the accidental union of 1603 as a basis for relations between Scotland and England. William III, preoccupied with his continental wars, continued the non-policy of neglect; but after 1690 the Scottish Parliament could take initiatives which would force Scotland back into the general reckoning at Court for the first time since the

1640s. It did so when it passed the Act of Security and the Act anent Peace and War in 1703. The language of the Act of Security is most revealing; demanding, as it did, 'in this session of Parliament there be such conditions of government settled and enacted as may secure the honour and independence of the Crown of this kingdom, the freedom, frequency, and the power of the Parliament, and the religion, liberty and trade of the nation from English or any foreign influence'.[2] The force behind this shrill demand was the possibility that a rebellious Scots Parliament would alter the succession settlement to ensure that the next sovereign of England would not succeed to the Scottish throne.

Scotland demanded attention because it was experiencing economic difficulty to such an extent that its ruling class began to fear for the social stability of the country. English efforts to suppress the commercial power of the Dutch Republic had forced Scottish merchants into the difficult process of readjusting to large-scale trade with England. The harvest failures of the 1690s resulted in famine every bit as intense as that suffered on the continent, causing massive social dislocation. The foundation of the Company of Scotland in 1695 was greeted by English obstruction, which prevented access to the money markets of London, Amsterdam and Hamburg. Scots bitterness knew no bounds when it became apparent that the Company's audacious attempt to trade beyond Europe, including their scheme for a colony at Darien, would end in failure. The Scottish commonwealth teetered on the edge of bankruptcy in 1700; bereft of economic assets, and barely able to feed its inhabitants.[3] Those who presided over its society felt themselves compelled to look beyond its borders for a solution.

These two problems, social and economic crisis in Scotland, and political conflict between the Scottish Parliament and the English government in London, were solved (for better or worse) by the negotiated union of 1707. By that settlement the political elite of Scotland gambled that the answers to their domestic problems lay in economic union with England; they paid for that choice by surrendering their legislative sovereignty in parliament assembled. The rights and wrongs of that choice thankfully lie outside the scope of this book; for it can safely be assumed that the subject will continue to receive more than enough attention; but the fact that the settlement of 1707 stopped at legislative unity is of central importance to the work which follows.

The Scottish judiciary was safeguarded specifically by article nineteen of the Treaty of Union, though a loophole was left for civil appeals from the Court of Session to the House of Lords. Local heritable jurisdictions, a feudal legacy, were continued 'as Rights of Property' by article twenty of the Treaty, thus perpetuating the vast influence of the great Scottish landowners. More important, and more positive, was the continuation of the Scottish supreme courts of Session and Justiciary (and the minor consistorial and admiralty courts) at Edinburgh to administer Scots Law, which was to remain separate and distinct from English Common Law. The Court of Session consisted of fourteen Lords of Session sitting individually in the 'Outer House' as 'Lords Ordinary', and collectively (under a fifteenth judge, the Lord President) in the 'Inner House' as a court of appeal. Six of their number (the Lord Justice Clerk and five Lords of Justiciary) *usually*

also served in the Court of Justiciary, which sat as the supreme criminal court of the land, from which there was no appeal. The Lords of Justiciary, two by two, went out on one of three circuits twice a year, each sitting in three county towns as an intermediate court of appeal for criminal offences.

While the Scottish judiciary had been protected in the Treaty of Union, executive government was mentioned only at the end of article nineteen, which allowed the Queen and her successors to continue a Privy Council in Scotland until 'the Parliament of Great Britain shall think fit to alter it'. The Parliament of Great Britain saw fit to abolish it in its first session. Thus the nature of executive government in Scotland was an area of the Union settlement very open to change; and it remains so, as events contemporary to the composition of this book illustrate only too well.

The constitutional settlement of 1707 made Scotland and England one state; but constitutional law could not resolve the manifest social, economic and cultural differences between the two countries. Sophisticated methodology is not required to state that fact. One can point to the flourishing national institutions of the law, the church, and the universities in eighteenth-century Scotland; one can point to Scottish local government, the Scottish electoral system, the Scottish banking system, and the metropolitan society of Edinburgh; negatively, one can point to the national animosities which came to be represented by the Jacobite pretenders, the Duke of Cumberland, Lord Bute, and John Wilkes. National distinction was not only present, it was pronounced.

Government had to reflect this situation in its administration of Scotland. Special arrangements were made for the Scots in the departments at London, where most Scottish business involving the central government was left to representatives of that country. In Scotland itself a separate administrative structure, part provincial and part colonial, began to evolve at Edinburgh; and Scottish local government continued to evolve in a unique way. By and large Scottish government has been treated as a kind of twilight zone in British historiography, consigned to oblivion, along with Scottish affairs in general. Very little is known about Scottish government after 1721. It is time to poke into the darkness and attempt to discern the bare bones of Scottish government as it evolved in the eighteenth century.

Government from London

In 1708, against the wishes of the ministry, the new Parliament of Great Britain abolished the chief executive organ of government in Scotland, the Scottish Privy Council. This action had been urged on Parliament by the dissident Whigs of the Squadrone (a group of Scottish Country Whigs), in the hope that it would break the power of those in Scotland who had previously been identified with the Court, though some Scots (such as the Earl of Marchmont) genuinely believed that a separate Privy Council did not conform to the true spirit of 'completing the Union'.[4] Thus there came to be one British Privy Council sitting in London which included the surviving Scottish officers of state: the Keeper of the Great Seal in Scotland, the Keeper of the Privy Seal in Scotland, the Lord Justice General, and the Lord Clerk Register.[5] Government policy in the eighteenth century, however, was not formed in the Privy Council but in the Cabinet; real decision making was restricted to the so-called 'Inner Cabinet', which did not include a Scot until late in the century.[6] Table I shows the King at the apex of executive government, which was the constitutional situation, but in practice neither Queen Anne nor any of the Hanoverian Kings took a sustained interest in Scotland. The only exception to this general rule was George II's understandable distaste for Scotland after the 1745 rebellion; yet even then the hard line taken by the King and the Duke of Cumberland did not greatly influence the policy adopted by the King's First Minister, Henry Pelham.[7] The Inner Cabinet, usually dominated by one minister, determined issues of policy, which were then presented to the monarch 'in the closet' (i.e. in private conference) by the First Minister. This was the situation in regard to major policy decisions, but Scottish business was seldom considered of sufficient importance to merit cabinet-level discussion. As a result individual government departments had much influence in the ordinary administration of Scottish affairs.

The major departments of central government in eighteenth-century Britain were the Secretaries of State, who dealt with home and foreign affairs; the Treasury, busily expanding its influence and power over the course of the century while finding the financial wherewithal for Britain's wars with France; the War Office, which ran the army; and the Admiralty, which administered Britain's growing navy. Each of these departments should have dealt with the Scottish business that came their way as they dealt with their other domestic business, but in practice they were preoccupied with more important affairs, and Scottish matters were largely neglected.

Most Scottish affairs, particularly in peacetime, were the province of one of the Secretaries of State or the Lords of the Treasury. Day-to-day business was carried out by three or four clerks, supervised by an under-Secretary, in the Secretary's Office; and by about a dozen clerks, supervised by two Secretaries, in the Treasury.[8] Very few of them understood Scottish business. 'I find all the inferior agents about both offices [Secretary of State and Treasury] extremely ignorant about the common course of Scotch business,' Gilbert Elliot observed in 1761.[9] Recommendations had to be given in to the clerks at the Secretaries' office exactly as they would appear on a complete warrant, for the clerks did not know the correct form or the names of the offices.[10] Appointments were misplaced and forgotten, records and correspondence were lost. The same situation existed at the Treasury. 'If you have any of the clerks of the Treasury in pay you should desire him to call on the Duke [of Newcastle, then First Lord of the Treasury] and mind him,' Allan Whitefoord wrote to the Earl of Loudoun in 1760, 'if you have no such resident you must often fail when otherways you would succeed.'[11]

At most times from 1708 until 1725, and again briefly from 1742 until January 1746, there was a separate Scottish Secretary of State. He was officially a third 'British' Secretary of State with responsibility for home and foreign affairs, but in

Table I: *The Government of Scotland, 1707-1765*

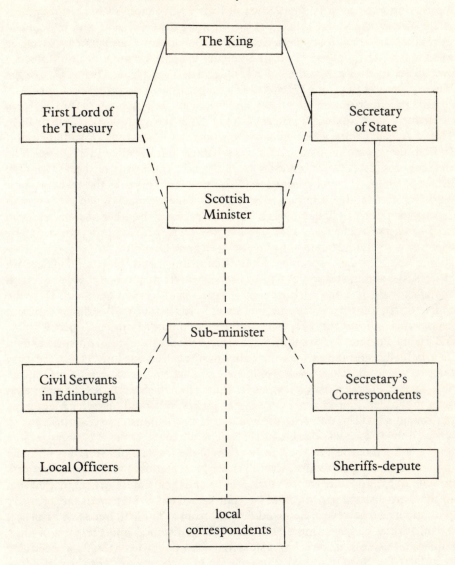

————: Formal Government
– – –: Influence

practice confined himself to the Scottish business of the Secretaries' office.[12] This meant that judicial appointments, presentations to parishes in the gift of the Crown, the disposal of Crown offices in Scotland (many of them sinecures), and the correspondence with the Crown officers in Scotland all went through his office. Yet, crucially, the officers of the revenue, the army, and navy in Scotland were all outside his jurisdiction, hence his influence over government patronage was limited. At times the Scottish Secretary exercised a great deal of influence over all Scottish affairs, as the Duke of Queensberry did from 1708 to 1710 or the Duke of Roxburghe from 1716 to 1720; at other times a Secretary could not even control the distribution of offices and pensions which came within his own department, like Roxburghe from 1720 to 1725 or the Marquess of Tweeddale in 1745.[13] At such times the Secretary was no more than a minor administrator. Indeed, there were no plans to force Tweeddale out of office in 1746, when he suddenly resigned, only to reduce his influence, and in the next few years the Prince of Wales' following intended to restore him to office in the event of a new reign, but not to give him power beyond his department.[14] When there was no Scottish Secretary of State his work was done by one of the other Secretaries; from 1725-1742 and again from 1746-1754 by the Duke of Newcastle, thereafter by whoever held the Secretaryship for the Northern Department.[15]

The Treasury was responsible for the Scottish revenue, the salaries of Scottish officers, the administration of Crown property in Scotland, bounties for Scottish manufacturers, and the appointment of customs officers in Scotland. Over the course of the century it became increasingly important in British government from both a political and an administrative standpoint.[16] Both Sir Robert Walpole and Henry Pelham, for example, used their control of the department to extend their influence and power over the entire ministry. A First Lord of the Treasury came to have some claim to lead a ministry, even when, like Newcastle or Grafton, he did not sit in the House of Commons. Quite often the Secretaries of State would defer to the First Lord's wishes in Scottish affairs. When Edinburgh's Member of Parliament sought to influence the appointment of a minister to a Scottish parish of which the Crown was patron, in 1756, he wrote to the Duke of Newcastle (who was First Lord of the Treasury) rather than to the responsible Secretary of State: 'I well know my Lord Duke, that all these presentations, in the execution pass through My Lord Holdernesse's office, but at the same time, I'm not ignorant that all these are order'd and directed by your Grace only.'[17] At times the Treasury even attempted to govern Scotland directly from Whitehall, but as we shall see, the difficulties of governing Scotland at such a distance, and the press of more important business, made it impossible for such a policy to be totally successful.[18]

In fact, the Scots required a sub-system of lobbyists to steer their business through the small but inefficient bureaucracy at Whitehall, while the English required advice on Scottish conditions and customs. The result was the emergence of the Scottish 'manager' or 'minister'; terms that represented the two aspects of his unofficial office; for while a Scottish minister represented Scottish interests within the Government, a Scottish manager was expected to keep Scottish M.P.s and Representative Peers on the government side of the division

Table II: *Government from London: Departments of State*

The Treasury
The First Lord and four ordinary Lords of Treasury supervised the Treasury's subordinate boards in Edinburgh. One of the Treasury clerks was responsible for Scottish appointments.

The Secretary of State
There was a third, Scottish, Secretary in the following years: 1708-11, 1713-14, 1714-15, 1716-1725, 1742-46. From 1725-42, and again from 1746-54, Scottish business was in the care of the Duke of Newcastle, who was Secretary of State for the Southern Department from 1724-48, and Secretary of State for the Northern Department from 1748-54. Thereafter Scottish affairs were the responsibility of the Northern Secretary until 1782, when they were transferred to the new Home Department.

The Secretary of War
The Commander in Chief of the Forces in Scotland corresponded with the Secretary of War as well as the responsible Secretary of State. All military commissions passed through the Secretary of War's office, including those for Scotsmen and the Scottish regiments.

The Board of Admiralty
The responsibilities of the Lords of Admiralty over naval affairs were equivalent to those of the Secretary of War.

---

lobbies. From 1725 until 1761 Archibald Campbell, Earl of Ilay (and after 1743, third Duke of Argyll), exercised much influence over Scottish affairs without ever being made a Secretary of State. He provides the model for any abstract notion of a Scottish minister in the period before 1780. His family represented the largest and most influential aristocratic interest in Scotland in the early eighteenth century, a fact which encouraged Sir Robert Walpole to seek a political alliance with Ilay and his brother John, second Duke of Argyll, in 1725. In return for most government patronage in Scotland, they kept most of the Scots M.P.s behind Walpole. In the process Ilay ceased to be his brother's political lieutenant and became one of Walpole's associates, even after Argyll broke with the minister in 1737. During this period Ilay was more a manager than a minister, but Walpole fell from power in 1742, and the next year Ilay succeeded his brother as third Duke of Argyll. As the wealthiest peer of Scotland and an experienced politician, his voice in Scottish affairs could not be ignored. He submitted recommendations for offices, he advised the ministry on its election plans, and he received supplicants in Scotland during his annual summer visits to Edinburgh, Glasgow, and Inveraray. He came to gain, as Lord Milton wrote, 'the attention and confidence of his fellow subjects; and without the advantages of a minister, bestowed upon him a very high degree of ministerial power'.[19]

Most English ministers found it convenient to delegate Scottish patronage to a Scots politician resident in London, and to seek his advice on Scottish elections; but Argyll was unique in achieving a position of real power, using his independent political base in Scotland as a means of exerting influence over government policy. The problem thus revolves around the representative and managerial aspects of the minister's place. In some ways the situation was similar to that of a modern Secretary of State for Scotland. Tom Johnston achieved a remarkable amount of independence as Secretary of State during the Second World War, and William Ross became an accomplished defender of Scottish interests within the Labour government of the 1960s, while on the other hand Scottish Secretaries of the late 1940s and the 1950s tended to be mere administrators of policy handed down to them.[20] Argyll, like Tom Johnston, was extremely successful in making government work in the interest of Scotland. Something similar could be claimed on behalf of Henry Dundas at the end of the eighteenth century. The nature of the constituency has changed but the constitutional tension has remained.

The eighteenth-century Scottish minister carried a certain amount of authority in Parliament, where Argyll in particular served as a spokesman on Scottish legislation and Scots appeals to the House of Lords.[21] After Argyll's death in 1761 the Duke of Newcastle urged the Earl of Bute to give at least one of Argyll's old offices to the third Earl of Marchmont, reporting to the Earl of Hardwicke that: 'I insisted on his use in the House of Lords, both on extraordinary days, and for carrying on common business, which was a very necessary thing.'[22] Marchmont eventually did become Keeper of the Great Seal in Scotland, and in fact did spend quite a bit of time in the Lords on Scottish business. The formidable figure of Lord Mansfield, however, prevented Marchmont from ever achieving anything like Argyll's [Ilay's] influence in the House when he was Walpole's minister. As both an exiled Scot and an eminent judge, Mansfield was credited with an authoritative knowledge of Scots law by the rest of the Lords, who as a whole respected his opinions over Marchmont's.[23] It was Mansfield who was responsible for overturning the Court of Session's rulings against fictitious votes,[24] and it was Mansfield who gave Boswell, in 1772, 'a disagreeable feeling of his supreme power over the property of Scotland'.[25]

The Lord Advocate spoke for the government in the House of Commons, however, even when James Stuart Mackenzie had been set up as Scottish minister by the Earl of Bute in the early 1760's. The Advocate was usually the author of Scottish legislation, responsible for introducing it, and at times also served as a kind of government whip for Scottish M.P.s.[26] Thus when the Scottish M.P.s held a meeting on the militia issue in 1762, a measure which the 'Old Corps' whigs in the ministry opposed, the attendance of Lord Advocate Miller distressed the Duke of Newcastle because it indicated ministerial support for the measure.[27] G. W. T. Omond's thesis that the Lord Advocate was always Scottish minister was partly the result of a misunderstanding of the office's status in the eighteenth century, and partly the result of reading the mid-nineteenth-century standing of the Advocate back into the previous century.[28] By acting as a parliamentary spokesman the Advocate did possess ministerial authority over Scottish legislation, and when he acted as a whip for Scottish M.P.s he acquired a certain 'managerial' role as well. But both of these roles were confined to the House of Commons before 1782. The representation of Scottish interests within the executive bureaucracy, and the management of the Scottish electoral system for the government, were functions which before 1765 were carried out by persons other than the Lord Advocate. The men who fulfilled these functions longer than all their predecessors and successors put together were the third Duke of Argyll and his sub-minister, Lord Milton.

The role of the Lord Advocate has never been confused with that of the Scottish manager when historians have considered Scottish electoral politics, particularly in reference to the activities of the second Duke of Queensberry, Ilay/Argyll, and Henry Dundas. The nature of a Scottish manager's activities, however, has not been understood as clearly. The work of Dr. W. Ferguson and Dr. R. M. Sunter[29] has shown us that his electoral work really consisted of balancing the claims of several local factions in such a way that one of two objects was attained. The more active managers (like Queensberry or Ilay) wished to maximise ministerial influence, while others (like Ilay in his later years as Duke of Argyll) merely wished to buttress or at least recognise the dominant interest in a locality. This meant controlling the distribution of government patronage. The Scottish minister advised the British Secretaries of State on the disposal of crown offices in Scotland and advised the Treasury on the disposal of appointments in the Scottish customs establishments; though some families, such as the Campbells in the early part of the century, or the Earls of Marchmont and the Dundas's of Arniston in mid-century, succeeded in obtaining direct access to the ministers.[30]

As there were very few people in the London offices who knew anything about Scotland or Scottish offices, an appointment had to be carefully shepherded through the bureaucracy by an interested party or it would be laid aside and lost. This task of calling at the offices at least once a week to check on the clerks and speak with the minister took up most of Ilay's time, even when he had become Duke of Argyll, and James Stuart Mackenzie operated in much the same manner. It was a thankless task. 'Alas!' Andrew Fletcher wrote to his father in 1754, 'many of our countrymen imagine that it only costs their friends a word to provide for them by which means the most substantial favours are undervalued . . .'[31] Nor was it always easy to coordinate Scottish business. 'Your Lordship has no conception what it is to settle business of this kind, betwixt a Secretary of State, and a first Lord of the Treasury, whose hours, situations, and engagements, are so different and remote . . .,' Gilbert Elliot complained to Lord Milton in 1761.[32] Later great Scottish politicians like the Duke of Queensberry, the Earl of Loudoun, and Sir Lawrence Dundas, would call round the government offices on behalf of their own friends,[33] but no Scottish politician had anything like Argyll's or Mackenzie's authority until the rise of Henry Dundas.

This mundane aspect of even the most successful Scottish minister's life

contrasted strongly with the viceregal status with which he was credited in
Scotland. The Scots, it seems, wanted a Viceroy: Dr. Riley writes of Walpole
being 'the prisoner of Scottish expectations' when he designated Ilay as his
Scottish lieutenant in 1725.[34] How else can one explain the accounts of Argyll's
power given in the memoirs of Alexander Carlyle, John Ramsay of Ochtertyre,
and Thomas Somerville?[35] Yet there were constant attempts to go over the head of
the Scottish minister and deal with the Treasury and the Secretaries directly,
particularly by Scottish Members of Parliament. Thus Alexander Hume
Campbell, M.P. for Berwickshire, and his brother, the third Earl of Marchmont,
would negotiate directly with Henry Pelham or the Duke of Newcastle if they
desired a favour;[36] or Gilbert Elliot would personally call on the Treasury, as well
as James Stuart Mackenzie, in an attempt to secure a Commissioner of Excise's
place for a Roxburghshire friend.[37] The success of these efforts depended on the
English ministers themselves. If they were on good terms with the Scottish
minister, or if they needed the support of Argyll's personal parliamentary
following, they would discourage such activity; if they resented the position of the
Scottish minister, as Newcastle did in 1755 or Grenville did in 1765, they would
disregard the Scottish minister's recommendation in favour of another applicant.

While the Scottish minister was generally credited with an overall
responsibility for Scottish affairs, in practice this responsibility had to be
exercised almost entirely by personal influence. Even more than other ministers,
because his position was unofficial, it was that much less secure. For example,
groups in Scotland like the Convention of Royal Burghs or the Commissioners for
the Annexed Estates made additional provision for their relations with the
government. The Convention would dispatch personal representatives to London
to lobby for matters which it viewed as important to the interest of the country,
such as an extension of the daily post to Scotland or the renewal of the bounty for
the export of coarse linen cloth. Their representatives would contact the Scottish
minister and other Scottish politicians in London, but they would also establish
direct communication with English ministers and English politicians of influence.
The Convention, the Annexed Estates Commission and other Edinburgh boards
all employed London agents to oversee their affairs at the Treasury.[38]

There were two perceptions of the Scottish minister. In London, many
Scottish M.P.s and other great Scottish aristocrats resented his authority and
constantly attempted to undermine his credit with the ministry for much the same
reasons that the members of the Squadrone party had urged the abolition of the
Scottish Privy Council in 1708, arguing that it ran against the spirit of the Union to
set up one Scot above the rest and invest him with special powers, or as Duncan
Forbes put it in 1725: 'if any one Scotsman has absolute power, we are in the same
slavery as ever . . .'[39] This sentiment found much sympathy in English ministers
such as the Duke of Newcastle and the Earl of Hardwicke, who thought it
dangerous to devolve power in any meaningful sense to a Scottish politician; hence
the Earl of Breadalbane's report to a friend in 1765 that the Marquess of
Rockingham had told him

that it was the opinion of the King's servants and of many Scotch noblemen and commoners that there ought to be no ministry for Scotland, but that all the business of the United Kingdom should go thro' the same channel. He [Rockingham] added that the opinion of the great officers of Scotland would naturally be asked on many occasions, but that a particular minister for that department was not intended.[40]

On the other hand the landed gentry, the ministers of the kirk, and the merchants of Scotland seemed to desire their own representative in London; it was not just eighteenth-century manners which led at least some commentators to refer to Argyll as the 'father' of his country when he died in 1761.[41] They wanted order, they wanted to know where to apply for patronage for their younger sons, and above all, they wanted efficient government. Thus John Mackenzie of Delvine, an Edinburgh Writer to the Signet, called for a renewal of the Argathelian system in 1770:

> Best depend on it, more mutinies will now arise in this quarter, unless some man of esteem, possessed of property beyond the Tweed, be it the Duke of Argyle, Ld Frederick [Campbell], Lord Marchmont or whom the premier for the time pleases, be pitched on to hear & soften many idle murmurs for which any man's shoulders are overloaded who has much more interesting matters hanging on them — ... Scotland for anything I know does best under an aristocracy — that, under Ilay was long & pretty regular — the best tradesmen generally know best how to chuse their tools.[42]

The advent of Henry Dundas as a British politician of note was welcomed by many Scots, not for party-political reasons, but because Dundas's prominence insured that Scottish problems and issues received the attention of the government. As the fifth Duke of Argyll commented in 1787, in connection with some business of the Highland Society:

> The affairs of Scotland have at this period a little better chance of being attended to, than ever was the case before, or perhaps will be again, from the peculiar influence of one of our countrymen [Henry Dundas] with the minister.[43]

The same difficulty exists today, despite the vast expansion of the political nation, in relation to the role of the Secretary of State in Scottish government, for the more power is devolved to a modern Secretary from Whitehall, the more he would resemble his eighteenth-century predecessors, the Scottish ministers.[44]

Government in Edinburgh

Government in Edinburgh during the eighteenth century remains something of an enigma to historians. Its nature is difficult to discern because abolition of the Scottish Privy Council in 1708 removed its natural focus; yet Edinburgh was patently a centre of government. The major courts of Session, Justiciary and Exchequer and the minor Commissary and Admiralty courts provided employment for a native legal elite. The General Assembly of the Church of

Scotland met annually in Edinburgh, as did the Convention of Royal Burghs, providing national forums for the church and the merchant oligarchy of the burghs; and the Scottish Board of Customs, Board of Excise, Post Office, Board of Trustees for the Encouragement of Fisheries and Manufactures, and Commissioners for the Annexed Estates all dealt with various economic and administrative problems, as did the Barons of Exchequer in their administrative capacity. Socially, the city remained the focal point of national life for a Scottish elite. In addition, just as there were official and unofficial aspects to Scottish government in London which overlapped and sometimes competed with each other, so those who maintained close communications with people of influence in London acquired a very real, yet unofficial, status in Edinburgh.

The figure of an unofficial minister resident in Edinburgh has sometimes been called a *sous ministre*, a term used by Robert Chambers in several of his works published in the nineteenth century.[45] The term is actually another rendering of the more pedestrian appellation of sub-minister, first used by John Home in his *History of the Rebellion in the Year 1745.*[46] Both terms refer to someone in Edinburgh who acted as a delegate for and channel of communication with the Scottish minister in London.

The most obvious example of such a minister was Andrew Fletcher, Lord Milton of the Scottish Court of Session, who served as the third Duke of Argyll's trusted lieutenant from 1725 to 1761. Milton was a remarkable man, with a natural talent for political compromise and the detailed everyday drudgery of administrative matters which gave him considerable success in business, administration, and electioneering. Argyll secured his appointment to the bench in 1724, and later promotion to Lord Justice Clerk in 1734. His finest moment came after the 1745 rebellion, when his natural humanity, fortified by a sound political instinct, led him to advocate mercy for the defeated Jacobites, thereby bringing down on himself the enmity of the Duke of Cumberland and the army. He was rewarded for his services to the government during the rebellion, when he was virtually in command of civil administration in Scotland, by being made Keeper of the Signet in 1746, a sinecure which had always previously been attached to the office of the Secretaries of State.[47] In 1748 he received the Signet for life, at the same time resigning his office of Lord Justice Clerk, though remaining on the bench as an ordinary Lord of Session.

Milton continued with his primary occupation of managing the Argathelian interest (Argyll interest) in Scotland after his resignation as Justice Clerk, especially in the administrative world of Edinburgh, where he exercised considerable influence on the Board of Trustees and the Commission of Annexed Estates. He was also very prominent in the evolution of Scottish banking, contributing much to the policy and prosperity of the Royal Bank, as well as playing a leading role in the foundation of the British Linen Company in 1746, where he continued to exercise much influence almost to his death. 'Let it be remembered to his honour,' John Ramsay of Ochtertyre observed, 'that he never took a hammer to break an egg — that is, he never had recourse to harsh or violent measures when it was not absolutely necessary.'[48]

Like Argyll, Milton's singularity raises questions about the nature of Chambers' term of *sous ministre*. Yet while Milton was unique in the amount of power and authority he wielded, there can be no doubt that up until 1765, certainly, there was always someone like a sub-minister in Edinburgh.[49] Some did not act for the Scottish minister, such as Baron John Scrope of the Court of Exchequer, an Englishman, who definitely acted in a ministerial capacity for the Treasury from 1708 until his departure, in January 1724, to become Walpole's closest assistant at the Treasury itself, where he continued to take an interest in Scottish administration.[50] It was no coincidence that Milton emerged as a prominent figure in Edinburgh after Scrope's departure. At other times the Earl of Mar, the Duke of Montrose, the Duke of Roxburghe, and the Marquess of Tweeddale kept political-cum-administrative agents in Edinburgh during their tenures as Secretaries of State.[51] Much later, after the third Duke of Argyll had died, William Mure (like Scrope a baron of the Court of Exchequer) became the acknowledged representative of the Bute interest in Edinburgh, particularly while James Stuart Mackenzie acted as Scottish minister between 1761 and 1765.

After 1765 the functions of the sub-minister began to accrue to the Lord Advocate. The improved postal service (daily posts between London and Edinburgh began in 1763) and the genial qualities of the approachable Henry Dundas made it possible to make a direct approach to the Scottish minister for patronage. Improved transportation and communication made it possible for the Lord Advocate to attend to his duties in Parliament and serve as a sub-minister for the government during that part of the year when he was resident in Edinburgh. If Scottish affairs required particular attention, as they did at the time of the French Revolution, the Advocate would remain in Edinburgh to direct the government's activities rather than attend Parliament. The Lord Justice Clerk and Barons of Exchequer, willing to act in an executive capacity earlier in the century, came to feel that such activity compromised their judicial status. By 1804 Lord Advocate Charles Hope could claim, in a speech to the House of Commons, that the duties of all the old Scottish officers of State had 'devolved' on the Lord Advocate: 'To him all inferior officers look for advice and decision; and with the greatest propriety, it may be said that he possesses the whole of the executive government of Scotland under his particular care.'[52] Thus the administrative activity of Scrope, Milton and Mure became the province of the Lord Advocate and the Solicitor General, acting under the authority, if seldom the supervision, of the Home Secretary.

What did a sub-minister do? His principal function was to serve as a point of contact in Edinburgh for those who wished something of government; whether it be patronage or government action.[53] It is important to remember that there were two aspects to the post: a political one which entailed the coordination of various local interests and the wishes of the ministry in London, and an administrative one which consisted in forwarding information to the Scottish minister in London, and sometimes the English ministers themselves. Officially, the government's correspondents were supposed to act as its eyes and ears in Scotland, but in practice any sort of remotely controversial intelligence had to go through private channels.[54] Only Milton efficiently operated as a political agent, for by the end of his active life he had built up a national network of correspondents. Thus only he operated as a truly representative minister, serving as a channel of communication for Scottish opinion, particularly in the fifteen years which followed the 1745 rebellion. The other sub-ministers were largely administrators serving the managerial needs of government in London.

How did a sub-minister, in particular Milton, exert his influence? He built up a system of followers in the administrative world of Edinburgh, among the minor officers of the Courts and the boards. The College of Justice (the Courts of Session and Justiciary), for example, harboured an enormous number of offices.[55] The Court of Exchequer was the same, attended as it was by officers such as the Auditor, King's Remembrancer, Treasurer's Remembrancer, and Clerk of the Pipe, many of which were sinecures executed by deputies.[56] Places in the Post Office, Board of Customs, Commission for the Annexed Estates, and all the others were awarded on the same basis. Milton's followers included William Jackson (Secretary for the Scottish Post Office), William Alston (Legal Agent for the Commission for the Annexed Estates as well as Deputy Auditor of Exchequer), Richard Gardiner (Deputy Comptroller General of Customs), and David Flint (Secretary of the Board of Trustees for the Encouragement of Fisheries and Manufactures). There were others as well.[57] The administrative world of Edinburgh did not lack that very essence of political patronage, jobs.

The official equivalent of the sub-minister was the Secretary of State's Scottish correspondent. Initially after the Union this function was carried out by the Lord Advocate, most efficiently by the elder Robert Dundas of Arniston under the Duke of Roxburghe and by Duncan Forbes under the Duke of Newcastle. Before 1745 the Lord Justice Clerk (the head of the Scottish Court of Justiciary) took a share of the correspondence when the Lord Advocate was absent from Edinburgh; after 1745, with the Lord Advocate preoccupied with prosecutions of Jacobites and preparation of extensive government legislation, the Lord Justice Clerk became the Secretary's principal Scottish correspondent.[58] Not surprisingly, it was Lord Milton's tenure as Lord Justice Clerk from 1734 until 1748 which witnessed the transfer of responsibilities. His important role in directing Scottish civil government during the 1745/46 rebellion demonstrated the Justice Clerk's superiority as government correspondent because of his constant residence in Scotland and his travel outside Edinburgh to the circuit courts of the Court of Justiciary. Milton's successor Lord Tinwald took responsibility for Scottish security, Justices of the Peace, supervision of the election of Representative Peers, and advised the government on crown presentations in the church.[59] Lord Justice Clerk Glenlee continued to correspond with the Secretary of State in the 1770s and 1780s, though in comparison with the decade after 1745 the volume of correspondence was negligible.[60] Similarly, the Commander-in-Chief of the Forces in Scotland corresponded at length with the responsible Secretary of State in the years following both rebellions, but by the 1760s such correspondence took place on little more than the level of courtesy, similar to the Secretary's correspondence with the King's Commissioner to the General Assembly of the

Church of Scotland.[61] Official Scottish correspondence remained at a token level until the troubles which followed the revolution in France, when the Lord Advocate became the government's principal correspondent.[62]

The administrative boards which met in Edinburgh consisted of those which drew their authority from the Treasury and those whose status was less precise, particularly the Board of Trustees, who drew their powers directly from the King. As such, it is they and not the Edinburgh correspondents who were the administrative ancestors of today's Scottish Office. Nevertheless, their efficiency in the eighteenth century was open to considerable doubt, for the boards, as the Earl of Marchmont complained, produced 'a negligence in the greatest number and let things fall by degrees into one or two hands covered under a set of respectable but unactive names . . . '[63]

The Scottish Court of Exchequer was pre-eminent among the Edinburgh boards in that it acted, in addition to its judicial capacity, as a kind of subordinate Treasury for Scotland. It administered the Scottish revenue, both income from taxes and Crown property, and paid the Scottish Civil List and other sums directed by the Treasury, such as the annual £10,000 to the Equivalent Company and £2000 to the Board of Trustees for the Encouragement of Fisheries and Manufactures.[64] Thus it was the Board of Exchequer, in the first instance, who undertook the administration of estates forfeited to the Crown after the 1715 and 1745 rebellions, and it was they who supervised the Scottish receivers of the various taxes, with the power to call any of them to account if they so desired.

There were five barons, with one of their number, the 'Chief Baron', presiding over his brethren, three of whom were Scots and the fourth English. Throughout most of the eighteenth century the Chief Baron was English as well, as the Treasury felt that this would maintain the court's efficiency;[65] yet the court was still usually under a cloud of disrepute at the Treasury, which was acutely aware of the large number of Scottish salaries and payments drawn on a very small revenue. Ironically, much of the trouble can be attributed to the inefficiency which resulted from the appointment of a series of bad English Chief Barons and Barons, as those English lawyers most keen to get on with a career in exchequer law naturally wanted to remain at the centre of their legal world at Westminster. The two chief barons who served from 1728 to 1756 were particularly bad, neither attending the court in its winter sessions,[66] and the court's reputation only began to recover with the appointment of Chief Baron Robert Ord, a Northumbrian who chose to live at Edinburgh (close by Dean Village) rather than attend the court irregularly.

The Scottish receivers[67] were as ripe for the politics of patronage as the customs. Most of the principal Receiver-Generals and Collectors of the various taxes treated their offices as sinecures and employed deputies, in the same manner as the non-judicial officers of the Court of Exchequer itself. Like the Paymaster General in England, these officers were free to lend the funds in their care for their own profit until the barons directed them to release the money or remit it to London.[68] The stamp and window tax establishments in particular provided extensive patronage, as there were fifteen or sixteen sub-distributors of stamps in Scotland as well as employees in the stamp offices at Edinburgh, while the two

Table III: *Government in Edinburgh*

Subordinate to the Treasury
  Boards:
    Barons of Exchequer

    Commissioners of Customs and Salt Duties
      (1707-1721, post-1742)

    Commissioners of Excise

    Commissioners of Forfeited and Annexed Estates
      (1716-1721, 1755-1782)

  Other Officers (all accountable to the Barons of Exchequer):
    Deputy Postmaster General (responsible to the
      Postmasters General in London who in turn
      were responsible to the Treasury)
    Collector of the Stamp Duty (responsible to the
      Commissioners of the Stamp Duty in London who
      in turn were responsible to the Treasury)
    Paymaster General Scotland
    Cashier of Customs and Salt
    Cashier of Excise
    Collector of the Land Tax
    Surveyors General of the Window Tax (post-1755)
    Collector of the Tax on Salaries and Perquisites
      (post-1758)

Outwith Treasury Control
  Commission of Police (1714-1782)
  Board of Trustees (post-1727)

Correspondents of the Secretary of State
  Lord Justice Clerk
  Lord Advocate
  Commander in Chief of the Forces in Scotland
  Lord High Commissioner to the General Assembly

Keepers of the Crown Seals in Scotland
  deputy Keeper of the Great Seal
  deputy Keeper of the Privy Seal
  deputy Keeper of the Signet Seal

Surveyors-General of the window tax supervised twenty district surveyors.[69]

The Barons of Exchequer, however, did not have authority over all the subordinate institutions of Treasury activity in Scotland, most importantly in the case of the customs and excise establishments. Day-to-day administration and most communication with the Treasury was undertaken by two boards of commissioners set up in Edinburgh after the Union; one for the customs and salt duties, and one for the excise duties. These boards and their officers were expected to raise substantial amounts of money from their English-style revenue systems, yet, particularly in the case of the customs, they were most open to political interference. Political needs triumphed over financial interests for the entire century.

The Board of Excise for Scotland was lucky in that, unlike the Board of Customs, it was able to appoint its subordinate officers without Treasury interference, which meant that those with political influence at the Treasury could not intervene in Excise appointments.[70] This is not to say that politics did not figure in the actions and appointments of the Scottish Board of Excise. The Treasury did appoint the officers of the central office at Edinburgh, which could be used for political purposes or as sinecures. The third Duke of Argyll's bastard son, William Williams, for example, held his place of Auditor of the Excise as a sinecure; and the Comptroller General of the Scottish Excise in the mid-eighteenth century was also a sinecurist, appointed by the interest of John Scrope.[71] Nor was it unknown for ministers to seek to influence the commissioners' choice of subordinates by making a recommendation to the board from London, 'which has been very often the Practice of late with those who have Interest,' claimed one Excise officer in 1761.[72] The commissioners were open to other influences as well in making their appointments, dividing the spoils equally. Thus in 1761 George Drummond appointed a Supervisor of Excise who had a vote in Stirlingshire to the well-paid post of General Supervisor, acting on the recommendation of Sir James Campbell of Ardkinglass, M.P. for that county and a supporter of Lord Bute and the Duke of Argyll. This appointment was made over the vigorous protests of Lord Kames, who wished to abolish all four offices of General Supervisor and use the salaries as part of the fund to encourage the linen industry, claiming that their work could be done by two clerks at a saving of over £500 a year.[73] Such decisions did not promote the greatest amount of efficiency, and the Treasury was often displeased with the operation of the excise in Scotland, but its method of trying to improve collection — the introduction of English commissioners — was just as much of a failure as it was in the Court of Exchequer.[74] In fairness to the board, there are indications of attempts to maintain the standards of their officers. In 1757 the commissioners wrote to the Duke of Argyll to protest the action of the Magistrates of Edinburgh in instructing their M.P. to solicit a Treasury order in favour of one of their number, Gilbert Laurie, to be first accomptant at the board.[75] At least some of the members of the board refused to appoint a man unless he was reasonably well qualified, according to George Drummond:

no man can be employed who has not been instructed — and no man who has been instructed, can be employed in a higher rank with us, who has not served a limited time in our lowest station, from which he can only be raised gradually.[76]

Attempts to reinstate dismissed officers also seem to have been discouraged by the commissioners.[77]

How successful were these efforts? It is very difficult to determine an answer. Since the Treasury did not have to warrant excise appointments, there is no way to trace them systematically, and the minutes of the board have not survived for the period before 1780; so against the evidence that some standards were applied, one must set the complaints of Commissioner Richard Dauber, a former Collector of Excise at Norwich, who commented on 'the idleness, irregularities and enormities of every sort of the officers . . . ',[78] and the difficulty of enforcing the collection of, for example, the tax on beer:

since the commencs of the new duty on beer, the Breweries in this country have entered into a combination to pay no more than sixteen pence a barrel for what they should pay 3s. 4 1/4d. for, and as they are countenanced in this by the Justices; we seem to be without any remedy, and therefore at present I am so set fast that I can neither act righteously or unjustly, if we direct the officers to alter their manner of charging and to return beer of a better quality, of a worse, we bring the guilt of Perjury upon them and ourselves, and ruin the Revenue past reparation; if we do not, we shall get no money, we have stated our Case fully to the Treasury and desired our Clauses to be enacted; but what avails Law where there is no body to execute it.[79]

Dauber, however, cannot be regarded as a completely unbiased witness. His brother commissioner, George Drummond, who had been involved in the Scottish revenue in one capacity or another since before the Union, complained in 1759 that

we have got one of the board, of late, who being a stranger to the country, has come, I am sorry now to find it, with strong prepossessions against it, and imagines that the smallness of the revenue here, when compared with England, proceeds chiefly from the fraudulent practices of the traders, and the negligence and connivance of the officers, and therefore is taking measures for increasing the revenue which I cannot approve of, and which I believe will not answer the end . . . violent and ineffectual measures . . . are taken, whereby both traders and officers are harassed, the trade is cramped, and the officers dogged and embarrassed in doing their duty, with unnecessary forms, and tedious and perplexed orders and instructions.[80]

One cannot measure the amount of tax which has not been paid, an ambitious enough undertaking for the present, let alone the past. Probably there was considerable amount of avoidance of duty, particularly on beer, the national drink; but whether more determined efforts to collect the excise taxes would have been successful, given the almost national scale of resistance, is doubtful.

If the Scottish Board of Excise was subject to political pressures, the Scottish Board of Customs was dominated by them. It was a bonanza for the politician. Each outport in Scotland had a Collector, a Comptroller, and a Surveyor, all paid £100 to £200 a year. The Collector in certain areas was also responsible for the collection of the salt tax. Underneath these offices were a number, sometimes a very substantial number, of salt officers, landwaiters and tidewaiters, who collected the salt duty and inspected goods at the port. In addition, aside from the officers at the central office in Edinburgh, there were two Inspector Generals of the outports at £130 a year, four general supervisors, and twelve riding officers who patrolled the country to try to detect goods which had been smuggled. All of the appointments to these offices had to be approved by the Treasury and all were open to political influence there.[81]

When a vacancy occurred, the board 'presented' a man to the post, which meant that he was to act in that office until a warrant was sent to the board from the Treasury either confirming their presentments or naming someone else to the vacancy.[82] These presentments and warrants were officially handled by one of the Treasury clerks delegated to deal with Scottish warrants. Unofficially, the commissioners were solicited by various parties attempting to secure a presentment for a client, or themselves, while some commissioners presented only those recommended to them by their political patron. Some commissioners with political connections then sent lists of the presentments with an explanation of each individual case to someone in London with influence at the Treasury, where interested parties called at the Treasury to solicit for their own nominees.[83] 'Your Lordship must be sensible that it may frequently be necessary for the Duke of Newcastle, in consequence of personal applications made to him here, to appoint other persons to these vacancies,' one of the more conscientious commissioners was reminded in 1755.

The customs appointments were the Scottish minister's (or his enemies') principal tool in demonstrating the support of the ministry for a particular local interest, and as such the fortunes of customs presentments at the Treasury were central to a minister's political power. If the First Lord of the Treasury had some arrangement with the Scottish minister, he would rely on the minister's advice in accepting or rejecting the presentments from Scotland. After Walpole left the Treasury, though, the transaction was rarely so simple, for both Henry Pelham and the Duke of Newcastle wished to have the support of all Whigs in Scotland. 'Mr. Pelham insisted that as we supported government, government must support our interest,' one of Argyll's enemies recalled in later years.[84]

Like the commissioners of excise, the customs commissioners and their officers faced an enormous administrative task, and one wonders whether it was possible to protect efficiently a coastline which, from the Shetlands to the Solway Firth, was a smuggler's dream and a customs officer's nightmare.[85] In 1761, for example, a customs collector at Dumfries reported to the commissioners that gangs of smugglers numbering up to fifty were travelling inland with their goods in defiance of the outnumbered customs men.[86] Smuggling on such a scale was not brought under control until the end of the century.

The extent of this activity, particularly in smuggling tobacco from America and wines and spirits from France, aroused the resentment of the English merchants who competed with the Scots. For most of the century the Treasury was under pressure from them to take some action against smuggling in Scotland. Walpole's action in creating a single British board of customs in 1723, whose members took it in turns to serve in Edinburgh, was an example of Treasury attempts to tighten up administration, but even this initiative failed, for after a few years of activity the new board lapsed into relative inertia. When Walpole fell from power in 1742, a separate Scottish board was re-established, with no greater or lesser effect on administration than before.[87] Quite simply, the problem of taxing Scotland efficiently and effectively seems to have been beyond the capabilities of eighteenth-century government.

In addition to the Scottish branches of the Treasury which were concerned with the collection of revenue, there were several Scottish commissions which were established to attempt to fill the vacuum left by the abolition of the Scottish Privy Council. They were largely concerned with Scotland's economic problems, in recognition of the gap that existed between England and Scotland in terms of economic development. They did play some role in the great leap forward in Scottish agriculture, textiles and transportation which occurred in the eighteenth century, although the precise nature of their contribution has yet to be adequately delineated. It was probably a modest one. Nevertheless, the commissions are interesting examples of government intervention in the economy in a century when such action was exceedingly rare; and they also played their part in the political system, for they too provided patronage for the politician.

The first, and most useless, of the Scottish commissions was the so-called Board of Police. In 1711 the Earl of Oxford (Robert Harley) attempted to revive the old Scottish office of Lord Chamberlain, and put it into commission as the Commission of Chamberlaincy and Trade. When it became clear that the idea would draw objections in Parliament, however, it was dropped.[88] The Whig successor to this scheme was the Board of Police, or, as it was termed in its 1764 commission, the

> Commission for preparing an account of the Papists and non-jurors, their person, interests, and circumstances; for preparing a state of the Highlands of Scotland, with their opinion thereupon; and for the consideration of means for employing the poor, and of proper methods of preparing highways, and making rivers navigable.[89]

The salaries of the commissioners, it should be noted, were paid by the English Treasury; they included a First Commissioner, five Lords, three Gentlemen, a Secretary, cashier, solicitor and doorkeeper.

The first commission of 1714 was given responsibility for making recommendations for the exercise of crown patronage in the Kirk, and for the disposal of the parliamentary fund which was meant to encourage the coarse woollen industry in Scotland; but later commissions for the board deleted these tasks. Even before the second commission of 1727, as Dr. Riley has commented, the amount of work accomplished was 'ludicrous'. After 1727 the commissioners' chief activity consisted in drawing their own salaries from the Treasury and appointing their officers. By the 1760s some members of the board did not even bother to take their oath of office after they were appointed, and in 1782 the commission was abolished as part of Whig economical reform.[90]

A new Scottish commission was constituted when George II became King in 1727, officially entitled the Commissioners and Trustees for Improving Fisheries and Manufactures in Scotland but soon popularly known as the Board of Trustees. It was created to administer a variety of funds granted to Scotland for economic development by the Treaty of Union and subsequent Acts of Parliament. A sum of £14,000 over seven years had been granted by the Treaty of Union, a further parliamentary grant of £2000 per annum had been made in 1718, and the malt tax of 1724 (12 *Geo.* I c.4) provided that any funds in excess of £20,000 annually from the tax were to be applied to the encouragement of manufactures in Scotland.[91] The Trustees themselves were largely drawn from the aristocracy and the bench, with a few Lothian gentry and Edinburgh merchants. They collectively invested the funds at their disposal (about £20,000 in 1727, supplemented by another £20,000 in 1737) and applied the income from their investments, as well as their annual £2000 from the Treasury and the surplus from the malt tax, to a wide variety of ends, but principally in order to encourage the linen industry in Scotland. They made a genuine contribution to the development of the Scottish linen industry in the 1730s and 1740s, though thereafter their efforts declined in overall effectiveness as the scale of the industry outstripped their resources.[92]

The Trustees themselves were unpaid, which may provide an explanation for their difficulty in achieving the quorum of five of the twenty-one. 'In these offices of trustees for the Manufactures there is no profit or reward,' Lord Milton explained to Gilbert Elliot in 1761. 'I found great difficulty to get a quorum except when there is some little office to dispose of.'[93] Milton's remark points out the political aspect of the board's activities. Their officers, particularly the 82 stampmasters of linen cloth, were useful sources of local patronage. In 1758 David Flint, the board's secretary, wrote to Milton that the stampmaster at Jedburgh had died, and the board had already received applications to replace him in favour of a wigmaker and a weaver there. 'There's but little to do there,' he went on,

> so any honest body may serve the cure. As it's one of the district which Mr. Fletcher [Milton's son] represents perhaps his friends might be obliged in the choice and the supplying the vacancy delayed till he and they are acquainted. Your pleasure shall make for some time stand still or run fast.[94]

There are many other examples of this aspect of the board's activity. In short, in a country that lacked offices, the trustees provided a lucrative and welcome source of patronage for anyone, especially Lord Milton, inclined to distribute them on a political basis.

From 1716 to 1725, and again from 1755 to 1784, there were commissions in Edinburgh dealing with estates forfeited to the Crown after the rebellions of 1715 and 1745. The two commissions had no relation to each other; the first being concerned with selling the estates in its care, the second with the more ambitious task of actually improving the highlands.[95] Little is known of the first commission other than that it supervised the sale of most of the estates forfeited after the 1715 rebellion to the York Building Company. Much more work has been done on the

C

second commission, which took over the administration of a number of the larger estates forfeited after the 'Forty-Five'

> for the purposes of civilizing the inhabitants upon the said estates, and other parts of the highlands and islands of Scotland, and promoting amongst them the Protestant religion, good government, industry and manufactures, and the principles of duty and loyalty to his Majesty, his heirs and successors, and to no other use or purpose whatsoever.[96]

The entire life of the commission falls within the period encompassed by this book, so the political aspect of its activities will be examined in subsequent chapters. It certainly suffered from over-management, with the commission spending perhaps a third of its funds in salaries to its officers.[97] Economically, the commission attempted much in the thirty-two years it existed, particularly from 1761 until 1774, but little was actually accomplished. The resources available to the commission could not support the ambitious undertaking it represented.[98]

Local Government

Central government largely limited itself to war and diplomacy in the eighteenth century, and raising revenue to support its activities. The rest was left to the locality, where public order was maintained, the land tax gathered, the poor cared for, the roads repaired and bridges built. Yet of course there was some interaction between central and local government, so it is therefore important to offer a brief synthesis of work on Scottish local government in the eighteenth century in order to provide a backdrop for much of what will be related below. Government generally recognised that the landed gentry should oversee their own county affairs; but in Scotland it retained the ability to exert its influence through the appointment of the Sheriff-depute, the Justices of the Peace and the Commissioners of Supply, just as it sometimes sought to influence the election of the county's Member of Parliament.

The county's government operated through five institutions: the Sheriff-depute, the Commissioners of Supply, the Justices of the Peace, the county freeholders, and the parish. Two of these institutions expanded their influence as the century went on, the Sheriff-depute and the Commissioners of Supply, while the J.P.s declined into general inactivity. The county freeholders and the parish heritors were specialised bodies who largely acted in a subsidiary capacity to the Commissioners of Supply. These are general trends; the specific local situation could vary widely from absolute inactivity to increasing initiative, but until more work has been done in the local records now centralised at Edinburgh's Register House, only a sketch of local government can be undertaken.

The most important official in Scottish local government by the end of the century was the Sheriff-depute. This was partly because of the government's reluctance to appoint Scottish Lords Lieutenant until 1794,[99] and partly because all Sheriffdoms came under the control of the Crown after the abolition of Heritable Jurisdictions in 1747. After that year all thirty of the Scottish Sheriffs-depute were appointed from the ranks of the Faculty of Advocates or, in certain cases, from prominent landed families, at a salary ranging from £150 to £250 per annum. A Sheriff was required to reside in his jurisdiction at least four months of every year and hold a regular court at the county town. In his absence, he appointed a Sheriff substitute (usually a writer [solicitor]) to act for him. He headed the principal local court, with primary jurisdiction over most civil cases, theft, assault, and disturbing the peace.[100] By giving some young advocates judicial experience, the Sheriffdoms served as a kind of training ground, or as Lord Milton put it, 'a seminary', for the Court of Session.[101]

An additional officer of the Sheriff's court was the Sheriff clerk, who was not appointed by the Sheriff but by the Keeper of the Signet. Thus while the signet seal was attached to the Secretary of State, the Sheriff Clerk was appointed by the Secretaries, but after that he was appointed by private keepers, including Lord Milton from 1746 to 1766, and Henry Dundas from 1777 until 1811.[102] The clerk not only kept the records of the Sheriff's court, but kept the records of the county freeholders' annual Michaelmas headcourt as well, and often acted as clerk for county election meetings.[103]

By no means all Sheriffdoms were run on ideal lines, however. In Ross, for example, Hugh Rose of Geddes refused to pay his substitute on the Isle of Lewis until the latter obtained an order from the Court of Session forcing him to do so.[104] The Sheriff-depute for Fife and Kinross in the 1750's, Mr. James Leslie, a brother of the Earl of Rothes, went mad and was confined to an asylum in London.[105] Lord Torphichen, Sheriff-depute for the county of Edinburgh, treated his office as a sinecure and left everything to his substitute, just as if the Act of 1747 had never been passed.[106] The frequency of a Sheriff's court and the attendance of the Sheriff varied as well. The Sheriff court at Stirling in the early 1760s met twice a week, yet in 1765 the Sheriff or his substitute in Haddington held their court only 34 times.[107] Most of these evils were the result of the influence still exerted over government appointments by the county magnate, best illustrated by the Banff affair of 1764 (see below p. 114). Lord Justice Clerk Glenlee complained to the Secretary of State in 1775 'that the great men of our own country in their applications do often pay more attention to their own political interest and connexions than to the King's service and the interest of their several counties'.[108]

The political status of the Sheriff-depute was enhanced by his additional duties as the principal local executive officer of the Crown. He carried out exchequer writs, accounted for Crown property in his jurisdiction, called jurors, received the writs for parliamentary elections, and helped set the price of grain. He also acted as a more direct link between the county and the government. It was most often the Sheriff who called county meetings, forwarded county petitions to London, and assumed responsibility for keeping the peace in times of civil unrest. He determined the day of the County's parliamentary election meeting, and he acted as returning officer for the county.[109]

Next in importance to the Sheriff were the county Commissioners of Supply, a group which had been responsible for the collection of the Scottish land tax since 1667.[110] In many cases, the same gentleman would be named as both a

Table IV: *Local Government*

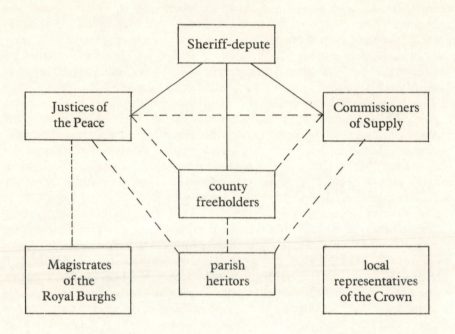

local representatives of the Crown:

    customs, salt and excise officers
    postmasters and stampmasters
    surveyors of the window tax (post-1755)
    linen stamp officers
    fishery officers
    factors of annexed estates (1746-1784)

————————: Formal Government

— — — — — —: possibility of intercurrent membership

Commissioner of Supply and a Justice of the Peace, but over the course of the eighteenth century the Commissioners came to dominate those functions they shared with the J.P.s. In addition to collecting the cess and other taxes, the Commissioners began to acquire responsibility for the repair of highways and bridges, apprehending and detaining criminals, and even providing a school for any parish which had not built one itself.[111] Yet the activity and efficiency of the

Commissioners varied from county to county, and in some of the smaller counties they met very infrequently.

The Commissioners of Supply had the advantage of superior organisation. There were more opportunities of revising the lists of commissioners and keeping them reasonably current, as they were named in the annual Act of Supply from lists handed in to the ministry by the county's Member of Parliament after each general election. They met more often than the Justices of the Peace because the Sheriff or his substitute had to call their meetings to secure the county's land tax, and other taxes such as those on windows, servants and horses. They also met more often after the Commissioners in some of the larger counties began to elect a convener who could call meetings independently of the Sheriff. It was the Commissioners of Supply who were at the head of the evolution, from about 1756, of the county meeting as a forum for landed opinion on local, Scottish and British issues.[112] It was a development which deserves much closer study than it has yet received.

The Justices of the Peace, as an institution, were imported from England by James VI and I in the seventeenth century as part of an attempt to use the landed gentry to reduce the power of the aristocracy. The attempt did not succeed, and the Justices as an active group existed only in Acts of Parliament.[113] The Justices of some counties became more active in the eighteenth century, however. Lanarkshire may serve as an example. Commissions were named at the beginning of each reign, and between 1739 and 1744, largely on the recommendation of the local M.P. National government only took an interest in their composition when Lord Hardwicke was Chancellor (1737-1756), usually leaving the inspection of recommendations to the Lord Justice Clerk.[114]

J.P.s were most uniformly effective in simple legal tasks such as granting licences, administering oaths, and regulating weights and measures. The poor were usually dealt with by the kirk sessions, leadership in road repair passed to the Commissioners of Supply, and after 1747 local criminal justice largely became the province of the Sheriff's court.[115] The frequency, after the Union, of circuits by the Lords of Justiciary twice a year to the north (Perth, Aberdeen, Inverness), west (Stirling, Glasgow, Inveraray), or south (Jedburgh, Dumfries, Ayr) had provided a criminal court of appeal outside Edinburgh. The introduction of reasonably efficient Sheriff's courts after 1747 made the existence of yet another criminal court superfluous. By 1784, Lord Justice Clerk Glenlee explained to the Home Secretary that

> by the establishment of the Sheriff Courts . . . and from other Causes, which I shall not Recite, the Commission of the Peace fell into Neglect. Many Gentlemen declined accepting, few or none attended the quarter Sessions, and of consequence, the regular appointment of Constables, fell into disuse, in Many Counties: So that the execution of the Law came to depend upon the Sheriffs & Magistrates of Burrows, and their officers . . .[116]

Most, if not all, Commissioners of Supply and Justices of the Peace were county freeholders; in fact in some counties the business of supply was transacted at the conclusion of the freeholders' annual Michaelmas headcourt. A freeholder was feudal superior of land valued at a rent of 400 pounds Scots a year, or 40 shillings Scots 'of old extent'.[117] This gave him the right to be placed on the roll of county freeholders and gave him the right to vote in parliamentary elections, though after the middle of the century the practice of creating nominal superiorities for political purposes undermined the old system. It was the Commissioners of Supply who assessed the value of land, although the freeholders themselves voted on whether an application for admission was legitimate or not. Another example of the overlap of different institutions was the raising of 'rogue money' for employing constables and maintaining a gaol. The freeholders' headcourt determined the rate, the Commissioners of Supply organised the collection, and the J.P.s employed the constables and built the gaol, at least in those counties where they were active.[118]

The parish was the most rudimentary of all the institutions of local government, concerned as it was with the provision of education and poor relief. The parish's kirk session, made up of the minister and the church elders, undertook much of the administration involved, but finances were the responsibility of the parish heritors. A heritor owned property in the parish. The cess he paid on that property helped to pay the minister's and the dominie's salaries, maintained the church building and the school, and in some cases provided funds for the relief of the poor.[119] Government willingly left education and poor relief to the heritors and their kirk session, but participated in parish life on another level, by virtue of the Crown's position as lay patron of more than a third of the parishes in Scotland. From 1689 until 1712 the kirk session and the heritors had jointly chosen the parish minister, but after that year lay patrons, including the Crown, had been restored by Act of Parliament. Yet the Crown's ministers trod softly in appointing parish ministers, as a general rule following the recommendation of the most substantial of the gentleman heritors, especially if they were resident in the parish.[120]

Aside from county government, there were sixty-six royal burghs in Scotland which under the terms of their charter enjoyed a measure of self-government. Each had a burgh council made up of merchants and tradesmen. The merchants' occupations could range from tobacco lord to draper, as long as they were a burgess, or freeman, of the town. The tradesmen, on the other hand, were organised into incorporations, each for a craft like shoemaker or smith, the number of organised crafts varying from town to town. The size of the council also varied from burgh to burgh; in Edinburgh there were twenty-five councillors until 1729, thirty-three thereafter; in Rutherglen there were nineteen magistrates and councillors, in Dingwall there were fifteen, and in Haddington there were twenty-five.[121] The number of magistrates also varied: from Edinburgh's seven to Rutherglen's four. The councils were all self-perpetuating, electing their own successors through a variety of devices, such as restricting the electorate to the outgoing council itself or having each member of council select burgesses to join the old council in electing a new one.

The burgh council set the watch, imposed standards of sanitation, regulated the town markets, administered the 'Common Good' (or feudal revenues of the burgh), and set assessments on the burgesses to supplement it.[122] Each burgh had its own courts, with its bailies as judges, but only Edinburgh's magistrates had a jurisdiction free from the local Justices of the Peace or the Sheriff-depute.[123] Burgh courts dealt with minor criminal offences, debts, claims for rent, evictions and bankruptcies. Their tax burden was assessed independently of the counties, a portion of the land tax being set on the burghs, and they were fortunate in having their own national organisation, the Convention of Royal Burghs, to look after their interests.[124]

After the Union the royal burghs of Scotland, with the exception of Edinburgh, were grouped into fourteen districts to correspond with the fourteen seats allocated to represent them. They thus became a unique sub-section of the political system, with a distinctive political behaviour different from that of English boroughs. While only a few of them, the most obvious example being Inveraray, were dominated by a patron, most town councils were out to make the best deal possible for themselves and their burgh with whoever was taking a political interest in their district.[125] In some, such as the decaying East Neuk burghs in Fife, this could mean corruption; in others, such as Aberdeen or Ayr, it meant a certain amount of respect for the integrity of the burgh.[126]

Scotland enjoyed a state of 'semi-independence' in the eighteenth century. Real power undoubtedly rested with the English ministers, but they had no desire to use it; and even on those few occasions when they chose to exert themselves, the Scots, particularly under Argyll and Milton, were strong enough to force compromises. The Union had destroyed a Parliament, but it allowed many different Scottish institutions to survive. These institutions and the society which supported them both flourished in the eighteenth century as the Scottish upper class strove, not for assimilation, but for parity with English society. Government mirrored the situation. Management there most certainly was; but it would have been very strange indeed if a country which was expanding its universities and towns, creating a modern transportation network, and transforming its agriculture, should abdicate all interest in government and politics.

Scots were not participating in British politics because such a politics did not exist. Scottish affairs and issues were largely separate and distinct and, in the period which is the subject of this book, revolved around the basic problem of national development. Most accepted the aim, but acute differences remained as to the methods and means. This tension underlay all of Scottish political life in the middle of the eighteenth century. Semi-independence (a quasi-Union?) allowed the Union settlement to work by providing a buffer between English government and assumptions, and Scottish institutions and society in general. The friction between the two provides the theme for much of what follows.

2

The Duke of Argyll and Scotland

Introduction: Court and Country[1]

THE 'Squadrone' had forced the abolition of the Scottish Privy Council in 1708. They were a small group of Scottish Country Whigs who were distinguished by family traditions of opposition to the Stuart monarchy and a close network of matrimonial alliances. They differed from most country Whigs in their determination to replace the Court party. Their identity of interest made up for their lack of numerical strength, as even in the Scottish Parliament the largest estimate of their strength had been twenty-four. In the first British Parliament their party numbered, at most, four of the sixteen Scottish Representative Peers and eleven of the forty-five Scottish members of the House of Commons.[2] Even in terms of their political power in Scotland, care should always be taken to distinguish between the Squadrone, the Scottish country party in general, and the Scottish Tories. The Squadrone's triumph over the Privy Council was short-lived, however, for it merely resulted in a more diffuse version of what had gone before. Lord Treasurer Godolphin decided to maintain the Scottish Court interest by obtaining the appointment of the second Duke of Queensberry as a third 'British' Secretary of State, with special responsibility for Scotland. For the next two years all Scottish affairs were delegated to Queensberry with minimal English intervention.

Apart from the administrative arrangements which involved Queensberry, it is important to note the immediate emergence of a separate Scottish political identity in Parliament, as described by Dr. Riley: 'any threat to what were thought to be Scottish interests at once united the Scottish members.'[3] One example was the response to efforts in Parliament to alter the Scots law of treason, which provoked unanimous opposition from Scottish M.P.s in deference to opinion in Scotland. Riley also notes the adoption of lobbying techniques by the Scottish Convention of Royal Burghs, another national institution which had survived the Union. It had begun as a forum for merchant opinion in Scotland, but after the Union it 'took a wider view of its sphere, and . . . endeavoured to promote industry and trade generally, both by direct encouragement and by applying for changes in duties, for bounties, drawbacks, etc.'[4] It concentrated, through its annual committee and the appointment of parliamentary agents, on ensuring that Scottish interests were represented, if not always honoured, in London.

Godolphin's arrangement of delegating Scottish affairs to Queensberry came to an end in 1710, when a Tory ministry took power in London with Robert Harley as the new Lord Treasurer. Harley went to the opposite extreme from Godolphin, in that he attempted to integrate Scottish patronage and policy with the government departments at London. At first Harley bypassed Queensberry as Secretary of State and attempted to deal with all Scottish business through the Treasury, consigning the Secretary's office to a subordinate role. After Queensberry's death in 1711 Harley (or the Earl of Oxford, as he had become in that year) hit upon the scheme of resurrecting the powers of the medieval office of Lord High Chamberlain of Scotland and putting it into commission. This would have created an additional subordinate board in Scotland which would complement the Barons of Exchequer, but the scheme faltered because of the difficulty of deciding just what its powers would be. When the Whigs eventually implemented the idea as the Commission of Police in 1714, it was little more than a pretext for additional Scottish sinecures.

Harley's attempt at dealing with Scottish affairs failed, Dr. Riley has written, because 'his policy put more work on his shoulders than he could carry.'[5] In 1713 he recognised this fact by appointing two Scottish subordinates: the Earl of Mar as Secretary of State and the Earl of Findlater (who had been known as the Earl of Seafield in 1707) as Lord Chancellor of Scotland. Oxford (Harley) had become engaged in a struggle with Viscount Bolingbroke for supremacy within the ministry, so the coming general election demanded an efficient system of management for Scotland if the ministry was to hope for success there. Oxford's appointment of Findlater and Mar was a recognition of the failure of his previous policy. The significance of his attempt at direct government in Scotland lay in its failure.

The Tory majority in Parliament displayed an inclination to interfere in Scottish affairs at the same time as Oxford was experimenting with direct administration. In 1711 the Greenshield case fulfilled the premise between the lines in the Treaty of Union by establishing the right of appeal from the Court of Session in Edinburgh to the House of Lords at Westminster. The case was particularly sensitive in Scotland because it involved an Episcopalian minister (Greenshield) prosecuted by the Presbyterian authorities in Scotland. This was followed by the Toleration Act of 1712, which extended freedom of worship to Episcopalians who would pray for the reigning monarch. Then there was the Hamilton affair of 1711, which prevented Scottish peers with British peerages from sitting in the House of Lords by virtue of those British (that is, post-Union) peerages.[6] The Duke of Hamilton had the misfortune to set the precedent by failing to secure his right to sit in the House of Lords as Duke of Brandon. There was also the 1713 House of Commons vote to apply the malt tax to Scotland, a measure which violated the Treaty of Union. This drove the Scots Representative Peers and Members of Parliament to hold a series of conferences which led the Earl of Findlater (he of the 'There's ane end to an auld sang' in 1707) to make a motion in the House of Lords to bring in a bill to dissolve the Union. The motion failed by four votes. It played a part in forcing Harley to appoint Findlater Lord Chancellor of Scotland.

After 1713 interest shifted away from Scotland, as the rivalry within the ministry between Oxford and Viscount Bolingbroke began to dominate all other considerations. The political crisis which followed the death of Queen Anne in 1714, as all political crises after the Union, pushed Scotland further into the background. The Jacobite rebellion of 1715 soon brought it back to the centre of attention. Yet the confusion in ministerial politics, with Whig nudging Whig for influence, prevented the emergence of any clear Scottish policy. Politics in England were complicated by rivalry between the new King and his heir apparent, the new Prince of Wales, and by rivalry between the chief Whig ministers: Sunderland, Stanhope, Walpole and Townshend. Politics in Scotland were complicated by rivalry between the Court party headed by the Duke of Argyll and the Squadrone, who had become attached to Stanhope and Sunderland. Political intrigue was rampant and pervasive. When the fortunes of Stanhope and Sunderland rose in the ministry, the leader of the Squadrone, the Duke of Roxburghe, was made third Secretary of State, and the followers of Argyll went into eclipse.

The fortunes of the Squadrone and the followers of Argyll (known as Argathelians) were determined by the resolution of the conflict between the English ministers. Sir Robert Walpole, a Norfolk squire with a flair for parliamentary business, was appointed First Lord of the Treasury and Chancellor of the Exchequer in April 1721, after the bursting of the South Sea Bubble. Walpole began to dominate the ministry by using his influence in the House of Commons and the power of the Treasury. It was at this time that the Squadrone, as represented by Roxburghe, made a basic miscalculation by backing Walpole's opponents within the ministry. As a result, Walpole looked to Argyll for Scottish support, and began by supporting Argyll's followers with Treasury patronage in Scottish elections. From this point onwards the Squadrone were to decline until their almost total eclipse in 1725.

Walpole's Scottish policy may briefly be described as identification with the house of Argyll; but, as J. H. Plumb has noted, 'They did not dispense the patronage, they asked for it.'[7] The second Duke of Argyll was a great and difficult man. As John Simpson has commented, 'it is hard not to sympathise with a man so evidently designed for a brilliant part, yet eternally at odds with the script, with his fellow players, and with himself.'[8] He and his brother Ilay formed an uneasy association under Walpole: the one the great Scottish magnate, the other at times almost a political hack. Blood was thicker than water, but it could not determine inclinations and taste: their grand niece recorded the family tradition that 'The Duke thought Lord Islay [sic] undignified and time-serving; Lord Islay thought the Duke wrong-headed and romantic.'[9] The Duke cut the heroic figure while Ilay cut corners with the ministry. Ilay was Walpole's agent in Scottish affairs. He could advise and oppose, but he carried out Walpole's wishes, much to the distaste of the Duke of Newcastle, whose jurisdiction as Secretary of State included Scottish affairs.

While the problem of distributing Scottish patronage was solved satisfactorily by Walpole, his political success was safeguarded by minimal government activity in Scotland. Walpole did take the initiative in Scottish affairs on three occasions; but the first two were motivated by political considerations, and the third was a mistake.

In 1723 English tobacco merchants, undercut by their Scottish rivals, demanded action against smuggling in Scotland. Walpole took the opportunity to stage an investigation of the Scottish Customs Establishment, which mollified the English merchants and gave him an opportunity to oversee a purge of Scottish customs officials. One result was a new customs commission for England and Scotland, whose members took it in turns to sit in Edinburgh to supervise the Scottish customs establishment. A second result was an increase of customs officers in sympathy with the ministry.

In 1725 English resentment at the low tax yield from Scotland, so low that it could not pay the Scottish Civil List, forced Walpole to allow a new malt tax for Scotland to pass through Parliament. The response in Scotland was immediate and intense. The 1713 tax had never been enforced because of its effect on the price of what was then the national beverage: beer. The announcement of the 1725 tax caused the Glasgow mob to run amuck, sacking the house of the Member of Parliament for the Glasgow burghs, Campbell of Shawfield, because he had supported the tax. The brewers of Edinburgh refused to brew until the tax was withdrawn, and took legal action to safeguard their position. Several prominent Squadrone politicians acted in sympathy with the protesters, including the recently dismissed Lord Advocate, Robert Dundas, and the Duke of Roxburghe, who still held office as Secretary of State.

The challenge to the government was met by the new Lord Advocate, Duncan Forbes, and by Lord Ilay in his capacity as Lord Justice General. The Magistrates of Glasgow were brought to trial for countenancing a breach of the peace, and the Court of Session ordered the brewers' petition to be burnt by the hangman at Edinburgh's mercat cross. Ilay's presence ensured that the Court of Justiciary would not display any sympathy for the protesters, despite the inclinations of Lord Justice Clerk Ormiston. Meanwhile Walpole took the opportunity to dismiss Roxburghe as Secretary of State. The Malt Tax may never have been completely paid (see Richard Dauber's complaint above, p. 18), but in appearance at least the will of the government was enforced.

There is surely some significance in the fact that Walpole did not again assert the power of central government from the crisis of 1725, which was used as an opportunity to break the Squadrone as a party, until 1737. Patronage was distributed, and opposition occurred, but government adopted a low profile while Ilay busied himself with political management designed to maintain as many Scottish ministerial votes in Parliament as possible. The Squadrone, or what remained of it, and the Scottish country Whigs increased their links with the English opposition, and caused Ilay some difficulty, but the ministry's arrangements for Scotland were not seriously pressed until 1737.

The Porteous Riot of 1736 weakened Walpole's Scottish arrangement by dividing Argyll and Ilay, and threatening Ilay's status in Scotland. The 'riot' was in fact nothing of the kind, but the execution by the Edinburgh mob of the Captain of the Edinburgh Town Guard, Porteous by name, who had ordered the Guard to fire on the crowd at the public execution of a smuggler in April 1736.[10] Porteous was condemned to death by the Court of Justiciary for his actions. The Edinburgh mob took the law into its own hands after Queen Caroline, as Regent, had granted a stay of Porteous's execution. The result was outrage in London at this breakdown of law and order in Edinburgh, and the introduction of a punitive bill in Parliament against the privileges of the City of Edinburgh. Walpole countenanced the bill; and though Ilay argued against the measure, he did not oppose it. Argyll, on the other hand, engaged in forthright opposition. He was not alone. The ministry was ultimately forced to backtrack in the face of near unanimous opinion in Scotland, and Edinburgh escaped severe penalties.

The damage had been done, however, for Ilay's prestige in Scotland was reduced by this demonstration of the limitations on his influence with the ministry. At the time, he boasted to English acquaintances that 'I have contrived it so that if my brother should run mad, and break with the Court, there are not three people in Parliament who will follow him unless I go along with them',[11] but in fact when his brother did break with the ministry in 1739, Ilay's influence in Scotland was severely curtailed. Argyll stood out for political independence and Patriot principles during the general election of 1741; his adherence gave the disparate opposition in Scotland enough strength to secure more than half the country's seats in the House of Commons, which substantially contributed to Walpole's inability to maintain a parliamentary majority, and his subsequent resignation in 1742.

There can be little doubt that Ilay was Walpole's servant in Scottish affairs: 'My Brother, Ilay, wants to make all his friends Tools to Walpole because he finds his ends in so doing,' Argyll wrote to one of his nephews in 1741, ' . . . My Brother Ilay prefers his Places to all other Considerations; friendship, Honour, Relation, gratitude & Service to his Country Seem at present to have no weight with him . . .'[12] The nature of his relationship with Walpole, however, must be explored further before the exact nature of Scottish government during Walpole's ministry can be determined. The important point is that Scottish affairs between the 1715 and 1745 rebellions rarely required the attention of the First Minister. We have seen that Walpole set Scottish policy when he had to; but it seems likely that the rest was left to Ilay under only the most general supervision.

The crucial question is the source and nature of political power in Scotland. One can adopt one of three perceptions of Scottish politics after the Treaty of Union. It can be argued, using the crises briefly described above as evidence, that the Scottish allies of a given ministry merely carried out instructions from their English masters. Alternatively, one can argue that Ilay bowed to the inevitable when faced with English pressure, but otherwise carried out his own policies in order to cope with the needs of the Scots political nation, a group which had not yet been integrated into an anglicised political system. Lastly, one can adopt the interpretation presented in this book, that Scottish ministers were responsible to their English superiors, but that the relationship was not one-sided, or based on deceit; that the Scottish manager represented Scottish interests within the government, sometimes successfully and sometimes unsuccessfully.

We are examining the unequal relationship between two separate entities. To state that one entity, Scotland, was subordinate to the other does not solve the puzzle. There was and is a large grey area open to negotiation, in which the subordinate party's acceptance of its position does not imply submission or assimilation. Rather than emphasise the submissive aspects of Scottish government, it may be useful to examine the Scots' maintenance, by negotiation, of a separate political identity. This is a much abused term, but it is here taken at its most simple meaning: separateness.[13] It must be understood that the nature of this separate identity is not comprehended here, only its existence. The existence of that identity, in all its complexity, was revealed when government was forced to re-evaluate Scotland's place within the Union in the aftermath of the 1745 rebellion.

The Duke of Argyll and the 'Forty-Five

Archibald, third Duke of Argyll, was 61 years old when he inherited his brother's dukedom in 1743. He had never been an impressive man visually; he was short, walked with an unattractive limp, dressed carelessly and, according to Horace Walpole, spoke in a high, unpleasant voice. His education in Scotland and Holland had been that of a lawyer, and he looked the part. The figure which peers at the present day observer from his portraits does not so much resemble a wealthy duke as a pawky lawyer, a judge perhaps, patiently sitting for his portrait and never getting the pose just right. The delicate Lord Hervey compared him to 'a pedantic, dirty, shrewd, unbred fellow of a college', and even Argyll's secretary joked that he looked more like a regent of Marischal College, Aberdeen than the Regent of the realm he was when the King departed for Hanover.[14]   His historical reputation has been affected by the contempt with which he has been portrayed in the published papers of Hugh, Earl of Marchmont, and the memoirs of John, Lord Hervey, and Horace Walpole, all of whom have been much consulted by historians. Their views are best represented by Horace Walpole's oft-quoted verdict that Argyll 'had so little great either in himself or his views, and consequently contributed so little to any great events, that posterity will probably interest themselves very slightly in his fortunes'.[15] The Scots themselves viewed Argyll in a different light, represented by John Ramsay of Ochtertyre's memory of him as 'not only the wisest and greatest Minister, but also the most enlightened patriot, Scotland has produced'.[16] A view generally followed, in less ecstatic terms, in the various histories of Scotland.

All accounts of Argyll's personality agree that he was intelligent. The Earl of Granville once said to him that 'there may have been cleverer, or quicker men, but I never knew a man who had less rubbish in his understanding.'[17] He was a patron of science and the arts, an amateur inventor, and a dabbler in astronomy, mathematics and botany. He was a dedicated improver who several times undertook the challenge (at Whitton in Surrey, the Whim in Peebles, and Inveraray in Argyll) of developing a desolate property into a good estate. He was also a lover of books. By the time of his death he had accumulated one of the largest private libraries in the kingdom, building a handsome home for it on Argyll Street in London which gave his house there its unofficial title of 'the Library'.[18]

But above all else Argyll was a politician. 'How can a man whose mind seems to have been framed for the enjoyment of such agreeable and innocent amusements bring himself back to town and engage in a scene of public business and the intrigues of a C[our]T?' one young M.P. wondered in 1743.[19] Argyll's precise, incisive, yet unimaginative mind seemed to glory in the labyrinth of Georgian politics. Politics was the great game, reflected in his use of metaphors from his favourite parlour diversion, whist. His intellect contented itself with the study of human nature and the mastery of the intricate political machinery of the day without ever questioning the values of the structure. Dr. Ferguson put it best when he suggested that the greatest mechanical invention in Argyll's collection was the system of management he constructed in Scotland.[20] Within these narrow limits he was supreme.

Argyll's political career seemed at an end when he succeeded to his dukedom in 1743. He had a huge estate to administer; and his political mentor and master, Sir Robert Walpole, had been forced from the government in 1742. A rival, the Marquess of Tweeddale, had recently become Secretary of State with authority over Scottish affairs. Argyll himself felt weary and wanted to retire. As he wrote to his friend Lord Milton:

> I am now too old and have too great a stake to wish to set myself up again as a Cock to be thrown at, and farther I have not health and constitution and I shall not have time on account of my private affairs, and my amusements to cater into any political scheme that required application, attendance or bustling, and every year at my age I must expect to be less capable of it![21]

'If I act temperately it must be a very odd ministry who will not be civil to me,' he added in another letter written at the New Year, 'and if I act otherwise, I should put myself to a great deal of trouble for really I don't know what.'[22]

His fond resolutions were altered by the 1745 rebellion, which broke out while Argyll was himself in Scotland at Inveraray, traditional seat of the chief of the Campbells. Unsure of government support, and remembering the events of 1715, when his brother had been politically outmanoeuvred in London while outmanoeuvring the Jacobites in Scotland, Argyll departed for London. The sneers of Horace Walpole[23] never for a moment took into account the fact that there was no one in Scotland at the time of the rebellion with the authority to raise the loyal clans or even a lowland militia.[24] Argyll's lieutenant, Lord Justice Clerk Milton, took charge of Scottish civil government in the absence of initiative from the Lord Advocate, while in London Argyll finally obtained the King's permission to raise troops in his own county as hereditary Lord Lieutenant.[25] Secretary Tweeddale, in contrast, tried to minimise the threat from the rebels; 'called them rabble, and it was a farce';[26] with the result that he was disgraced after the battle of Prestonpans established the rebellion as a serious threat. In January 1746 he suddenly resigned his office.

This development did not mean that Scottish affairs were then formally handed over to Argyll, who was never made Secretary of State. A different kind of rival emerged in the person of the Duke of Cumberland, victor of Culloden and hammer of the highland clans. On leaving his command in Scotland in July 1746, Cumberland expressed his feelings toward Scotland in a letter to the Duke of Newcastle:

> I am sorry to leave this country in the condition it is for all the good that we have done has been a bloodletting, which has only weakened the madness, but not at all used [it up] and I tremble for fear that this vile spot may still be the ruin of this island and of our family.[27]

Cumberland's severity would ultimately provoke a reaction against him in England, but in 1746 and 1747 John Bull was in no mood for mitigation; and Cumberland found sympathisers in the ministry, most notably Newcastle and Hardwicke. Even more important, Cumberland communicated his distaste to his father the King, who demanded that his ministers be severe with the rebels.

In this atmosphere Argyll's influence did not count for much, particularly in view of the fact that Cumberland and the army felt that Argyll's friend Milton, as Lord Justice Clerk, was obstructing the course of the law by adopting a conciliatory attitude towards those with Jacobite connections. George II began to refer tetchily to Argyll as the 'Viceroy' of Scotland, refusing to see him in the closet or recognise him at court.[28] Cumberland chose five new Scottish Representative Peers in 1747 and intervened in several other Scottish parliamentary contests. Henry Pelham at the Treasury had consulted Argyll on the Scottish elections, but the duke himself delayed his annual visit to Scotland, he informed Milton, because

> I should only draw crowds of people about me & make a most wretched figure, by being neither able to reward, punish nor in some cases to protect my friends, all which would appear in a more glaring light if I was now at Edinburgh than here at London, ... I might easily have made matters worse, but not better, ...[29]

Argyll's attitude towards Hardwicke's 1747 bill for the abolition of heritable jurisdictions in Scotland further eroded his credit with the ministers. He knew that in Scotland the measure was seen as part of English punishment for the rebellion, and argued that the measure should be delayed until national animosities had time to cool. This was presented as obstruction and opposition by Argyll's enemies — with some success, for Argyll's friends in the House of Commons opposed the measure. In the Lords, the duke's long explanation of the constitutional history of the jurisdictions was not well received. 'The D. of A[rgyll] made the most exotic speech I ever heard,' a hostile Scottish M.P. wrote to Lord President Culloden, 'had I not been informed before that he was to speak for the bill I should have thought from his facts and reasonings that he intended to vote ag't it.'[30] Partially as a result of this, when Newcastle drew up the list of the new Sheriff-deputes for the King's approval, he took the recommendations of the

Commander-in-Chief of the Forces in Scotland, and not those of Argyll and Milton.[31]

At the end of 1747 the death of Lord President Culloden (Duncan Forbes) created a keen competitive atmosphere amongst the various parties interested in Scotland as they jostled each other to obtain the post for their own candidate. At the same time, a subtle shift of power occurred within the ministry. The Earl of Chesterfield, an enemy of Argyll's, left the ministry in February 1748, and at the same time the failure of the Dutch to meet the military commitments of their alliance with Britain gave increased strength to those within the ministry who favoured peace. These changes in the balance of the ministry enabled Henry Pelham to effect a compromise calculated to maintain Argyll's willingness to cooperate with the government while making it clear that he did not dominate its Scottish policy. Argyll's recommendation for a replacement of Culloden was rejected in favour of Robert Dundas of Arniston, an ex-Squadrone politician then in correspondence with Lord Hardwicke. But Argyll was kept reasonably happy by the provision made for his closest associates: Lord Milton, who had been finding the burden of being Lord Justice Clerk increasingly wearing, was allowed to resign and at the same time had his office as Keeper of the Signet made a life appointment, and Charles Erskine, Argyll's nominee for the Lord Presidency, succeeded Milton as Justice Clerk. In addition, Argyll's personal secretary John Maule was made a Baron of the Exchequer, while his replacement, Milton's son Andrew Fletcher (just returned as Member of Parliament for the Haddington district of burghs), was given the reversion of a lucrative Exchequer office.

Pelham pieced this compromise together at roughly the same time as the signing of the preliminary peace treaty at Aix-la-Chapelle. The advent of peace marked the beginning of Pelham's supremacy within the ministry as Newcastle's diplomacy became less important than his brother's plans for financial reform. The strain of this adjustment was such that for a while there was a real danger that Pelham and Newcastle would break with one another, and for a time in 1748 they actually ceased to communicate. Cumberland also quarrelled with Newcastle in 1748, and so lost much of the influence he had formerly wielded over the ministry.[32]

Pelham had found Argyll 'compliant' in helping him with the 1747 elections, and saw no reason to antagonise so important a man 'if he does the King's business well, and in a manner inoffensive to those who are known friends to the King'.[33] He continued to consult Argyll on Scottish affairs and to take his recommendations into account, but at the same time Pelham recognised the interest of Argyll's Whig opponents, still generally known as the Squadrone. The Earl of Marchmont, for example, a dedicated enemy of Argyll's, told Pelham in one interview that there was no Squadrone, for if there was, it would have a head. 'He said he knew no heads of it,' Marchmont recorded, 'but the tails of it made a great bustle and were very violent.' Pelham told him that he favoured taking advantage of Argyll's credit and abilities, 'and without acting offensively let in others'.[34] By 'others' Pelham meant the other Scottish peers and their followers, whether from families which had been connected with the old pre-Union

Squadrone or not. Whether what Pelham attempted to practise in London ever became accepted in Scotland is another matter; but it was true that session gowns, sheriffdoms, other Crown legal appointments, and places amongst the sixteen representative peers were awarded on a broader basis. 'Though I have great regard for his grace and think him the most able, and willing to serve there as any in Scotland,' Pelham explained to Hardwicke in 1753, 'yet I do not think it necessary always to have his *fiat* in the disposition of offices.'[35]

Later, when Pelham turned his attentions to financial reform, he began to build up his own network of adherents in the subordinate boards of the Treasury at Edinburgh, though again, their effectiveness was open to doubt. After 1751 he secretly corresponded with Baron Edlin of the Court of Exchequer (an Englishman) on Scottish affairs. In the same year he appointed another Englishman, Corbyn Morris, as Secretary of the Scottish Board of Customs, for the express purpose of collecting information on the Scottish revenue. David Bruce, surveyor of the forfeited estates for the Barons of the Exchequer, was privately employed by Pelham as a spy, and Robert Dundas, son of the Lord President and former Solicitor General under Tweeddale, corresponded with Pelham on the problems of the Scottish revenue.[36]

Even the administrative officers of the Crown in Scotland were detached from Argyll's influence. Lord Justice Clerk Tinwald had a long history of attachment to Argyll's interest, but after his appointment to office he made great efforts to be all things to all factions, especially the English. He continued his association with Argyll and Milton to a certain extent, but in addition began to correspond with Pelham, Newcastle, Hardwicke, and the Dundas family. Lord Advocate Grant also had an Argathelian past, but quarrelled with Lord Milton in 1747 and drew off from his former connections, moving into a closer association with the Dundas family. Grant limited his political activity as well, confining himself to those activities which fell strictly within his competence as Lord Advocate, in which sphere he worked under the direction of Lord Chancellor Hardwicke.[37]

Only Argyll and Milton had the prestige or inclination to risk whispered insinuations of Jacobitism or collaboration. Only they were willing to try to influence government Scottish policy, rather than blindly obey it as proof of their loyalty to the Crown. They had been active in Scottish government for over twenty years, and Argyll had been a prominent Scottish politician for twice that time. As Keeper of the Great Seal he held an office formerly held by the Lord Chancellor of Scotland; as Lord Justice General he had the right to preside over the Court of Justiciary; as one of the last Extraordinary Lords of Session (none had been appointed since 1724) he had the right to sit with the Lords of Session. He was a lawyer and judge as well as the wealthiest peer in Scotland. Milton was not only Lord Justice Clerk until 1748; his new office of Keeper of the Signet was formerly part of the prerogative of the Scottish Secretary of State. Thus the two men had a considerable amount of official status even though they lacked the kind of authority possessed by an actual Lord Chancellor or an actual Secretary of State.

Argyll and Milton saw no profit in marking out the old Jacobite families for persecution, taking a cynical view of those, like a certain Provost of Montrose, who was 'so great a Whig that he calls everybody Jacobite whom he does not like'.[38] 'The Whigs on Queen Anne's death pushed matters too high chiefly to secure and maintain their interest at Court,' Lord Milton later wrote, 'whereas if they had dealt with some moderation there would not [have] been [a] first or second Rebellion.'[39] This should not be seen as any obvious kind of nationalism, as both favoured assimilation with England and harboured visions of a completed Union. Sir John Sinclair, for instance, recorded that Argyll actively promoted 'a resemblance or identity of language' between Scotland and England, in the conviction that Scots would eventually die away.[40] The two men did not oppose the implications of the Union, but they did oppose crude political repression. Instead they favoured gradual change and economic improvement, which led to their involvement in the foundation of the British Linen Company, in plans for a commission to civilise the Highlands, and in proposals for the improvement of the city of Edinburgh. 'GOD, taking Pity upon us, raised up these two eminent Patriots, in Defence of their Country,' the parish minister of Saltoun recalled at Lord Milton's funeral.[41] God may have played a part in the process, but Pelham's willingness to use the Argathelians gave them their opening and allowed them to use their influence to forward eventual assimilation rather than immediate incorporation as an object of government policy.

Argyll and Milton received great credit for their vision from many Scots at the end of the century, but in their own lifetimes they faced much obloquy and abuse from the south. The most dangerous attack on them came in 1752, when the administration finally introduced its bill to annex the highland forfeited estates to the Crown. The origins of the bill went back to 1747, when Lord Milton, with the help of some other judges, began to draw up a scheme for the acquisition of large tracts of the Highlands by the Crown. At Hardwicke's insistence, well-known anti-Argyll figures such as Lord Arniston and the Earl of Findlater were included in the deliberations, but even so, there were many delays. The major stumbling block seemed to be the Treasury's reluctance to assume reponsibility for the debts burdening the estates forfeited to the Crown after 1745; indeed, some of the coolness between Milton and Tinwald and Grant may have stemmed from the legal officers' support of the Treasury. Finally, however, Pelham, Hardwicke and Grant drew up a bill which embodied a less ambitious version of Milton's plan; the commissioners of the estates would not be paid, there would be no further purchases of estates, and fewer forfeited estates would be annexed than were initially proposed.[42]

Other problems awaited the project after its introduction in Parliament. Pelham and Grant got it through the Commons unscathed, although the opposition vociferously denounced it as a Scotch job which would reward the Scots for rebellion. Worse was still to come. The Duke of Bedford had recently been forced from office by Newcastle and was eager for revenge; the Duke of Cumberland remained a bitter foe of Milton and Argyll and was seeking a means of striking at them: Cumberland, through Horace Walpole, arranged the conveyance of information supplied by his Scottish connections which intimated that Argyll was protecting Jacobites who held government offices in Scotland.[43] Bedford dramatically repeated these charges in a speech he made against the annexation bill in the House of Lords, and demanded an investigation. This assault caused considerable consternation to the supporters of the government. Argyll gave a subdued reply to Bedford which Walpole described as weak and disappointing; the knowledge that Bedford was clearly speaking for Cumberland, Argyll wrote to Milton, prevented him from too vehement a reply 'that I might have been engaged in an altercation with one too much above me'.[44] Newcastle, by seeming to accept the truth of the charges, gave them greater credibility, but Hardwicke succeeded in pushing the bill through the Lords and into law. Cumberland, determined to strike, then gave a copy of his information to his father, who demanded that Pelham conduct an investigation. The accusations, however, were wildly inaccurate; the list of suspected Jacobites, for example, was headed by Lord Milton's name. The King departed on a summer visit to Hanover with Newcastle in tow as attendant Secretary of State. By the time he returned, Pelham had assembled an impressive report which absolved Argyll of all guilt in the affair. The only permanent harm done was the cancellation of a journey to London by Milton to discuss the administration of the annexed estates with the ministers.[45]

Pelham had stood by Argyll and the principle of caution and compromise above all else. He was exploring ways of extending the authority of the ministry in Scotland, but at the same time he would not allow Argyll or the Scots in general to be marked out and abused. It was not so much that he and Argyll were allies as that they were agreed they could 'do business' with one another; so Argyll was given the opportunity to represent Scottish interests while his Scots aristocratic rivals stumbled against one another in their rush to be more English than the English themselves. He had become an elder statesman who could indulge in the luxury of threatening retirement if he was not appreciated sufficiently.[46] Pelham's death in 1754 and the attempt by the Duke of Newcastle to take his brother's place upset this arrangement and created another period of uncertainty.

The English Ministers and the Duke of Argyll, 1754 — 1760

The death of Henry Pelham arguably marked the end of the era of absolute Whig supremacy in British politics under the Hanoverians. The relatively coherent political group which Walpole had created and Pelham had preserved began to disintegrate; extra-parliamentary opinion began to assume greater importance; Britain entered a new series of wars with France for dominance in world trade; and the pace of social and economic change at home began to quicken. These shifts and adjustments were reflected in the unstable political situation which prevailed at Westminster for the next fifteen years. Political groups were nebulous and just as dependent on the personalities of their leaders as the issues on which they agreed. An entire generation of important and talented Whig politicians followed Pelham to their graves in the period, causing further disruption at a time when personal leadership was so important in politics. The career of the elder Pitt — brilliant, sporadic, inconsistent, and unreasonable — expressed the possibilities and problems inherent in the age. The old party talismans were gone; Whig and Tory were almost meaningless labels; court and country only slightly more meaningful; the new words were trade, commerce and empire — an Englishman's liberties and the rights of the King.

Of course these very general trends only became apparent in later years. At the time of Pelham's death his brother, the Duke of Newcastle, was faced with the task of reconstructing the ministry after the death of its most important member. Despite the betting at White's on Pall Mall over which Member of the House of Commons would take the Treasury ('Fox against the field'), Newcastle persuaded the King to allow him to assume Pelham's place at the Treasury. For thirty years he had been one of the Secretaries of State under Walpole and Pelham; and his personality has been vividly described in countless works on eighteenth-century British history: 'Upon the whole, he was a compound of most human weaknesses, but untainted with any vice or crime,' was Lord Chesterfield's judgement. The modern historian with the closest and most complete knowledge of Newcastle the man, Sir Lewis Namier, wrote perhaps the most interesting assessment since Chesterfield:

> With an abundant substratum of intelligence and common sense, he looked a fool, and with an inexhaustible fund of warm human kindness and sincere goodwill, he acquired a reputation for dishonesty.[47]

He was a good minister but a dead loss as a leader; his consuming fear of responsibility and neurotic need for approval made him a bad First Minister. He would not hold the place for long.

Newcastle's relations with Argyll had never been cordial. After the abolition of the appointment of a Scottish Secretary of State in 1725 much Scottish business came into Newcastle's department, where he jealously asserted his position against the sly operations of Ilay. There is evidence of friction between Ilay and Newcastle under Walpole in the 1730s: Lord Hervey's memoirs record that Queen Caroline scolded Newcastle for intriguing against Ilay 'to do disagreeable things to him and make it impossible for him to carry on the King's business in Scotland'.[48] Newcastle continued to distrust Argyll after Walpole's fall, disapproving of his return to London in 1745, cooperating with Cumberland in the period immediately after the rebellion, and in 1752 even pressing within the ministry for action against Argyll, arguing 'that if the duke of Argyle was suffered to do wrong, it would fall upon you [Pelham], or me'.[49] As he wrote when he received news of Argyll's death, he felt that the Scottish duke

> was entirely directed by, or subordinate to, highland influence, and that . . . he always retained that principle which obliged him to have recourse to and depend in some measure upon great highland families who had been declared enemies to the government.[50]

Somehow Argyll was not a true Whig in Newcastle's eyes; that is, an English Whig. Newcastle had no first-hand experience or knowledge of Scotland and was particularly dependent on the anglophile Scots M.P.s and peers in London for information, many of whom were eager to add to his convictions that Argyll was working against the aims of the ministry in Scotland.

We have seen that Pelham believed that he could continue to employ Argyll and at the same time broaden the foundation of government in Scotland to include other political interests as well. Newcastle believed, however, that his brother had indulged the Scottish duke too much; that the 'highland interest' he believed to exist was still entrenched in Scotland. During Pelham's last illness, Newcastle and the Earl of Hardwicke successfully blocked the second of Argyll's attempts to obtain the Lord Presidency of the Court of Session for Charles Erskine, the then Lord Justice Clerk. They secured the place for Robert Craigie, former Lord Advocate under Tweeddale, largely because of his reputation for political independence.[51] Newcastle also personally persuaded General Humphrey Bland, who had served with Cumberland during the rebellion, to take up the appointment of Commander in Chief of the Forces in Scotland.[52]

Yet Newcastle could take little action in the general election of 1754 because he had only moved over to the Treasury just before the dissolution of Parliament. Pelham had already made the ministry's arrangements and Newcastle had time merely to make minor adjustments; Argathelians were generally successful in the larger county contests in Scotland, winning disputed elections in Ayrshire, Aberdeenshire, Lanarkshire and the county of Stirling.[53] Newcastle even gave Argyll a thousand pounds from the Secret Service fund to keep Sir Lawrence Dundas out of the Linlithgow district of burghs.[54] He did intervene in the elections for the northern highlands, however, probably out of suspicions about Argyll's 'highland power'. Letters from London ensured the defeat of Argyll's candidates in two closely run contests for the northern district of burghs and the county of Ross;[55] while Argyll obliged Newcastle by helping to secure the Inverness district of burghs for John Campbell of Calder, whose place on the Treasury Board was needed for Newcastle's friend Lord Dupplin.[56]

Argyll was not completely at ease with the new situation. He had his doubts about Newcastle, writing to Milton that he was 'much afraid that business will not go well on, merely for want of capacity and of making a due distribution of power'.[57] This referred to Newcastle's problems in finding a suitable leader of the House of Commons as much as it did to his Scottish policy, but it did soon become apparent that Argyll's position was being undermined. Newcastle consistently denied any design of supplanting Argyll while he was at the Treasury, insisting that he was merely continuing the policy of distinguishing 'between entire submission and proper regard'.[58] His concern for the well-being of the King's other friends in Scotland, however, began to be interpreted both by Argyll and his enemies as an attack on his power.

One of Newcastle's first initiatives had been an attempt to persuade the Earl of Hopetoun back into public life as an adviser on Scottish affairs. He offered him the place of King's Commissioner to the General Assembly, worth £1000 a year. Hopetoun was closely connected with the Dundas's of Arniston and other old Squadrone families, held a lucrative sinecure on the Board of Police, had the dominant political interest in Linlithgowshire, and was linked to the wealthy Duke of Queensberry through the recent marriage between his daughter and the Duke's heir. Unfortunately for Newcastle, Hopetoun refused to accept the appointment for more than one year, preferring to keep to his splendid country house near South Queensferry.[59] The very fact that Newcastle had asked Hopetoun to enter into correspondence, however, was talked around Edinburgh and weakened Argyll's influence. There is no direct evidence that this happened but it would conform to the general behaviour of the anti-Argyll faction in Edinburgh at this time, and help explain, for example, why General Bland went to such unprecedented lengths to honour Hopetoun that May: lining the High Street with troops to salute him with the colours, and ordering the Commanding Officer of Edinburgh Castle to wait upon the Earl to receive his commission. 'Ld. Hopetoun's recommendations will go a long way here,' the Earl of Granville reported to the Marquess of Tweeddale from London.[60]

Newcastle had more success with Hopetoun's nephew, Lord Deskford, eldest son of the Earl of Findlater. Deskford was a talented but mercurial man who was an old school friend of Newcastle's nephew Lord Lincoln. Taking advantage of his father's friendship with Cumberland and Hardwicke, he had been very active on the Board of Trustees after the rebellion and a keen participant in the discussions over Milton's plan for the forfeited estates. He was very ambitious and saw Argyll as an overmighty subject who stood in the way of his own public career; as the grandson of the famous Lord Chancellor Seafield he considered that he had a right to participate in the government of the country. Years later an acquaintance recalled his most serious flaw:

> Often have I seen him preside among his Inferiours with very Just advantage & was a mighty useful Country man in a variety of Respects — But as he felt with too much anguish this plain Truth That favour especially at Courts is not always the portion of Men of Skill He would too frequently Debate (agreeable to some modern Philosophy) what nothing but pride or folly will Impung —[61]

Newcastle, however, was eager to draw Deskford into his orbit, and appointed him a Commissioner of the Customs with the promise of a salary more than double that of the other Commissioners.[62] Newcastle no doubt hoped to gain a talented follower and a competent customs commissioner; Deskford and his friends in Edinburgh hoped for more than that. He told Lord Milton that Newcastle meant him to lead the Board of Customs, and others assumed that his appointment was meant to bring him to Edinburgh so he could lead the Commission for the Annexed Estates when it was formed.[63]

Later that same summer Newcastle gave William Grant his 'double gown' as Lord of Session and Justiciary, and appointed the Dean of the Faculty of Advocates, Robert Dundas, as Lord Advocate. Argyll agreed to Dundas's appointment, as he had agreed to Deskford's, but as he had once before commented, a request from Newcastle varied little from a command.[64] Dundas was just as talented and just as ambitious as Deskford, and just as jealous of Argyll's authority in Scotland. He was closely connected with Hopetoun,[65] and related by marriage to Findlater, so he was naturally in communication with Deskford. He eagerly entered into his new office, writing to the great men of the country to ask their help, entering into correspondence with Newcastle, undertaking a tour of the Highlands to familiarise himself with that part of the country, and commissioning Alexander Webster's survey of the country's population.[66]

Even the appointment of Lord Justice Clerk Tinwald's son James Erskine as a Baron of Exchequer, which Argyll favoured, had also been sought by anti-Argathelians such as the Earl of Breadalbane and Lord Dupplin. Newcastle's request that Erskine correspond with him, and Erskine's obedience, indicated a greater interest in the doings of the Scottish Exchequer from the Treasury and could not help but pull the Erskines slightly away from Argyll.[67] Lastly, Newcastle's behaviour over the by-election in the Elgin district of burghs, caused by William Grant's elevation to the bench, was a further blow to Argyll's prestige. He insisted that Andrew Mitchell, whom Argyll had successfully excluded from the Aberdeenshire seat at the general election, succeed Grant. Argyll tried to give tacit support to another candidate, but Lord Deskford's residence in the district enabled him to frustrate these efforts by getting Newcastle to write directly to Argyll in favour of Mitchell. The Scottish duke could not defy the English one.[68]

Newcastle began to construct a more ambitious network of correspondents in Scotland than those Pelham had maintained. General Bland, Commander in Chief of the Forces in Scotland, was writing frequently to the duke and to Hardwicke, complaining of the obstruction of Argyll's friends:

> I think Oliver Cromwell has set us an example of how to bring this country under the obedience of England, and which render'd the People happy ... and if some more of his rules were followed by the English Ministry in what relates to this country it would produce the desired effect.[69]

Deskford, Dundas and the new Lord President were also all writing letters south, sometimes to Newcastle but more often to Newcastle's chief lieutenant on the Board of Treasury, Lord Dupplin. Dupplin had been educated in England, and sat in Parliament for Cambridge, but his father, the eighth Earl of Kinnoul, held extensive estates in the Tay valley near Perth. He was a fussy and long-winded man, but his ability to master detail made him a capable bureaucrat; Romney Sedgwick accurately described his personality when he wrote that Dupplin was called a fool because the word 'bore' had not yet come into usage.[70] His letters to Scotland gave credence to the rumours of a new 'Scotch ministry', particularly when he wrote in terms similar to an April 1755 letter to Dundas, which spoke of Newcastle's regard for 'his particular friends', and claimed that Newcastle would 'always distinguish them from others with whom it may be proper and adviseable for him to act in order to carry on the King's service'.[71]

Yet throughout 1754 Newcastle was assuring Argyll that there was no intention of excluding him from Scottish affairs. He and Argyll corresponded throughout the summer while the latter was in Scotland; Newcastle informed him of

Deskford's appointment, and consulted him on each of the several vacancies which occurred on the bench at that time, as well as discussing Dundas's appointment as Lord Advocate, and the affair of Andrew Mitchell's return for the Elgin district of burghs. Newcastle seemed genuinely appreciative of Argyll's accommodating stance in regard to Mitchell's election, as well as his responses to Newcastle's other proposals. Argyll made no complaints, constantly agreed, and even referred to 'my scheme of keeping peace amoung the Kings friends in Scotland' when approving two judicial appointments in the interest of the Duke of Queensberry and the Marquess of Tweeddale.[72] On one point only did he not meekly defer. Newcastle several times referred to enforcement of the law, probably reflecting the influence of the information General Bland was sending south; that revenue laws and the legislation passed after the rebellion were not being enforced, and that the will of the government was otherwise being ignored. 'Your Grace hints at many other defects in the execution of the Laws besides that of the Window Tax,' Argyll wrote, 'you'll forgive me to say I really don't know them, . . . the Laws in general have never been so well executed as at present.'[73] Thus an element of friction remained, despite the superficial harmony.

Argyll arrived back in London at the end of November to find a situation of extreme political confusion. The prospect of a conflict with France in North America loomed ahead while the House of Commons reeled along without leadership or direction — 'a rope of sand', in one member's words.[74] Newcastle was attempting to dominate the entire ministry, with Hardwicke and Dupplin as lieutenants, and ciphers everywhere else. Argyll at first wished Newcastle well, 'for I don't love his enemies', but by Christmas began to be convinced that Newcastle really was planning to erect a new Scottish ministry, though Newcastle himself continued to deny such a project.[75] His response was to become more closely connected with Henry Fox, who had come to a form of agreement with Newcastle in late November but who was still far from satisfied with the treatment he had received. Like Pitt, they resolved to cause as much difficulty as they could for Newcastle in Parliament, in order that they might be better appreciated by the duke.

Pitt and Fox wrecked the ministry's plans for the parliamentary session by constantly harassing and humiliating the man Newcastle had made leader of the House, Sir Thomas Robinson. Argyll made his own contribution to the shambles. He helped bring about the introduction of a bill for a renewal of the Scottish linen bounty, although Newcastle had made it clear that he wished the affair delayed for another year, giving Fox and Pitt the opportunity to criticise the ministry for the delay (see below, p. 70), and Argyll's friends in the House of Commons also supported Fox in opposition to Newcastle over the Mitchell election petition, which took the ministry over a month to carry.[76] But perhaps the most embarrassing incident which resulted from Argyll's dissatisfaction concerned the introduction of a bill to extend the period whereby Sheriffs-depute in Scotland held office at the King's pleasure rather than for life. A clause in the 1747 Act abolishing heritable jurisdictions had set a period of seven years, which Hardwicke and Lord President Glendoick wished to extend to another fifteen years because of their conviction that the Sheriffs would become political agents of the aristocracy if they served for life. The bill also marked the debut of Robert Dundas as a speaker in the House of Commons; but the attention of the House was drawn, not to Dundas, but to another young Scottish M.P., Gilbert Elliot. Elliot, at that time connected with Argyll, gave a brilliant speech opposing the measure on the grounds that it was contrary to true Whig principles.[77] Although the bill passed, the period of extension granted was only seven years, and the debate had been so embarrassing that the government dropped its other Scottish legislation for the session. 'This shows the Duke of Argyll and Duke of Newcastle are at variance,' Lord Marchmont wrote to one of his friends in Scotland.[78]

Newcastle was inclined to agree. 'I saw last year the consequence of having the Duke of Argyll my declared enemy,' he wrote to Hardwicke in October 1755, 'which left me in reality only three [Scottish] friends that I could absolutely depend upon, viz. the Advocate, one Colville, and Mitchell at Brussels. My Lord Duke went all round the compass to hurt me.'[79] The English duke's response was to protest, yet again, that he planned no measures against Argyll and that Argyll's anger was misplaced, but in Edinburgh a very different situation prevailed. Gilbert Elliot described the state of affairs in Scotland in a letter to Lord Bute written in August 1755:

> In this country things proceed much as they have done for some time. Lord Deskford, Lord Advocate, Hopetoun and etc. are supposed to be most in confidence, those who look for favours, or dread being blighted with Jacobitism apply there. The little hangers on of that knot trumpet everywhere their great power, and every letter from a Dupplin, Ch[ancell]or, D[uke] of N[ewcas]tle, are talked all over the town. The Trustees, the Commission for the Forfeited Estates, the General Assembly, the nomination of Sheriffs, Judges and etc. are the great objects of attention. I suppose in the election of Magistrates for this town [Edinburgh], in the filling up some little offices named by some of these boards, and in bestowing Crown presentations, some of these operations will appear.[80]

When the parliament adjourned in the spring of 1755, Argyll felt that Newcastle's protest of innocence had 'arisen more from the precarious circumstances of the present connections than reflection or friendship'.[81] However, he could take comfort in the fact that some of his old rivals were more jealous of Deskford and Dundas than they were of himself. The Marquess of Tweeddale, for example, had held aloof from the new party; Argyll endeavoured to improve on this while he was in London by supporting Tweeddale's follower Thomas Hay when his nomination to the Court of Session was challenged, and by helping Tweeddale secure a place on the Board of Police for his brother Lord George Hay.[82] The Earl of Marchmont, with Argyll's friend the Earl of Home challenging his control of Berwickshire, took advantage of the friction in Edinburgh by making an attempt to insinuate himself with the duke and Lord Milton. Marchmont was convinced that he would have a much better chance of obtaining places for his friends and safeguarding his county interest by an alliance with Argyll, on the grounds that 'there is no trust to be put in the Duke of Newcastle.'[83]

There is also some evidence to suggest that an approach was made to Argyll in the summer of 1755, by Gilbert Elliot, on behalf of the new faction forming around William Pitt and those attached to the young Prince of Wales. Elliot was well placed to make such an approach, as Argyll had secured his election to parliament in 1754; and he had become friendly with Argyll's nephew the Earl of Bute, who was becoming increasingly influential in the household of the young Prince at Leicester House. Uncle and nephew were not on the closest of terms but their family relationship provided some basis for a connection. One of Elliot's letters at least hints at such an attachment:

> The thoughts of gaining P[it]t I own pleases me beyond measure, . . . For my own part, I can see but one distress that can befall me in my little political capacity — were our great Man [Argyll], to persevere in a connection not less disagreeable to me than it is to you, — but this I think can scarcely happen, or if it should, the circumstances may probably make it easy for me to act a right part, without incurring the imputation of ingratitude —[84]

It was certainly true, in any case, that the Leicester House group were claiming that Argyll would join them when they took up opposition in October 1755, before Argyll reached an accommodation with the ministry through Fox.[85]

Newcastle, very aware of the danger of losing Argyll, was increasingly apprehensive about the upcoming session of parliament, particularly as the issue of the Hessian subsidies already looked as if it would give the opposition a ready focal point on which to concentrate their efforts. The King was also changing his attitude toward Argyll, seeing in him a potential means of influencing the newly emergent Lord Bute. As a result, more regard was paid to Argyll's recommendations for offices, and more important still, the 'King's friends' in Scotland were instructed to demonstrate their willingness to cooperate with Argyll. In the middle of June, for example, the commissions for four new members of the Board of Trustees arrived in Edinburgh, and of the four Newcastle originally intended to appoint, only the Lord Advocate was actually named; two of the other three were identified with Argyll, whereas none had originally been intended.[86] A month later Newcastle informed Lord Advocate Dundas that his recommendation for a sinecure could not be honoured, as Argyll pressed his own nominee so strongly 'that it would be breaking with him to give it any recommendation but his own'.[87]

The most striking development of all was Lord Dupplin's letters to Deskford and Dundas at the end of July, written on instructions from Newcastle, asking each of them to wait upon Argyll when he arrived in Edinburgh and to show him all possible regard while he was in Scotland. As Dupplin wrote Deskford:

> In the distribution of offices in Scotland the Duke of Newcastle has showed and is determined to show an impartial regard to merit and the friends of the government. Whatever jealousies (well or ill founded) there may have been in former times, they cannot now subsist in the minds of any man. At the same time I think that the Duke of Argyll from his rank, his property, his abilities, his experience in business and his extensive connections must and will always claim a great degree of regard and attention, from any minister with whom he acts, and I know it is the Duke of Newcastle's wish to give it him. Though it might be an error in policy to carry on the

affairs of Scotland entirely *by* one hand yet to carry on the business of government *with* the Duke of Argyll will in my poor opinion be wise, prudent, and necessary. I do not know whether I explain myself clearly, but to my own comprehension the distinction is obvious. There is a great difference between entire submission and proper regard.[88]

'I have obeyed the Duke of Newcastle,' Robert Dundas wrote to Andrew Mitchell, 'though in my life I never did anything with greater reluctance for many very good reasons'; Deskford reported to Newcastle that he had 'carried civility as far as possible'.[89] But Newcastle was left in doubt as to the effect of these efforts, for unlike the previous summer, he and Argyll were not in correspondence.

In the meantime Newcastle was spending the summer months frantically trying to reconstruct his ministry before the autumn session of parliament. Finally, frustrated in his efforts to gain Pitt, he won the support of Fox by promising him office as Secretary of State. Argyll, in the fortunate position of remaining an unknown quantity while he was in Scotland, received letters from Bute, Fox and Newcastle concerning the new arrangement, each trying to gain his interest. His replies to all three survive, cautiously and deliberately phrased to suit the expectations of each correspondent. Most interesting is his letter to Bute, which comments that Fox's and Newcastle's interpretations of their agreement, as each set it out in their letters to him, were almost totally different: 'I should be apt to think this agreement will be so far from lasting that it will molder away very soon.' Fox received a friendly letter promising him support and assuring him that his former Scotch baiting had been forgotten on account of the support he had given the Scottish linen industry the year before. Newcastle, on the other hand, received two letters, the first pressing for the resolution of several Scottish affairs Newcastle had delayed, the second virtually demanding a specific appointment. Newcastle's capitulation was total. All of Argyll's demands were met.[90]

This marked the end of Deskford's and Dundas's attempts to circumvent Argyll. By the end of 1755 Robert Dundas, in financial difficulty after losing control of his recently deceased wife's fortune, was actively seeking Argyll's aid in an application for a government pension.[91] Lord Deskford was hurled into political oblivion; by the end of 1755 he was informed that he had to leave the Board of Customs because Argyll had demanded it.[92] The administrative world of Edinburgh was Argathelian once more, yet Argyll faced continued difficulties in London. Fox helped to improve relations with Cumberland, but Argyll and Newcastle still quarrelled. 'I am very willing to assist the D. of Newcastle if he will let me,' Argyll had written Milton after he had arrived in London in the autumn of 1755, but such willingness did not last long. Newcastle continued to snipe at Argyll by maintaining an unpredictable attitude towards Scottish patronage, sometimes disregarding Argyll's recommendations, at other times delaying appointments so long that Argyll interpreted his actions as obstruction.[93]

At the same time Newcastle expected Argyll to serve as a political agent. In December 1755, he enlisted Argyll's services to help obtain the office of Lord Clerk Register of Scotland for Alexander Hume Campbell, brother of the Earl of Marchmont and M.P. for Berwickshire. Hume Campbell had been approached by Newcastle with a view to augmenting the ministry's sorely pressed spokesmen in the House of Commons. An able lawyer and a talented speaker, the Scottish M.P. demanded a lucrative office in return for his active support. Newcastle refused to consider an English office but instead hit upon the idea of persuading the Marquess of Lothian to resign his office as Lord Clerk Register of Scotland in exchange for a large pension. Argyll was expected to persuade Lothian to agree to this, but was loath to do so because the office had traditionally been reserved for peers, and because he distrusted Hume Campbell and his brother, despite their recent efforts at conciliation with him. His prevarication annoyed Newcastle but could not frustrate his design, though in fact Hume Campbell proved to be of little use to the ministry after obtaining his life office, partially because of difficulties in his personal life.

The ministry's attempt to use Argyll to lure Lord Bute away from Leicester House proved to be even more provoking for all concerned. When Newcastle had written to Hardwicke in October 1755 about Argyll's terms for supporting the ministry, he noted that 'The King wants me to employ him to get *a certain Lord of his country*.'[94] Prince George had just come of age and the King was obliged to appoint a princely household for him; George naturally wished his mentor Bute to have a prominent place in that household; but the King wanted Bute's influence over the Prince reduced, if possible by persuading him to accept a pension. Newcastle and Hardwicke encouraged the King's inclination, Fox and Argyll opposed it. The King insisted, and negotiations were carried out in the summer of 1756 in a rather byzantine fashion, with Attorney General William Murray approaching Argyll, who then approached Bute. Ultimately it was not Bute who was won over to the ministry, but Argyll who began to think of cooperating with Bute and Pitt. Disappointed with Newcastle's attitude toward the problem, he left London for Scotland after the failure of the negotiations; when Bute's letter informing him of his appointment as Groom of the Stole to the Prince reached him at Inveraray, he replied that 'the common phrase of wishing joy, is too weak for what I mean.'[95]

By that time Fox had in effect resigned. The war was going badly and the trial of Admiral Byng for failing to relieve Majorca made the ministry appear worse than incompetent; consequently the next session of parliament had become a forbidding prospect for a minister. One of the government's most able spokesmen in the House of Commons, William Murray, was going to the bench as Lord Chief Justice, and Fox was fed up with Newcastle's refusal to give him real authority in the ministry; as a result he requested a less responsible office in October, leaving Newcastle without a leader of the House of Commons only weeks before the new session.

The only practicable alternative to Fox was Pitt, who had made it abundantly clear that he would not serve with Newcastle. Even the King had to face the fact that Pitt had to come into office, and if this meant that Newcastle had to go out, that price had to be paid. The Duke of Devonshire agreed to take the Treasury, and room was found in the administration for some of Pitt's followers and a few Leicester House men; Hardwicke retired, although no successor was appointed as

Lord Chancellor, Robert Henley becoming Keeper of the Great Seal. Pitt himself succeeded Fox as Secretary of State for the Southern Department. Pitt had triumphed, or so it seemed, and the political world waited expectantly, and a bit apprehensively, to see what would happen.

Argyll followed Fox. As he wrote to Fox in November 1756, just before Newcastle's resignation:

> I own freely that I have for some years been sick of business; want of favour (to say no worse) in the Closet, and the low regard, if not contempt, I met with in other places, had driven me to an inclination to retire out of the kingdom. I have indeed been much easier since you have had the Seals, and should have been more so, if you had been the Home Secretary [Secretary of State for the Northern Department].[96]

Newcastle's departure caused Argyll little sorrow, but when he returned to London he at first kept his distance from the new minister, waiting upon Newcastle at his levees and siding with Fox in a dispute with Pitt over a parliamentary by-election.[97] In the meantime the King attempted, in early December, to delegate Scottish affairs to the Secretary of State for the Northern Department, the Earl of Holderness, who wrote to the Lord Justice Clerk to that effect; but within weeks it became apparent that the King's wishes could not be carried out. Holderness's letter is little more than an historical curiosity.[98]

As Pitt became more enamoured of the idea of raising highland troops for the war effort, so Argyll began to become influential in the ministry and in the cabinet. Argyll's nephew Bute was in alliance with Pitt, and thus served as another link with the new minister, reversing the situation of the previous summer. A month after Holderness's letter the Lord Justice Clerk received a letter from another correspondent which informed him that 'the man of the Library is at present in more power with regard to our country than ever I knew him'; shortly afterwards Lord Marchmont wrote that 'there is no doubt but the Duke of Argyle should be applied to directly from Scotland, as he has more to say now than ever, and an application directly to him will be most effectual'.[99] Pitt was preoccupied with the war and his effort to win it. He needed troops; and with his political background, he could hardly call for the employment of mercenaries. Argyll, with Fox and Cumberland as intermediaries, offered the perfect solution: highland regiments. In return Argyll was allowed to dispose of the officers' commissions as he saw fit. By March 1757, helped by a highland famine, two entire regiments had been recruited: 'some of the John Bulls cannot believe that such a body of men could be raised in so short a space,' Argyll's secretary reported to Lord Milton.[100]

Treasury affairs, on the other hand, were not in Pitt's department and did not interest him; they were left to the Duke of Devonshire. Devonshire's Chancellor of the Exchequer, Henry Legge, appears to have been on good terms with Argyll, who had once mentioned him to Fox as a suitable First Lord of the Treasury. This connection probably explains Argyll's increased influence at the Treasury, which consulted him on new measures of taxation for Scotland, and on a large number of Scottish customs appointments which were made in February 1757.[101]

The King, encouraged by Cumberland, sacked Pitt in March 1757. Argyll does not seem to have been dismayed by this development, for he expected Fox to replace Pitt: 'Here is a new ministry again,' he wrote Milton, 'I wish they may be able to stand it, for I am now not only perfectly well with Mr. Fox, who must be a minister, but with the Duke of Cumberland . . . in this new sunshine everything will be easy, as long as the public fair weather lasts.'[102] He eagerly set out to aid Fox, even serving as his ally's agent in an unsuccessful attempt to persuade Gilbert Elliot to remain at the Board of Admiralty if Fox formed a ministry.[103] It was around this time that Fox made his remark 'that the Duke of Newcastle should be Minister for England, the Duke of Bedford for Ireland, and the Duke of Argyll for Scotland, professedly and independently'.[104] Perhaps the knowledge that Fox favoured such an organisation of the ministry fuelled Argyll's desire to help bring him back into prominence; James Grenville wrote Lord Bute, then endeavouring to bring Newcastle and Pitt together, that

> the Duke of Argyll is propagating with all possible industry that matters are entirely settled between Fox and Newcastle. The whole Fox party the same thing. Lord Barrington vows to me nothing is more false, and that to his knowledge the reverse was true this morning.[105]

Thus when it became clear that Newcastle and Leicester House (with Pitt) would form the ministry, and exclude Fox, Argyll naturally became pessimistic about his own position, informing Milton on 11 June that 'Scotland will in all probability be directed by Lord Bute, you will be surprised to hear that he has not been near me these six weeks.'[106]

Bute's lack of attention can no doubt be explained by his wish to bring about a very different kind of ministry to the one envisaged by Argyll, but the duke's fears proved unjustified, for the new coalition ministry led by Pitt and Newcastle generally adopted the *modus vivendi* of early 1756 as its method of handling Scottish affairs. Argyll was allowed to recommend for most customs and other minor appointments while, at Newcastle's insistence, more substantial Scottish places were distributed on a wider basis. The great task of waging war and raising the money to pay for it pushed Scottish affairs to the background, with the single notable exception of military recruitment in that country. In this sphere Scotland became very important to the war effort, furnishing twenty-six new regiments from a population of only one and a quarter million over the course of the war, not to mention English regiments sent to Scotland to recruit up to strength.[107] In addition, the press act was implemented on a national basis every year from 1757 until 1759, and the navy allowed considerable leeway in pressing men from the east coast ports.[108] The Scottish courts, in an excess of British patriotic zeal, refused to act as a curb on the military's activities.[109] The principal political beneficiary of this development was Argyll, despite his opposition to the worst of the abuses which resulted; his virtual control of the large number of military commissions that were given to Scotmen in these years greatly extended his political influence in Scotland.[110]

Although the direction of domestic affairs was largely left to Newcastle during the coalition ministry, the duke had little chance to establish a Scottish policy. He certainly never attempted to use Lord Mansfield as a Scottish minister, an historical myth which originated in Lord Campbell's *Lives of the Chief Justices of England*.[111] Argyll's importance in helping to raise Scottish troops put him beyond Newcastle's capacity to cause damage. Even the King had been won over by this time, mostly by Argyll's aid to his beloved army. 'It is very well known,' Newcastle remarked in 1760, 'what additional credit the Duke of Argyll has gained for these last two or three years in the closet.'[112] The English duke's statement was supported by an incident which took place in the summer of 1760, when Newcastle hesitated over the Duke of Atholl's proposal to allow his nephew John Murray, son of the famous Jacobite Lord George Murray, to stand for the county of Perth in the general election. Argyll went straight to the King and obtained his consent without waiting for Newcastle, an action that would have been unthinkable before the war.[113] Nor did Argyll have to fear Cumberland, who had retired from public life after the uproar that followed his signature of the Convention of Klosterseven in 1757, which neutralised Hanover in the continental war, causing the King to repudiate it and Cumberland together.

Newcastle was always ready to complain about Argyll, but never to take action against him. The Earl of Marchmont rightly dismissed his talk against Argyll after 1757 as 'the mere talkative gratification of silly anger that would go no further'; Newcastle himself admitted that he was '*seemingly*' on good terms with Argyll, 'having let him dispose of almost all the places in Scotland'.[114] As Dr. Ferguson has commented, during the coalition ministry 'Argyll was stuck with the ministry and they with him.'[115] The King, Bute, and Pitt saw no reason to antagonise the Scottish duke, so Newcastle was unable to carry his jealousy any further. And in a sense Argyll and Newcastle were fellow spirits; Britain was engaged in a worldwide war while Argyll and Newcastle, creatures of habit and their Walpolean education, continued the old game. When it came time for Newcastle to begin shaping the government plan for the 1761 election, although Robert Dundas sent him information, it was Argyll who had the final word on the arrangements for Scotland.[116]

3

The Duke of Argyll and the Duke of Newcastle:

four case studies in mid-eighteenth-century administration in Scotland, 1754-1760

THE political differences between the Duke of Argyll and the Duke of Newcastle after the death of Pelham were basically concerned with the nature of Scotland's relationship with the national government. Newcastle, like Pelham before him, saw his task in terms of incorporating Scottish affairs into the structure of national government at London; this meant eliminating, in fact as well as in theory, any Scottish minister or Secretary of State at London. He wanted to complete the Union. He felt that 'Scotland ought to be treated as part of the United Kingdom under the same constitution, and governed by the same laws in most material points',[1] but he felt that Scots were not obeying the laws; and that as long as there was a minister, a 'viceroy', or anyone else standing between the King's ministers and the Scots there was little chance of enforcing the law in Scotland as it was enforced in England. One can point to numerous inconsistencies between this stated belief and Newcastle's actual actions, notably his behaviour after the 1745 rebellion and during the Scots application for a militia in 1760, but this behaviour reflected Newcastle's fear of the Jacobite threat rather than any feeling of hostility toward Scotland. His hostility was reserved for those Scots, like Argyll or Lord Bute, who prevented him from interfering in Scottish affairs.

The importance of Robert Dundas and Lord Deskford in 1754/55 was that they openly attempted to present themselves as servants of Newcastle himself, not of any Scottish rival to Argyll. This fact may help to explain the hostility felt towards them by the Marquess of Tweeddale and the Earl of Marchmont, who at the end of the day banded together with Argyll to restrain them, or in Deskford's case, to bring him down. Both of them aspired, or had aspired, to replace Argyll, not to dispense with the position he held. Deskford and Dundas were genuinely different: a point well illustrated by General Bland's letter of introduction for Dundas when he first went up to Parliament:

> Neither the Favours, nor Frowns of the great Men in this Country, can byas him from telling the Truth, or sway him from pursuing the true interest of great Britain; and as he owes his promotion strictly to your Grace, and not to any Cabal or Faction here, he will adhere strictly to your measures, knowing the interest of Scotland to be inseparable from that of England: And who ever goes about to divide them, he looks upon as an Enemy to great Britain and our Happy Constitution.[2]

It was this idea of 'bringing Scotland within the workings of the constitution', to use Henry Cockburn's later phrase, that the small coterie of aristocrats who supported Dundas and Deskford wanted to implement under Newcastle's patronage. As we have seen, their chance proved to be short-lived, but it did prove to be a harbinger of things to come. To appreciate the challenge to Argyll, and its failure, we must make a detailed study of the actual operation of government in Edinburgh and London from 1754 to 1760, for administration reflected the shifting political fortunes of Newcastle and Argyll at Westminster.

Legal Patronage and Legal Appointments, 1754-1760

Politics and the Law were almost inseparable in eighteenth-century Edinburgh. If they were more intertwined in Scotland than in most societies, perhaps it was because of the executive vacuum which existed in Scottish government. On a simpler level, there was much legal patronage to be had and much political influence was exerted at London to secure it. Scottish judges were particularly political in contrast with other societies, not only in their decisions but by their participation in the electoral system. Judges were county freeholders; they served on government commissions; and as Sheriffs-depute they sometimes acted as very forceful representatives of the Crown. This aspect of the Scottish judiciary was of course alien to the English tradition and easily shocked English sensibilities. The best way to combat the trend would have been the restoration of the Scottish Privy Council in Edinburgh and the provision of increased powers for the Justices of the Peace at the local level; but this positive approach was not likely to occur to eighteenth-century ministers; instead, the English government began to attempt to appoint judges who would avoid political activity. This did nothing to solve the problem of the lack of executive government in Scotland, but it did increase the stature of the Scottish bench.

By some trick of fate there were more legal vacancies in Scotland during the Newcastle ministry (excluding the first appointment of Scottish Sheriff-deputes in 1747) than there had been in all the time that had elapsed since the 1745 rebellion: there were seven vacancies on the Court of Session in 1754-55 compared with five from 1745 to 1754. This phenomenon presented Newcastle and Hardwicke with a unique opportunity to transform the Scottish bench. Tables IV-VI have been drawn up with a view to illustrate just how far the First Minister and the Lord Chancellor took advantage of this opportunity.

Certainly Newcastle and Hardwicke did not have a favourable view of the Scottish bench in 1754. They had heard accusations of Jacobitism in the judiciary, and of obstruction and neglect. Another of General Bland's strongly phrased letters reinforced this impression, when he delivered the following assessment after the death of a prominent Scots judge in 1754:

> All the Cabals and disorders in this Country, have been owing to the Disunion of the Judges, who instead of looking up to your Grace and the rest of His Majesty's English Ministers, have

E

Paid their Court to the great Men here who recommended them to their Employments, and
enter'd into the Private Piques and disagreements of those their supposed Patrons, and thereby
neglected the King's and the Publick Business shamefully. I beg Pardon for making use of this
Expression, but as I have been an Eye Witness of the Facts, I cannot avoid telling the Truth.
Some of these Judges are still on the Bench, who from a Piece of popular Vanity, call themselves
Patriots, and too often oppose the Court Measures Right, or Wrong, . . .[3]

Bland argued instead for Judges and a Lord Advocate who were directly
connected to the Crown; and at least partially because of his influence Lord
Chancellor Hardwicke obtained the appointment of Robert Craigie as Lord
President of the Court of Session two months before Pelham's death in 1754.
Bland was probably also influential in the appointment of Robert Dundas, son of
Craigie's predecessor, as Lord Advocate the following summer.

Neither man had any doubt about the reason for his appointment, particularly
in regard to the highlands and 'highland influence'. Craigie's first letter to
Hardwicke after his appointment assured the Chancellor of his zeal for any
endeavour to subvert the 'barbarity' of the highlands, and Robert Dundas's first
action after taking office as Lord Advocate was to embark on a highland tour 'as
that country is now so much the object of the attention of His Majesty's servants in
England'.[4] William Grant had been promoted to the Courts of Session and
Justiciary expressly for the purpose of making a vacancy for Dundas, for though
Grant had ceased to become an intimate of Argyll, Hardwicke had been
disappointed with his performance in Crown business.[5] A similar, though less
successful, appointment was that of Robert Pringle as a Lord of Session in the
summer of 1754. Pringle had been recommended to the Duke of Newcastle by the
Duke of Queensberry, enthusiastically supported by the Earls of Hopetoun and
Findlater. Newcastle wrote to Lord Deskford that he hoped Pringle's
appointment would convince 'the King's friends in Scotland' (i.e. Hopetoun,
Deskford and Dundas) 'that the greatest regard is had to their recommendations'.[6]

Argyll's response was interesting. Newcastle was consulting him on all
appointments, though it was made clear to him that others were to be humoured as
well: he made no objections to Pringle's appointment, and Grant's appointment
and that of James Erskine as a Baron of Exchequer were entirely agreeable to him.
He did attempt to complicate matters by encouraging the Marquess of Tweeddale
to recommend Thomas Hay, formerly deputy Keeper of the Signet during
Tweeddale's time as Secretary of State, for several of the vacancies which arose, a
development which was not happily viewed by the Hopetoun circle. It was surely
one of their group who, referring to himself as a 'true Whig', forwarded
information to Lord Chancellor Hardwicke which charged that Hay was a
Jacobite sympathiser.[7] 'I suspect that some of your old friends who are mine too
would almost rather see this fail,' Hay wrote Tweeddale, 'and indeed everything
you should carry on with the Duke's [Argyll's] concurrence, rather than see you in
any friendship, so deep is old animosity on both sides.'[8] The affair drove
Tweeddale closer to Argyll after Hay was cleared of any wrongdoing by reports
from the Lord President and the Lord Justice Clerk, for Newcastle and the King

had almost withdrawn Hay's appointment without making an investigation, while Argyll continued to defend him.

At the same time Argyll was directly striking at the Earl of Findlater by complicating the appointment of a new Sheriff-depute for the county of Banff in succession to Robert Pringle. Lord Findlater confidently expected Newcastle to appoint George Cockburn of Ormiston, son of the famous Lothian improver, maintaining that 'a Lothian whig of a family that never varied from the Protestant interest since the reformation is much fitter to execute the laws in this county than any northern highlander.'[9] However, Findlater was not identified with the county's M.P., James Duff (later Lord Fife); and by strange coincidence, Duff began to press Newcastle to appoint David Ross, younger, of Inverchassly, a lawyer from Tain closely associated with Argyll.[10] Newcastle wished to oblige a new Member of Parliament and wished to make a friendly gesture to Argyll after forcing him to support the return of Andrew Mitchell to Parliament, so Ross was eventually appointed. 'It will be an act of friendship to the Duke,' Lord Dupplin wrote to Lord Deskford (Findlater's son), 'not to put him upon refusing this recommendation of Lord Braco [Duff's father], who is a man of some consequence, and it will be at the same time a civility to the Duke of Argyll.' Findlater was furious; despite efforts at mediation by Hopetoun, Hardwicke, Andrew Mitchell, Dundas, and even Deskford, he refused to attend Parliament in his capacity as a Representative Peer.[11] Thus Argyll retrieved some of his prestige in the north of Scotland while at the same time spreading dissension amongst his rivals.

The Scottish legal appointments that passed the seals in 1754, then, while showing an active determination on the part of Newcastle and Hardwicke to support their friends in Scotland, also show that they did not intend to mark out Argyll entirely, but to carry him along in support of their policy by granting enough of his requests to keep him satisfied. The difference from Pelham's former policy appears to be only one of degree. Their failure to communicate their intentions to their supporters in Scotland is illustrated by the accusations against Hay and the behaviour of Findlater. Argyll, on the other hand, superficially accepted the emphasis of the English ministers while attempting to persuade others to press recommendations in competition to those of Newcastle's friends.

The next summer there were again a large number of legal vacancies to be filled, but this time Argyll's relationship with the ministry was more uncertain. Argyll had a candidate of his own for a gown: Lord Milton's son-in-law John Grant; but Newcastle, unlike the previous summer, was not corresponding with him, and his recommendation was neglected. Those appointments which were made, however, were much more apolitical. The two new Crown lawyers, for example, were to some extent bipartisan appointments. It had been evident for some time that something had to be done about the Solicitors General who were meant to carry on the Crown's legal business in the absence of the Lord Advocate. In 1746 the place had been divided in two, partially because of the volume of legal business facing the Crown, and partially to reconcile a conflict of interest between the Duke of Argyll and the Duke of Cumberland. Unfortunately neither Argyll's choice

Table V: *Legal Appointments, 1754*

date	office	appointee	interest	predecessor
Feb.	Lord President	R. Craigie of Glendoick	Hardwicke	R. Dundas of Arniston
Feb.	Lord of Session	A. Boswell of Auchinleck	Argyll	D. Erskine, Lord Dun
July	Baron of Exchequer	James Erskine	Lord Tinwald, Argyll, Lord Dupplin	James Kennedy
July	Sheriff-depute of Perth	John Swinton	Earl of Breadalbane	James Erskine
Aug.	Lord of Session & Justiciary	W. Grant of Prestongrange	Argyll, Newcastle, Hardwicke	P. Grant, Lord Elchies
Aug.	Lord Advocate	Robert Dundas	Newcastle, Hardwicke	William Grant
Oct.	Lord of Session	R. Pringle of Edgefield	Duke of Queensberry, Hopetoun & Findlater	A. Leslie, Earl of Leven
Oct.	Lord of Session	T. Hay of Huntington	Marquess of Tweeddale, Argyll	J. Pringle, Lord Haining
Dec.	Sheriff-depute of Banff	David Ross	James Duff, Argyll	Robert Pringle

(Alexander Home) nor Cumberland's (Patrick Haldane) proved to be especially proficient in performing his business; by 1755 both were weary after a very long term in a demanding office. Haldane was an elderly man, and had made enemies through his efforts to get into Parliament in 1754, so he was pensioned off at £400 a year. Home, a friend of Lord Milton's, was given a place as one of the principal clerks of Session.[12] Hardwicke, Lord Advocate Dundas, Lord Milton and Argyll all agreed that a single Solicitor was best, and that of the lawyers at the Scots Bar only Andrew Pringle or Thomas Miller were able enough to serve well. Pringle was Sheriff-depute of the county of Selkirk, where he had made great efforts on Argyll's behalf in the last election. Miller was also a Sheriff-depute, and had connections with the merchant community of Glasgow as well, serving as town clerk there. By all accounts both were extremely competent lawyers; as Argyll remarked to Milton when he recommended them, 'its very singular that the Advocate has also mentioned the same two gentlemen as worthy of being taken notice of.'[13] Pringle was made Solicitor while Miller, more closely identified with Dundas, succeeded Patrick Haldane as Solicitor for the Board of Excise.

The summer's judicial appointments were made independent of Dundas's or Argyll's recommendations, in favour of those who had been unsuccessfully recommended for the vacancies of the summer before. Andrew Macdowal was Lord Prestongrange's (William Grant's) brother-in-law and author of a noted work on Scottish law which Chancellor Hardwicke has greatly admired.[14] Patrick Wedderburn, father of the future Lord Chancellor Loughborough, was recommended by the Earl of Morton on account of his long service at the bar. Though Morton was connected with Newcastle and Hardwicke, he was not on close terms with Hopetoun, Deskford and Dundas.[15] George Carre was the nominee of the imperious Earl of Marchmont, then playing a double game by insinuating himself with both Newcastle and Argyll. Carre's appointment, by provoking a row between Marchmont and Lord Advocate Dundas over a sinecure office held by Carre, acquired some political significance because it temporarily forced Marchmont closer to the Argathelian camp.[16]

In contrast with the summer appointments, those made in October 1755 very much reflect the influence of Argyll as a result of the promotion of his ally Henry Fox. Though Robert Ord, the Northumbrian appointed Chief Baron of the Court of Exchequer, had an English patron in the Earl of Carlisle, from Argyll's point of view he was certainly preferable to the other candidates, Alexander Hume Campbell and Baron Smith of the English Court of Exchequer. Ord would later prove to be a reliable friend of Lord Milton and Baron Maule once he had arrived in Edinburgh.[17] The second appointment to the Court of Exchequer was directly in Argyll's interest because he had demanded it as part of the price for his support of the ministry over the coming session of Parliament. There had been many rival recommendations by the Lord President, General Bland, and the Earl of Findlater; but Argyll's recommendation of John Grant was phrased in such a way that it was made mandatory. 'Your Grace's favouring me in this instance,' he wrote to Newcastle, 'will be of one peculiar advantage to me, that it will help to silence those who have endeavoured to make the world believe that your Grace has not that regard for me, which you are so kind to say you have.'[18] Lastly, Argyll was able to frustrate Robert Dundas's attempt to secure the Sheriffdom of Selkirk for his uncle. Dundas had gone to extraordinary lengths to obtain the place, even accusing the county's Member of Parliament, Gilbert Elliot, of recommending a man with Jacobite sympathies; but Newcastle needed Argyll and Elliot and appointed accordingly, though his prevarication over the appointment confirmed Elliot's desire to join the opposition.[19]

The following summer Newcastle was so preoccupied with the war, and attempts to strengthen his ministry, that he made no appointment to the vacancy which had arisen in the Court of Session after the sudden death of Patrick Wedderburn, although the Earls of Findlater and Hopetoun had a candidate for the gown.[20] Newcastle kept them happy by finally giving the Sheriffdom of Banff to George Cockburn, as James Duff had followed Pitt into opposition during the preceding session of Parliament. David Ross was given the Stewartry of Kirkcudbright, probably for fear of offending Argyll by not making some provision for him, but a man with an estate in Ross would hardly find Kirkcudbright a convenient county in which to serve.[21] Argyll's influence appears to have strengthened after Newcastle left the ministry in November; the following month he persuaded the Earl of Holderness to appoint Lord Milton's nephew, George Brown of Coalstoun, to the session place that Newcastle had left vacant and to give Brown's Sheriffdom in Angus to John Campbell of Stonefield, who was connected with both the Duke and Lord Bute.[22]

The change in emphasis in the distribution of legal patronage between 1754 and 1756 is quite striking. Whereas at first the ministry's appointments could easily have been interpreted as an attack on Argyll's influence, the following summer a more even-handed approach was adopted, succeeded by a series of appointments in the autumn which were obviously made in Argyll's interest. The high hopes held by the 'King's friends' in 1754 had proved cruelly disappointing. In contrast, there were much fewer vacancies in the Scottish legal profession during the coalition ministry, and when it did come time for a redistribution of places in 1759 and 1760, the emphasis was on the Crown's legal officers rather than the bench itself.

Table VI: *Legal Appointments, 1755-1756*

date	office	appointee	interest	predecessor
May 1755	Solicitor General	Andrew Pringle	R. Dundas, Argyll	P. Haldane, A. Home
May	Solicitor to the Excise	Thomas Miller	R. Dundas	Patrick Haldane
July	Lord of Session	A. Macdowal of Bankton	Hardwicke	T. Hay, Lord Huntington
July	Lord of Session	P. Wedderburn of Chesterhall	Earl of Morton	H. Dalrymple, Lord Drummore

Table VI: *Legal Appointments, 1755-1756, cont.*

July	Lord of Justiciary	Lord Auchinleck	Argyll	H. Dalrymple, Lord Drummore
July	Lord of Session	G. Carre of Nisbet	Earl of Marchmont	J. Sinclair, Lord Murkle
Oct.	Chief Baron of Exchequer	Robert Ord	Earl of Carlisle, Hardwicke	John Idle
Oct.	Baron of Exchequer	John Grant	Argyll, Lord Milton	Sir John Clerk
Oct.	Sheriff-depute of Selkirk	William Scott	Gilbert Elliot, Argyll	Andrew Pringle
Oct.	Sheriff-depute of Berwickshire	Sir John Stewart	Earl of Marchmont, Hume Campbell	George Carre
Oct. 1756	Stewart-depute of Kirkcudbright	David Ross	Findlater	Thomas Miller
Oct.	Sheriff-depute of Banff	George Cockburn	Findlater	David Ross
Dec.	Lord of Session	G. Brown of Coalstoun	Argyll, Lord Milton	P. Wedderburn, Lord Chesterhall
Dec.	Sheriff-depute of Angus	John Campbell	Argyll, Lord Milton	George Brown

It was during the war years of the coalition ministry that Lord Advocate Dundas and Lord Milton became great rivals in Edinburgh legal circles, each with a following of his own. As John Dalrymple of Cranstoun, a young lawyer with some ties to Milton, described it:

Even Lord Milton & Lord Advocate have their writers (i.e. attorneys), bailies, ministers (i.e. clergymen), pretenders to pretensions, who set them against one another[.] They detest one another on account of hostilitys which each would very willingly commit, but which in many cases neither the one nor the other ever thought of. As for them the Seeing it diverts one. They have both very good mutton & claret, & perhaps if hostilitys were to cease, even we, who are quite indifferent as to the fate of the warriors, might suffer in the unhospitable harmony.[23]

Each promised his followers legal advancement through his influence with the ministers in London; Dundas primarily through his connection with Newcastle, Milton primarily through his connection with Argyll.

When the ministry did have to make an appointment in 1759, after the death of Lord Kilkerran, it was very surprising that the vacant 'double gown' of Session and Justiciary did not go to Dundas. He was the natural candidate; for many Lord Advocates, like his predecessor Grant, retired to the bench when a double gown became available. It was obvious that Dundas had his eye on the Lord President's chair that his father had formerly occupied, but there was nothing to stop him from taking a double gown to gain experience on the bench before the place of Lord President became available. Probably he did not want Andrew Pringle to become Lord Advocate because of his Argathelian connections; he wrote to Hardwicke to declare that he thought Pringle should have the gowns for reasons which he would tell him when he came up to attend Parliament.[24] It is likely that these reasons not only referred to Pringle's bad health but to his political connections as well. An additional benefit, from Dundas's point of view, was that Pringle's promotion would open the way for Thomas Miller to become Solicitor General and next in line for promotion to Lord Advocate, and Dundas had always had some hopes of gaining Miller.[25]

The next year Dundas, having given yet another demonstration of his loyalty to Newcastle and Hardwicke by speaking against the Scottish Militia bill in the House of Commons, was rewarded with the Lord Presidency of the Court of Session. By this single appointment alone the court was to be transformed into an efficient legal machine and the Dundas family interest established for good and all. Dundas probably thought that he had arranged his succession as well, with Miller replacing him as Lord Advocate and one of his depute Advocates, James Montgomery, becoming Solicitor General; but Argyll and Lord Milton were to show that they were capable of at least limiting Dundas's plans.

For one thing, Lord Milton had been attempting to gain Miller as well; he and Argyll offered him their interest both when the Solicitor's place came up and when Dundas retired to the bench, and Argyll was closely connected with the same Glasgow merchant set that employed Miller as their town clerk. 'I am sure I wish I saw more of our friends upon the list of promotions,' Charles Townshend wrote to Milton in March 1760, 'but doubtless you yourselves know the advocate best, and my fears may be groundless' — which would seem to imply that Milton did not consider Miller attached to Dundas.[26] Furthermore, they were able to obtain a new division of the Solicitor's place to gratify one of their friends, and make Miller promise one of his depute's places to another of their connections. These developments occurred despite strenuous efforts by Miller and Montgomery to

Table VII: *Legal Appointments, May 1759-March 1760*

date	office	appointee	interest	predecessor
May 1759	Lord of Session & Justiciary	A. Pringle of Alemore	R. Dundas, Argyll	Sir James Fergusson, Lord Kilkerran
May	Solicitor General	Thomas Miller	R. Dundas, Lord Milton	Andrew Pringle
May	Solicitor to the Excise	John Dalrymple	Argyll, Lord Milton, Charles Yorke	Thomas Miller
March 1760	Lord President	R. Dundas of Arniston	Newcastle, Hardwicke	R. Craigie of Glendoick
March	Lord Advocate	Thomas Miller	R. Dundas, Lord Milton	Robert Dundas
March	joint Solicitor General	James Montgomery	R. Dundas	Thomas Miller
March	joint Solicitor General	Francis Garden	Argyll, Lord Milton	Thomas Miller
March	depute Lord Advocate	John Dalrymple	Argyll, Lord Milton	James Montgomery
March	Sheriff-depute of Peebles	Alexander Murray	R. Dundas	James Montgomery
March	Sheriff-depute of Kincardine	James Burnett	Argyll, Lord Milton	Francis Garden

avoid such a settlement which included a journey to London in person to argue their case for a single Solicitor. Nothing they could do, however, could prevent Argyll from getting Francis Garden, the future Lord Gardenstone, made joint Solicitor General with Montgomery.[27]

Dundas and Milton between them made the recommendations for all the Scots legal appointments made in 1759 and 1760, while Newcastle and Argyll negotiated the actual dispensation of the offices in London. The figure of Thomas Miller, however, illustrates that it was the politicians who sought out the good lawyers, not talented lawyers the politicians. Similarly, Robert Dundas was a talented lawyer and an able man; and even Argyll seems to have been willing to attempt some sort of working relationship with him, even if Milton and he were rivals.[28] The politics behind the appointment of a man like Miller as Lord Advocate were very different from the politics behind the appointment of Dundas, for all his talents, in 1754. Dundas was a politician while Miller was sought by politicians. There was much significance in the difference.

A close study of the legal patronage of the 1750s indicates that while the Scottish judiciary and legal officers of the Crown were undoubtedly political, the fears expressed by General Bland, Newcastle and Hardwicke in 1754 seem to have been grossly exaggerated. They were undoubtedly successful in reducing the Duke of Argyll's influence on the legal profession, with the exception of the semi-administrative Court of Exchequer, but they really did very little to change the bench and the legal community in Scotland aside from encouraging Robert Dundas. Lord President Glendoick proved to be a broken reed, bankrupt in leadership, organisation and energy: if Dundas shone after his appointment to the President's chair, part of his lustre was the result of the contrast with his predecessor's dullness.[29] Likewise Hardwicke's appointment of Macdowal, according to Ramsay of Ochtertyre, could hardly be considered a step towards the revitalisation of the judiciary;[30] and Robert Pringle, appointed by the interest of Hopetoun and Findlater, left even less of a mark on the bench. It was Dundas alone, as Lord Advocate and Lord President, who forwarded the Whig ideal of expanding English influence.

The Scottish Revenue, 1754-1760

The Duke of Newcastle was determined to be a good First Lord of the Treasury, perhaps because there had been so many critics of his decision to succeed his brother in that department. Part of this effort was his attempt to strike a tough stance on corruption and the use of influence in the revenue. He refused to reinstate political appointees dismissed by subordinate boards of the Treasury, for example; and there is even some evidence that Newcastle was thinking of broader reforms such as the purchase of the Isle of Man, a notorious smugglers' den, at that time owned by the Duke of Atholl.[31] Another part of Newcastle's effort to make a mark at the Treasury was an attempted reformation of the Scottish revenue.

The new First Lord was convinced that the charges made by the Duke of

Bedford in the House of Lords in 1752 were true; that tax evasion was endemic in Scotland and that many of the officers employed by the revenue were not only corrupt, but Jacobite sympathisers as well. Lord Dupplin set out Newcastle's criticisms in a letter to Lord Deskford in September 1754:

> Certain it is that from the notorious abuses in the collection of the revenue and the manifest unwillingness that is shown by the people in general in that part of the Kingdom to pay any taxes at all, great prejudice has arisen to the Crown, dishonour to the country, and discouragement to the honest merchant ... The shifts that have been made to avoid the payment of some taxes has indeed brought reproach upon our country and justly created much dissatisfaction in this part of the United Kingdom. [32]

There had been charges against Scottish revenue officers brought before the English Board of Excise and the Treasury that winter, after a Scottish excise official named James Mackay had claimed that Jacobites still remained in the service. The investigation which resulted ended in the dismissal of several officers, though some of Argyll's friends doubted the validity of the charges. Gwyn Vaughan, a Commissioner of Excise in England, had heard Mackay's charges but remained unconvinced:

> Calling Jacobite has made many a man's fortune in my time, there are certainly such in Scotland, and in England, but I believe many a man is called so, that with as much justice be called son of a whore; ...[33]

In addition, Newcastle had noted that the window tax which had been instituted in 1747 was still not being collected in Scotland, and demanded a series of accounts for it and other taxes from the Court of Exchequer in Edinburgh. The Barons of Exchequer, three of whom were very elderly, and another inexperienced, did not respond in a satisfactory manner, convincing Newcastle that abuses in the subordinate branches of the Treasury in Scotland were indeed widespread and that the Barons of Exchequer were failing in their duty to supervise the collection of the revenue there.[34]

The first action Newcastle took to attempt to improve the administration of the revenue was to persuade Lord Deskford to agree to accept an appointment to the Board of Customs in Edinburgh, where a place had just fallen vacant by the death of Lord Ross. Deskford, 'naturally indefatigable', as Gilbert Elliot called him, accepted after receiving assurances that his salary would be augmented to suit his social station.[35] He was interested in government, intensely ambitious, and saw the Board of Customs as a short stop on the road to better things, telling one of his new colleagues 'that he wanted to go to school to learn the business of the country, and would be obliged to me for a lesson, but that he did not think he would be long with us'.[36] Newcastle saw Deskford rather as an active commissioner who would take charge of the revenue: 'His Grace means that you should put yourself at the head of reforming the abuses in the revenue and that the English Commissioners should co-operate with you,' Lord Dupplin wrote to him when he arrived in Edinburgh to take his seat at the Board in November 1754.[37]

Yet it was these very English Commissioners who isolated Deskford and rendered most of his efforts ineffectual. The Secretary of the Board of Customs, Corbyn Morris, was one of Pelham's appointees, and though he proved to be Deskford's closest ally, they were not always on the best of terms. Three of the other four Commissioners were English. Mansfeldt Cardonnel and Alexander LeGrand were former Customs Collectors who had been promoted to the board but whose zeal for the collection of the revenue had been tempered, perhaps, by long residence in Scotland; Cardonnel was a leading citizen of Musselburgh and LeGrand a prominent landowner in Leith.[38] Both were made of less assertive stuff than Deskford. The third English Commissioner was very different. Joseph Tudor had been Morris's predecessor as Secretary to the Board, and appears to have had some connection with Hardwicke; indeed Newcastle especially recommended him to Deskford before the latter took up his place, Dupplin writing that Tudor was 'the most proper person in whom your Lordship may place a confidence'.[39]

But Deskford and Tudor were just not meant to like one another. Perhaps Tudor was jealous of the new Commissioner, perhaps Deskford was too forward too soon. In any event, by December 1754 General Bland had written to Newcastle charging that Tudor was organising a 'plot' to exclude Deskford from customs affairs.[40] 'Mr. Tudor has good parts, but rude manners,' Deskford later concluded, 'the truth is Mr. Tudor is naturally insolent and overbearing, and it will not be easy to get him perfectly to correct that.'[41] By December of 1754 Deskford was writing to Dupplin about the 'most uncomfortable situation the Duke of Newcastle has put me into', explaining:

> everything at the Board of Customs is by the opinion the other commissioners have of his interest at London intirely under Mr. Tudors direction, and Mr. Tudor in order to establish his credit with London makes it his business to forward every unpopular measure here, and at the same time, to sacrifice the interest of the revenue, and every thing else to the Duke of Argile, whose interest at London he expects will help him to a place at the Board there — ... There is no possibility of doing with Mr. Tudor without absolutely submitting to him, which I will not continue to do, as I do not think his sistem either honourable for me or for the Duke of Newcastle's interest.[42]

As a result the conduct of business at the Board of Customs that winter consisted of one row after another over various affairs that came before the board, with Deskford writing a steady stream of letters to Lord Dupplin and Newcastle in an attempt to get the Treasury to reverse the board's decisions, while Argyll defended them in London. In December, for example, Deskford wrote to Dupplin that the Collector of Customs at Dundee, 'little better than an Idiot, absolutely unfit for the management of almost any port', was being protected by Commissioners Tudor and Campbell because they said they had no authority to take action against him. 'But I know well and so does everybody,' wrote Deskford,

> that the real reason of protecting this man and keeping that Port in the most scandalous confusion is that some years ago the Collectors wife was whore to the Duke or Argile and therefore let the revenue suffer as much as you please, this man must not suffer ——[43]

There were additional difficulties over the appointment of one Inspector General by the board and the proposed dismissal of another. The Treasury had ordered that an actual account of exports and imports be drawn up for the use of the Board of Trade. Tudor and Deskford's Scottish colleague, Colin Campbell, decided to use this order as an opportunity to provide for Campbell's son Archibald by asking the Treasury to appoint him Inspector of Exports and Imports at £100 per annum. Deskford denounced the plan as a job as soon as he heard of it, and in protest refused to sign the request to the Treasury; instead he wrote a protest to Newcastle urging that the request be refused. This Newcastle did not do, but he did have the Treasury Board rebuke their subordinates for submitting a report which did not have the signatures of all the Commissioners.[44] The other office, this one Inspector General of the Customs in Scotland, provided a similar but lengthier cause of conflict. There were two Inspectors, one of whom, Walter Grosett, had been one of Lord Milton's close aides during the rebellion in 1745; afterwards he had been promoted from Collector of Customs at Alloa to Inspector General as a reward for his service. His health had suffered, however, and he went abroad to Italy to convalesce; by the time Deskford arrived at the board, Grosett had been in Italy for six years. Deskford supported a move in 1754 by LeGrand to dismiss Grosett, but Argyll in London was able to persuade the Lords of the Treasury to continue to direct the Scottish Board to grant him a leave of absence.[45]

Two other quarrels developed during the spring of 1755. One was over Tudor's proposal that the board purchase the Duke of Argyll's yacht for use as a customs cutter: 'as good a battle as I have seen at our Board,' Colin Campbell declared to Lord Milton.[46] The other concerned George Douglas, Justice of the Peace and Sheriff Substitute at Fort William; and spy for General Bland. This became a test of strength between the General and Argyll; Bland, supported at the board by Deskford, claiming that Douglas was indispensable; Argyll and Colin Campbell supporting the Collector of Customs at Fort William, who wanted Douglas charged as a smuggler. Bland claimed that the object 'was to make me appear little and insignificant in this Country'; and certainly, Argyll did make Douglas's dismissal as Sheriff Substitute one of his conditions for continuing to support Newcastle in October 1755.[47]

In all of these conflicts Newcastle and Dupplin were willing to make gestures of support for Deskford, but they could not or would not give him influence at that board. Dupplin even attempted to reconcile Tudor and Deskford in the summer of 1755, when Deskford was instructed to pay his respects to Argyll during his annual visit to Edinburgh. This was done without much conviction on either side. When Fox became Secretary of State it was evident Deskford would have to go, for Argyll hated him: the Duke harboured more hostility toward the young aristocrat than he ever did toward Dundas. Newcastle was made to promise that Deskford would retire.[48] Once this promise had been obtained, Colin Campbell was instructed to renew his previous practice of sending up lists of all vacancies and presentments in the customs to Argyll — a strong indication that Argyll had regained his influence over Treasury appointments.[49]

Efforts were at first made to arrange an exchange of offices between Deskford and the holder of one of the Scottish sinecure offices; but Lord George Hay (a Gentleman of Police), George Dundas (Master of Works) and Lord Belhaven (General of the non-existent Scottish Mint) all declined the honour. Deskford had agreed to go, but wanted a pension or a place as compensation for his trouble; Argyll just wanted Deskford to go. After April 1756 Deskford ceased to attend the board at all and retired to his father's estates in the northeast. Newcastle and Argyll continued to quarrel over the provision to be made for him until the end of the reign; Deskford in the meantime continued to draw his salary as a member of the board.[50] The death of Colin Campbell in 1758, and the illness of LeGrand, forced Newcastle to appoint another commissioner to keep the board quorate. Significantly, that new commissioner was an Argathelian ex-Lord Provost of Edinburgh, Robert Montgomery, who assumed Campbell's former task of keeping Milton and Argyll informed of customs vacancies and presentments.[51]

Newcastle's efforts to transform the other principal subordinate boards of the Treasury in Scotland, the Barons of Exchequer and the Commissioners of Excise, were almost as unsuccessful if not as unfortunate politically as his meddling in customs affairs. The Board of Excise appears to have been inactive in the years following the rebellion; at least the Earl of Morton's letter recommending Patrick Wedderburn, the board's secretary, for a Court of Session gown claimed that he had time to maintain a practice at the Bar in addition to his secretary's duties, 'as there is not a great deal of Business at that board'.[52] Newcastle probably saw this as his chance to improve the Excise in the same manner as he was trying to improve the Customs, so when Wedderburn was appointed to the Session in the summer of 1755, the English Board of Excise was asked to recommend a proper person to become secretary of the Scottish board 'and also to succeed as a Commissioner of that revenue in case of a vacancy'. They responded by recommending Richard Dauber, Collector of Excise at Norwich.[53] The appointment of Thomas Miller to replace the elderly Patrick Haldane as the board's solicitor can also be interpreted as an attempt to increase the activity of the board.

Dauber went to Scotland and became acquainted with Deskford during Deskford's second, and last, year of attendance at the Board of Customs;[54] unfortunately, his subsequent career at the Board of Excise in many ways resembled Deskford's at the Customs. A vacancy did not occur on the board until 1758, when Newcastle did honour his promise and make Dauber a Commissioner; but, like Deskford, he was left isolated and unsupported. The secretary who succeeded Dauber in 1758 was an English placeman with Argathelian connections who soon became an absentee.[55] Argyll was able to circumvent Newcastle's intentions to appoint an English lawyer to succeed Miller when the latter became Solicitor General;[56] and the other four Commissioners were not sympathetic to Dauber's activities. The other English Commissioner at the board, Rhodes, was an invalid; two of the three Scots, Udney and Cochrane, had been appointed as a result of political agreements, and generally they followed the lead of the third Scot at the board, George Drummond.[57] Like Tudor and Deskford, Drummond and Dauber clashed over the direction of policy. Drummond appealed to Argyll, and Dauber appealed to Newcastle; by 1758 there was little action Newcastle could take to support his erstwhile *protégé*. Argyll complained vehemently of English interference in the activities of the Scottish board: 'I told him [Newcastle] that Sir R. Walpole never did it, and that it would ruin the Revenue,' Argyll wrote Milton. 'I would have you acquaint George Drummond of this that he may act accordingly.'[58] After a few attempts to begin a direct correspondence with the Treasury, Dauber gave up; by 1761 he was unsuccessfully trying to secure a place in England. Newcastle's departure from the Treasury in 1762 completed his isolation.[59]

Newcastle's efforts to improve the Court of Exchequer were more successful, and less obnoxious to the Argathelians. In March 1754, when Newcastle arrived at the Treasury, only one of the five Barons, Argyll's ex-secretary and close friend John Maule, was regularly attending his duties as a judge and an administrator. The Chief Baron, with the unfortunate but appropriate surname of Idle, spent most of his time on his estate in Yorkshire. Barons Kennedy, Clerk and Edlin were all elderly and infirm; Kennedy had not attended since 1752, Clerk could attend only when his presence was absolutely necessary for a quorum, and Edlin, though healthy, was already seventy-four years of age. The failure of the Barons to account properly for their administration of the forfeited estates and the unsatisfactory state of the accounts they forwarded to London on the Scottish revenue had helped prompt Newcastle's determination to 'clean up' the Treasury's subordinate boards. However, it was so obvious that the problem at the Court of Exchequer was not corruption, but ancient and unhealthy Barons, that even Newcastle had to admit that this was the case.[60]

The appointment of three new Barons in 1754 and 1755 provided a remedy for Exchequer troubles in Scotland. Newcastle started by appointing the Lord Justice Clerk's son, James Erskine, in 1754, although this appointment owed just as much to a desire to mollify the Lord Justice Clerk after refusing him the Lord Presidency of the Court of Session a second time as it did to a conscious attempt to reform the revenue. Chief Baron Idle and Sir John Clerk did not die until the summer of 1755, by which time Newcastle had to appoint Argyll's man John Grant to succeed Clerk on account of the political situation. He had planned to replace Clerk with an Englishman and so alter the composition of the Barons from three Scots and two Englishmen to three Englishmen and two Scots.[61] His plans for the Chief Baron's place also went awry; one of the Barons of the English Court of Exchequer had been intended but the man refused to go; and the eventual appointee, Robert Ord, was different from his predecessor not only in his attention to his duties but in his willingness to consort with Maule and Lord Milton.[62] Politics aside, the simple fact that four of the five Barons were now middle-aged and healthy contributed much to the dispatch of Scottish Exchequer business for the rest of the reign.[63]

Significantly, the issue which had originally aroused Newcastle's displeasure — payment of the window tax in Scotland — was resolved in consultation with the Argathelians. William Grant (the new Lord Prestongrange and former Lord Advocate), Lord Advocate Dundas, and Argyll met in October 1754 to concert the heads of a bill to improve the collection of the tax; Dundas wrote up their deliberations and introduced a bill during the following session of Parliament. The collection of the tax was taken out of the hands of the Commissioners of Supply and a new service created, with two Surveyors General in Edinburgh and twenty local Surveyors in the counties; within a year the tax was being paid and collection was proceeding relatively smoothly. This solution also provided twenty new patronage places for the Barons of Exchequer to distribute; and John Maule and Lord Milton were not slow to take advantage of them. Thus the only constructive reform of the Scottish revenue during Newcastle's time at the Treasury was carried through with Argathelian help, and aided Argathelian interests by creating additional Scottish offices.[64]

Newcastle's intervention in Treasury administration in Scotland had been largely superficial and always sporadic. He most closely followed his declared policy of reform in consultation with Scottish interests in his dealings with the Court of Exchequer, more by accident than by design, best symbolised by the fact that Chief Baron Ord, an excellent appointment, was a second choice personally unknown to Newcastle. The Duke's well-meaning intervention in Customs and Excise affairs, through his appointments of Deskford and Dauber, was ill-considered, ill-supported, and probably harmful to the service. He set up agents in Scotland whose activities caused conflict and friction with their colleagues, and then by not supporting them he ensured that this disruption ultimately served no purpose. Part of this friction resulted from sending Englishmen to take Scottish revenue posts, which raised formidable difficulties of adjustment for the officers, and caused predictable resentment amongst Scots who coveted the places for themselves. Lord Milton put it as any politician would: 'These English Gentlemen taken all together have not the least Influence in Scotland, so that bestowing Scots Offices upon them is really curtailing the means by which the King and his Servants ought to preserve their Influence in Scotland.'[65] Argyll could use stronger language: 'one would think their heads were turned and that they want to try to what degree of ill humour they can bring the people of Scotland to.'[66] Bound up with the impatience of Argyll and Milton at the waste of potentially political appointments was the issue of national distinction which would come to preoccupy so many Scots by the end of the Seven Years War.

The Linen Bounty, 1754–1756

The renewal of the government bounty for the export of coarse linen cloth in 1756, a measure particularly tailored to the needs of the Scottish economy, offers a perfect vehicle for a detailed study of parliamentary relations between Newcastle and Argyll during the Newcastle ministry. Newcastle had to face a demand for government action from what might easily be called a Scottish lobby; Argyll was given and used an opportunity to demonstrate his ability to harass Newcastle; but in the process he did much to forward Scotland's economic interests by means of his very considerable political skill. It was also an episode which excellently illustrates the relationship between parliamentary action and extra-parliamentary pressure from Scotland.

Briefly, the background to the measure began in 1751, when Parliament renewed the previous bounty on the export of coarse linen cloth for the limited period of three years because of pressure from English fancy linen manufacturers, who resented the bounty as a piece of favouritism towards the Irish and Scottish manufacturers of coarse linen. When it came time to consider another renewal of the bounty, in the 1753/54 session of Parliament, Pelham refused to bring in a bill, offering instead the sop of a block grant of £3000 a year for seven years to the Board of Trustees to encourage the linen industry in the highlands alone. Argyll's attempts to intercede had resulted only in a promise to reconsider the affair after the general election of 1754; as a result, the linen bounty lapsed in the summer of 1754.[67]

The following autumn Argyll began to seek English support in Parliament for a new bounty, opting for a broad alliance of interests which would even include as allies the Lancashire and Cheshire manufacturers, who had prevented a renewal of the old bounty. The price he paid for forming this alliance was an agreement to include a reduction of the duty on imported linen yarn in the proposed bill, although this would almost certainly entail a reduction in the price of yarn; a measure that was decidedly not in the interests of those Scots, mostly in the northeast, who made linen yarn. As A. J. Durie has pointed out, the acceptance of these terms put the interest of Scottish linen manufacturers before those of the spinners; at the time it was thought that a reduction in the duty on linen yarn would reduce English demands for Scottish yarn and so leave it to the Scots at a lower price. It was perhaps no coincidence that Argyll and Milton were involved in the British Linen Company, a major manufacturer of coarse linen cloth.[68] Since the alternative concession was an extension of the bounty to fine linen as well, it may be that self-interest played a part in the choice of the terms Argyll worked out in London.

Newcastle, not surprisingly, held no strong views on a bounty 'that does not interfere with the manufactures of this country (England)',[69] but that qualification left considerable room for retreat. Many opponents of the removal of duty on foreign yarn were City financiers with much influence at the Treasury, which may explain Newcastle's desire to delay consideration of the bounty for another year. The Scots were pressing for immediate action; Dr. Durie has estimated that between one-third and two-thirds of Scottish looms were idle in the depression which followed the end of the bounty; exports of linen cloth fell by a third and production of the principal Scottish linen cloth, Osnaburg, fell by half.[70] A contemporary source, Postlethwayt's *Universal Dictionary of Trade and Commerce*, published in 1755, claimed that 'above eight thousand weavers are quite turned adrift, many of whom are sent to our plantations, many become soldiers both in the British and Dutch service, and some are gone into other employments of various kinds at home'.[71] An alarmed Convention of Royal Burghs sent William Tod (a manager of the British Linen Company) and Andrew Cochrane (Provost of Glasgow) to London to press for action in conjunction with their Irish counterparts.[72]

Some of the politicians who sympathised with their case had political reasons for attempting to secure a bounty in the parliamentary session of 1754/55. Fox and Argyll intended to bring in a bill for a linen bounty to embarrass the administration; and although they never carried out their threat, the ministry was still forced into an awkward position when Lord Strange (one of the county M.P.s for Lancashire) moved that several papers relating to the linen bounty be laid before the House in order that members might be prepared to act on the matter early in the next session. This gave Fox a chance to show that he favoured the measure, while Charles Townshend, and Pitt in particular, took the opportunity to display their disapproval of the ministry's attitude. Pitt declared that it was a much more important question than the election affairs which had consumed much of the House's time that session; and William Beckford supported the great commoner by patriotically declaring that since the bounty had ended he found it impossible to buy British linen for his slaves in the West Indies.[73]

Predictably, Newcastle's friends in Scotland were hostile towards these machinations. Lord Deskford informed Dupplin that he was not associated with the conduct of the Convention of Royal Burghs, which had been urged on by George Drummond and Lord Milton;[74] and Newcastle's friend Andrew Mitchell found himself neglected by the Convention's representatives in London. Mitchell disapprovingly reported to Deskford that

> Schemes & plans were laid between the Deputies, of the Scots and Irish, in conjunction with those of Manchester, by which the Manchester people would certainly have been benefited, but this is not all, it was made a tool of faction to distress your friend [Newcastle] Mr. F[ox] declared himself a great friend to Linnen &c &c as did several other people, the D. of A[rgyll] was naturally at the head of this, and it was a specious thing to draw in every body from a certain quarter, nay it was carried so far that I was told by Pr[ovost] Cochrane on the Saturday before that tho' the D. of N. had desired and insisted that it should be putt off, yet it was resolved by the Association to move the house to enquire into the state of Linnen &c which Ld Strange was to do. I confess I was greatly surprised with this as I saw where it tended, it was a direct attack upon the Minister, which would have occasioned great abuse & some distress, this appeared plainly in the manner of its going off, for when the motion was made for papers and some assurances were given of its coming on early next year, Mr. Wm. Pitt after declaring himself a warm friend to Linnen, shewed some bad humour, and if I may conjecture he wants only an occasion to shew more, . . .[75]

Mitchell may have questioned the motivation of the bounty's proponents, but they did force Newcastle to give the measure his attention. Newcastle, Dupplin and James West met with the agent of the Convention of Royal Burghs, William Tod, and James Oswald, M.P. for the Dysart district of burghs, and promised to give Treasury support to an effort to obtain 'encouragement' for the linen industry in the next session of Parliament. Newcastle even wrote to the Preses of the Annual Committee of the Convention, George Drummond, Lord Provost of Edinburgh, pledging the same thing. On two points, however, he would not agree with the Scots: he rejected the favourite Glasgow measure of removing the drawback (duty) on the export of foreign linen to America, and he refused to commit himself to the Mancunian idea of removing the duty on foreign yarn.[76] Yet Argyll made the latter demand a condition of his continued support for the ministry in October 1755: 'The whole Country [Scotland],' he told Newcastle, 'will insist for relief about the Linnen, the Bounty for 15 years & taking off the duty on Yarn imported will answer the end.'[77] This Newcastle agreed to do, but he would not consider Glasgow's proposals, nor did Argyll wish to push him. Drummond and Tod prevented the Convention from instructing them on this matter when they were appointed as its agents in London for the 1755/56 parliamentary session, even though this, according to Drummond, was what the Convention 'most wished for'.[78] 'Don't leave room for throwing up different schemes about this affair,' Newcastle told Drummond when he arrived in London in December 1755:

> fix on one and keep to it, don't let us be embarrassed with the Hamburg merchants in what we are to do for you — apply for the bounty you formerly had and the taking off the duty on yarn and I will give you all the support to carry it through which you can expect from me.[79]

Lord Dupplin introduced the new bill to the Committee of the whole House. The terms of the bill, of course, were a renewal of the bounty on coarse linen cloth for a term of fifteen years, and the removal of the duty on foreign yarn. It seems as if almost everyone agreed to extend the bounty on exported coarse linen cloth — even the London merchants were apathetic. Opposition to the bill was focused on the removal of the duty on foreign yarn. English opponents were essentially the agents of London merchants who imported finished German and Russian linen, whose trade would suffer if the yarn which made their cloth came into demand in England, as this development would inevitably raise the price of their own goods. They were quick to point out that allowing foreign yarn into Britain would depress the earnings of British spinners, and thus dampen the effect of the linen industry as an employer in the Scottish highlands.[80]

The actual parliamentary opposition, as it is identified in the *Parliamentary History* or in private correspondence, can be identified with trading interests. Sir John Barnard of the City was most often mentioned as an opponent, but Alderman William Baker and Alexander Hume were other City-orientated M.P.s who opposed. Robert Nugent's opposition to the bill might indicate that some Bristol mercantile interests were involved as well. Another strong opponent was George Amyand, himself a Hamburg merchant and brother of the then under-Secretary of State, Claudius Amyand. Two of Pitt's supporters, William Beckford and Thomas Potter, were for the bounty but could not accept the removal of the duty on foreign yarn, and spoke against it. William Tod also mentioned some opposition from Yorkshire M.P.s, probably on behalf of the woollen industry, in his correspondence with Lord Milton; and the Tories opposed on the grounds that the ministry was coddling the Scots. Taken as a group, this assemblage amounted to a substantial opposition.[81]

Lord Deskford was the most important opponent of the bill in Scotland. He had been very active in setting up schools in the northeast of Scotland to teach the spinning of linen yarn and saw the bill as a betrayal of the objectives of his work.

Others from this area of the country agreed, such as Andrew Mitchell or Deskford's mother, Lady Findlater, who was in London 'roaring out' against the bill, according to Milton's son, and attempting to persuade Members of Parliament such as Sir Ludovick Grant not to vote for the measure.[82] Deskford thought that if it came to a choice, those with influence in Scotland should have favoured employment over advantage to capital; but no matter how convincing his arguments, there was nothing he could do to counter the influence of Milton and Drummond with the Convention of Royal Burghs and the Board of Trustees. Both of these institutions followed the Argyll line. Deskford believed Milton and Drummond were merely seeking commercial advantages for their British Linen Company or even a monopoly over the production of yarn in Scotland — far too black a reading of their motives, yet possibly not completely incorrect: both Drummond and Milton were perfectly capable of mixing public virtue with private profit.[83]

Deskford began his opposition when he returned to Edinburgh from the northeast in the autumn of 1755 to find that, in his absence, the Board of Trustees had voted a resolution which was to be sent down to London in favour of removing the duty on foreign yarn. He demanded another meeting to reconsider the resolution; 'I never choose meetings but when your Lordship is within reach,' the Board's secretary plaintively wrote to Lord Milton, 'but if any member desires it I fancy I must warn a meeting for the day to which the Board stands adjourned.'[84] In the time before the meeting Deskford assembled General Bland, the Lord Advocate, and the Lord President in an attempt to reverse the previous decision. This they failed to do, but they did refuse to sign the resolution, which caused Tod some embarrassment when it was forwarded to London, as the absence of their signatures encouraged 'inferences and misrepresentations'.[85]

Deskford was not stopped by this defeat, according to Tod, who wrote to Milton that he was writing letters to Members of Parliament in London 'and making all the stir he can'.[86] Unfortunately for Deskford, Dundas was converted to the yarn proposal after he arrived in London and consulted Newcastle on the subject.[87] Efforts at opposition in Scotland were more successful. A petition against the duty-free yarn was drawn up in Edinburgh and forwarded to Dundas and William Alexander (the city's M.P.), both of whom refused to accept the petition and instead assured Argyll of their support. Yet Edinburgh was not alone; Dunfermline, Paisley, and Glasgow, all centres of Scotland's fancy linen industry, also sent petitions to Parliament against removing the duty on foreign yarn.[88]

Glasgow in particular seemed to harbour opposition to the bill. This was not a sudden development; the year before, when the Convention of Royal Burghs had sent one Edinburgh delegate (Tod) and one Glasgow delegate (Andrew Cochrane) to London, there seems to have been an unspecified difference of opinion between the two, probably over Glasgow's attempts to remove the duty on the re-export of foreign linen to America.[89] Andrew Fletcher had written his father that 'MR. TOD is the only active solicitor, for our GLASGOW friends are rather laughed at in their operations, and do not speak out the language of their constituents but throw the whole burden upon THE DUKE OF ARGYLL.'[90] Whatever the cause of that disagreement, in 1756 Glasgow's petition was accompanied by instructions to employ 'solicitors and able council' to attempt to obtain an extension of the linen bounty to cover fine linen, or if that could not be obtained, to limit the new bounty on coarse linen to a level lower than before and prevent the acceptance of measures for abolishing the foreign yarn duty. Andrew Fletcher's observations on these instructions reveal a possible influence: 'that the council were directed to abuse the British Linen Company and etc. shows the activity of DESKFORD'S emissaries, and that he has not stuck at anything to make his court.' Argyll made certain that no Scottish merchant in London would implement Glasgow's instructions, dismissing Glasgow's opposition as parochial and an improper reflection on his influence after he had so publicly associated himself with the proposed bill.[91]

Argyll's political coalition worked too well for opposition to have any effect. Although Lord Dupplin's enthusiasm flagged when he was made aware of Deskford's objections, Lord Strange proved an effective floor manager, ably assisted by Alexander Hume Campbell and James Oswald on behalf of the Scots. The most important support for the bill came from the unlikely duo of William Murray and Pitt, both of whom made strong efforts in the debate which preceded the closest vote on the bill. This was an attempt by Sir John Barnard to put off consideration of the bill by the House which failed by just 16 votes. Of the Scots, only Lord John Murray and Dupplin stayed away from the final division, and both had estates in an area dependent on the spinning of linen yarn as a cottage industry.[92]

Argyll's contribution to the renewal of the linen bounty cannot be doubted, as the letter Newcastle wrote to him after its passage makes clear.[93] Though some of his decisions in regard to the measure may have been doubtful, his achievement seems more laudable in retrospect: according to Dr. Durie, the effect of removing the duty on foreign yarn was much less than had been feared.[94] Again, Lord Deskford had taken a public-spirited path, but again a fruitless one. He could not know that the approaching war would ensure that little yarn was imported until 1760, and that even after 1760 spinners were not badly affected; whereas the absence of a linen bounty had most definitely been bad for the spinners because there had been no work for them. One wonders just what sort of action the government would have taken if Argyll had not indulged in pressure politics: the most likely answer, given the general performance of government, is no action. On this reckoning Argyll the politician scores higher than Deskford the public servant.

The Commission of Annexed Estates, 1754-1760[95]

Much time had elapsed since the passage of the Highland Annexation Act of 1752 by the time the Duke of Newcastle entered the Treasury, yet a commission to administer its terms had still not been appointed. Pelham had been forced to carry out an investigation of government in Scotland; the Treasury had been preoccupied with the general election; Newcastle was absorbed in foreign policy; and Pelham's death caused even more delay while the necessary adjustments in the ministry were carried out. There was an additional problem in the Treasury's hesitancy to proceed until the nature and extent of the debts which encumbered the estates could be determined exactly. One of the Treasury Secretaries had written in 1749 about 'a confirmed opinion here among sensible & impartial men, of collusions being universally practised in those estates'[96] — an opinion which had lingered on over the years, as Bedford's attack on the Annexation Bill illustrated. Yet progress on compiling a report to Parliament on the claims was limited, and such a report was still outstanding after Pelham's death.[97] Newcastle demanded an account of the forfeited estates, including those which were destined to be sold, as soon as he became First Lord of the Treasury; but the Barons of Exchequer, since 1746 responsible for the administration of the estates, could not respond until November 1754.[98]

This failure surely influenced Newcastle in his determination to appoint a commission for the annexed estates rather than leave them in the hands of the barons. Both General Bland and the Earl of Findlater had written very critical reports of the Barons' administration to Newcastle and Hardwicke, even accusing some of the factors who had been appointed of Jacobite sympathies. A new commission became part of Newcastle's and Hardwicke's planned reformation of the administration of Scotland: the aim was 'improvement'. William Grant, for example, just raised to the bench as Lord Prestongrange and keen to gain credit with Hardwicke, wrote to the Lord Chancellor that

> I had seen with Lord Deskford in the low country his various schools for knitting and spinning, and when afterwards I saw little flocks of idle children in the highlands my heart burned with desire that they might be usefully employed, and rejoyced in the prospect of that being set about by the plan to which your Lordship had so greatly contributed.[99]

Lord Dupplin stressed the 'weighty, extensive and various' business of the future commission in a letter to Lord Deskford written about the time the Barons of Exchequer submitted their account of the estates. The commission's task would be the 'settling and civilising that country (as chalked out in the Act of Parliament by outlines only)'. This policy, he wrote, was so plainly outlined in the act 'that it seems impossible to me for anyone to mistake it', but he did specifically mention the use of low leases to encourage the growth of a 'yeomanry', and the introduction of planned villages, manufactures, and work schools to change by degrees 'the face of the whole country'. In other words, the tacksmen were to be eliminated from highland society in the hopes of developing a deferential but relatively independent peasantry on the English model. Dupplin made no mention of leases to Lowlanders or Englishmen, as Pelham had suggested in Parliament when the Annexation Act was passed, nor does this idea seem to have been put forward by anyone else at the time; even the bombastic General Bland wrote to Hardwicke of 'making the Poor People Happy'.[100] It was cultural colonisation, not the physical variety, which Newcastle, Hardwicke and their Scottish friends viewed as the task of the commission.

From an administrative standpoint Dupplin envisaged a commission which would give directions and set out general policy, while their secretary would be responsible for the execution of the commissioners' decisions and, indeed, the working of the entire apparatus below the commission level: 'His attendance and attention,' wrote Dupplin, 'must be daily, constant and continual.'[101] Thus the ministry in 1754 visualised the Commission of Annexed Estates as a group of prominent and learned men who would periodically meet to determine all questions of policy, which their energetic secretary, obviously intended to be an important man, would then implement in the most efficient manner possible. These preconceptions, unfortunately, proved to be sadly unrealistic.

The appointment of the commission itself provided the first indications of what was to follow. Argyll and Milton were identified with 'highland power and highland views', so Newcastle naturally wished to keep their influence on the commission to a minimum.[102] Lord Justice Clerk Tinwald, Hardwicke, General Bland and Lord Deskford all provided lists of proposed commissioners for Newcastle; Lord Milton was to be left out, and so was the Duke of Atholl, who had too 'much of the highlander in him in every respect and would be strenuous in keeping up the distinction between high and lowland people', in General Bland's opinion.[103] Taking these suggestions into account, Newcastle and Hardwicke agreed on a draft commission which the King was to sign in the autumn of 1754; one which was at least half English in composition and included many Scots personally connected with Newcastle. Pleased with Argyll's subservient attitude over the summer of 1754, Newcastle showed him the draft commission when he returned to London in the autumn; Argyll predictably found the composition of the commission disagreeable, telling Newcastle that it gave credit to the rumours of a new 'Scotch ministry'. The commission was delayed over the winter as Newcastle attempted to retain Argyll's support in Parliament, so that when the commission finally arrived in Edinburgh in May 1755, there were significant changes in its membership. Some who had been included before, like Edinburgh's former M.P. James Ker, were left out; others who were identified with Argyll were included, such as Gilbert Elliot, Lord Somerville, Lord Cathcart, and of course Lord Milton. These adjustments explain the large size of the commission, for more were included than were dropped, but the effect was just the same. 'You will observe,' Argyll drily noted in a letter to Milton, 'that the list of the Trustees of the Forfeitures is not a little mended'; Lord Deskford complained that 'I think the majority as the commission stands, are not as it was last winter in the first scheme.'[104] The new commissioners are listed in Table VIII, along with their record of attendance over the next five years. Even with the changes made at Argyll's request, such well-known allies of Newcastle as Hopetoun, Deskford, Dundas, Bland, the Lord President, and Andrew Mitchell were all included. On the other hand, Argyll's close friends Lord Milton and Baron Maule were commissioners, with close connections with several of the others such as George Drummond or Gilbert Elliot; yet by no means were they a majority. The most noticeable feature of the commission, however, was its size; the number was unwieldy. As Lord Marchmont guessed (see above, p. 15), the board's activities were bound to fall to a small number of activists; the question was basically whether those activists would be !ed by Lord Deskford or by Lord Milton.

This division became apparent when the commission met and considered the appointment of its officers. Most important of all, of course, would be its secretary; and various candidates had already been put forward and discussed since it had become known that Newcastle was to appoint a commission. In 1752, when Lord Deskford and Milton had met to draw up proposals for a commission for the ministry, they had agreed that William Tod, one of the mainstays of the British Linen Company, would make a good secretary;[105] yet Deskford had reported to Lord Dupplin the winter before the commission was appointed that Bland, Dundas, Lord President Glendoick 'and a great many others' objected to Tod 'as belonging entirely to my Lord Milton'.[106] The favourites were on the other side of the Edinburgh political fence. At first Robert Dundas's friend David Moncrieff, deputy Remembrancer of Exchequer, began to make interest, but he was soon superseded by Corbyn Morris, secretary of the Customs, who promised to serve without pay if he could have two English clerks to help him.[107]

Hopetoun, Bland and Dundas soon got Deskford to agree that it would be best to have an Englishman made Secretary, on the pretext that an Englishman would be non-partisan, although of course the plan was really a calculated effort to reduce Lord Milton's influence.[108] They decided that the best way to accomplish this was to solicit Newcastle to appoint an appropriate Englishman, as he and Hardwicke had vetoed Morris's pretensions because of his responsibilities at the Board of Customs. They chose Stamp Brooksbank, son and namesake of the M.P. and Director of the Bank of England. Brooksbank senior wished to find a place to launch his son in life and had in fact earlier recommended him to Newcastle for a vacancy in the Scottish Court of Exchequer.[109] Newcastle and Hardwicke were thinking of implementing Baron Edlin's plan of making a third English baron in the Court of Exchequer; Brooksbank was a lawyer, had been recommended for a baron's gown, and was a relative of Hardwicke. In short, he would make an excellent candidate to succeed Baron Clerk if he was already in Edinburgh. In May 1755 Newcastle and Hardwicke promised Brooksbank a salary of £500 Sterling and possibly hinted at an Exchequer gown as well to encourage him to make the journey north.[110]

The new commissioners first met at the end of June 1755, when a full twenty of the twenty-eight named in the commission attended, a figure never again even closely attained by the board. Its first order of business was a letter from Newcastle recommending Brooksbank as a proper secretary, which came as no surprise to 'the King's friends'; but the proposal to pay him a salary of £500 a year came as very much of a surprise, as it would have to be paid out of the commission's already limited funds, and equalled the salary of an ordinary Lord in the Court of Session. 'How would it appear in the eyes of the world if the first step we took was to give our Secretary a salary equal to those of the Judges in our supreme courts?' Hopetoun wrote to Newcastle afterwards.[111] A committee was formed to write to Newcastle on the matter, probably at the insistence of Lord Milton; Baron Edlin later wrote to Newcastle in terms which suggest that there was some conflict involved in this decision: 'I was greatly concerned at our ill timed Economy, but nothing I think could have prevented its taking place, so great is the Aversion here, as I mentioned above, to foreigners as they look on us to be.'[112] Eventually, Newcastle and Brooksbank agreed to a salary of £300 from the funds of the annexed estates, augmented by a grant of £200 per annum on the Scottish Civil List.[113]

The other notable conflict amongst the commissioners over the appointment of their officers concerned their London agent. Lord Milton, with Argyll's approval, hoped to gain the appointment of George Ross, a Scottish merchant in London, who already served the Board of Trustees and the Convention of Royal Burghs as their London agent. It only made sense, Ross argued, to centralise the London business of Scottish organisations by employing the same agent.[114] There were strong objections to Ross from other quarters, however. 'As he is a Scotchman, and in with the Argathelian faction, I don't know how far your Lordship will think him a proper person to be employed in that station,' General Bland wrote to Hardwicke, 'not from his want of abilities; but that a certain leading Duke of this country would be immediately acquainted with all the transactions of the Board, even before the English ministers.'[115] This essential disagreement manifested itself at a meeting in late July, when Gilbert Elliot proposed Ross as London agent, only to encounter point blank opposition from the Lord Advocate. Lord Deskford countered Elliot by producing a letter from James West, one of the Secretaries of the Treasury, recommending Milward Rowe, a Treasury clerk who already served as London agent for the Treasury's subordinate boards in Scotland. In this, as in the appointment of Brooksbank, the Argathelians were outmanoeuvred.

The other places were distributed with less conflict. William Alston, a follower of Lord Milton's, was made legal agent; Dundas could make no headway in an attempt to replace him because Hardwicke had been impressed by some of Alston's legal work on the forfeited estates when the Barons of Exchequer were responsible for them. Lord Prestongrange obtained the place of General Inspector for his brother Francis Grant, who had previously served in the same capacity under the Barons of Exchequer with another colleague, David Bruce, whom Argyll had favoured for the place. The clerk was an employee of the Bank of Scotland, Alexander Williamson, appointed at the behest of the Marquess of Tweeddale.[116]

Of more immediate importance were the proposals for action put forward at the commission's first meetings. It appears that Deskford, Dundas and Hopetoun dominated the early meetings of the commission, directing Lieutenant Colonel David Watson (Deputy Quartermaster General of the Forces in Scotland) to survey the estates in the commission's care, and adopting Lord Deskford's draft instructions for the factors of the annexed estates, emphasising the policy of long leases and lighter rents with a view towards creating a prosperous, independent tenantry.[117] Other than those general decisions, there was not much else for the commission to do but wait for Watson to complete his surveys and collect the rent.[118] By the time the board was able to arrive at genuine proposals for the consideration of the Treasury, political confusion and the pressure of global war had rendered its significance small. The commission, in fact, became a dead letter for the rest of the reign.[119]

   This was partly because of a shift in the political balance of Scotland just before the board submitted its first report. Newcastle needed Argyll; therefore what Argyll said and wrote re-acquired some of its former importance. Brooksbank, who was naturally identified with Deskford and Dundas, was ordered to pay his respects to Argyll along with Deskford and Dundas in the summer of 1755. When it became clear to Deskford that he was to be eased out of official Edinburgh, he instructed Brooksbank to be more friendly to Lord Milton and took him to dine at Milton House. Thereafter Brooksbank spent more and more of his time in England seeking a new place, with Argyll's encouragement and help.[120] Deskford, who had attended every meeting of the commission, left Edinburgh for good in the

Table VIII: *The Commissioners of Annexed Estates, 1755-1760.*
Attendance figures, including attendance at meetings of the standing committee.

	1755	1756	1757	1758	1759	1760
Duke of Argyll						
Earl of Marchmont	1					
Marquess of Tweeddale	3	5	2			
Earl of Hopetoun	6	2				
Earl of Findlater	1					
Earl of Morton						
Lord Deskford	14	7				
Lord Cathcart						
Lord Somerville	7	9	19	6	4	5
Lord President Glendoick	14	17	20	14	7	2
Lord Justice Clerk Tinwald	10	15	12	8	4	7
Lord Chief Baron Idle	4					
Lord Milton	5	11	23	4	4	7
Lord Prestongrange	13	9	15	6	5	1
Baron Maule	9	15	19	5	4	6
Baron Edlin						
Lord Advocate Dundas	5	1	1		3	2
Commander in Chief of the						
Forces in Scotland, General Bland	10	7				
G. Elliot, M.P.	5					
W. Alexander, M.P.	6	3	3	9	1	5
C. Hope Weir, M.P.		2	8	2	2	3
J. Oswald, M.P.	3					
A. Mitchell, M.P.						
G. Drummond	10	7	10	13	8	7

Table VIII: *The Commissioners of Annexed Estates, 1755-1760.*
Attendance figures, cont.

	1755	1756	1757	1758	1759	1760
Lieut. Col. D. Watson	4					
M. Cardonnel, Commissioner of Customs	11	13	23	13	7	8
A. LeGrand, Commissioner of Customs	6		3			
J. Tudor, Commissioner of Customs	13	13	20	12	4	
Commander in Chief of the Forces in Scotland from 5 Nov. 1756, Lord G. Beauclerk		4	10	7	2	4

Total attendance	1755-56		1757-60		1755-60	
Earl of Marchmont	1					
Marquess of Tweeddale	8		2		10	
Earl of Hopetoun	8				8	
Earl of Findlater	1					
Lord Deskford	20				20	
Lord Somerville	16		34		50	
Lord President Glendoick	31		43		74	
Lord Justice Clerk Tinwald	25		31		56	
Lord Chief Baron Idle	4				4	
Lord Milton	16		38		54	
Lord Prestongrange	22		27		49	
Baron Maule	24		29		53	
Lord Advocate	6		6		12	
General Bland	17				17	
G. Elliot	5				5	
W. Alexander	9		18		27	
C. Hope Weir	2		15		17	
J. Oswald	3				3	
G. Drummond	17		38		55	
Lieut. Col. Watson	4				4	
M. Cardonnel	24		51		75	
A. LeGrand	6		3		9	
J. Tudor	26		36		62	
Lord G. Beauclerk	4		23		27	

SOURCE: SRO, Minutes of the Annexed Estates Commissioners, E 721/1-5.

spring of 1756 and never attended again for the rest of the reign.[121] General Bland had a stroke and retired to England; Lieutenant Colonel Watson was promoted to an English post; Dundas was too busy to attend; and Hopetoun and Findlater had followed Deskford in retiring from the board. The business of the commission, in fact, fell to a small group which included Milton, Maule, the Lord President, Lord Justice Clerk Tinwald, Prestongrange, George Drummond, Lord Somerville, and Deskford's former antagonists at the Board of Customs, Tudor and Cardonnel. Argathelians predominated, although from time to time there were divisions between them, as when Prestongrange, much to Argyll's disgust, attempted to secure leases of lands which had belonged to Jacobite relations of Baron Maule.[122] Yet even this group lapsed into inactivity by 1759, for although it required only five commissioners for a quorum, several times Lord Milton was the only commissioner to appear at meetings.[123] If anything, the elimination of divisions within the commission by the refusal of Newcastle's friends to attend should have made the commission more efficient.

There was some trouble on account of hostility to the commission in London, particularly after Deskford's star had waned, and Lord Milton began to become more assertive: 'Ld. Milton seems to take more upon him in the highland commission,' Deskford wrote to Dundas in February 1756, 'Ld. Tweeddale and the President complain of Tudor's insolence — The President says that he is to have a conference with the Chief Baron in which he intends to authorise him to report to the ministers.'[124] Andrew Fletcher's 1756 letters to his father noted proposals by Milton and Lord Justice Clerk Tinwald regarding the annexed estates: 'However it may be for the good of the service,' he wrote in February, 'yet the tyde runs so high that it would be in vain to propose it at present. As THE DUKE OF CUMBERLAND seems to have the ascendancy, every scheme that lessens the merit OF THE ARMY is discouraged and ridiculed.' Again on 2 March 1756 he observed, 'had GENERAL BLAND adopted any of these schemes, and sent them up as his own, perhaps they might be favourably received, but their coming from SCOTLAND is a dead weight against them.'[125] It appears that Cumberland's dislike of the Scots, and his influence (until 1757) with the King, resulted in the neglect of the commission in 1756. Cumberland, after all, had been behind the opposition to the original annexation bill. Others evidently shared his attitude: 'I hear thoughtless people without doors talking that there is no end of favouring Scotland and squandering our money upon them,' Baron Edlin wrote to Hardwicke in January 1756.[126]

Hostility to the commission in London does not explain the commission's inactivity after 1757, when Argyll's position within the ministry improved. The answer does not seem to have lain in preoccupation with the war, although this may have reduced any interest English ministers had in the commission, but in the demands made upon the commission's resources by the surveys and accounts of the estates which they had commissioned and by the debts which encumbered the estates.[127] The problem of the debts on the estates was most important. There were more than 1700 claims, all of which had to be considered by the Court of Session, with the Lord Advocate representing the Crown, and all of which were liable to appeal before the House of Lords. This was a very expensive and time-consuming business, a monument to the extreme love of litigation which gripped the landed classes of Scotland at the time. Perhaps the most damning indictment of William Grant's tenure as Lord Advocate was his failure to make real progress on the claims; correspondingly, the brightest achievement of Robert Dundas's six-year term as Lord Advocate was his success in dealing with most of them, even neglecting his parliamentary attendance in favour of this higher priority.[128]

As long as the question of the debts was outstanding the commission could not be sure of its available funds; there had been expectations in 1752 that the income from the estates would be enough to pay off the debts certified by the courts. The realisation that the commission could not even begin to pay off t estates' debts may have contributed to demands to sell the estates in 1757.[129] Some of these demands may even have come from Scotland, where Baron Maule reported that the creditors were restless at the lack of settlement. An important project, then, was to establish the precedent of Parliament providing funds to settle the estates' debts; Maule suggested that this be attempted for the Perth estate, the largest, most valuable, and most debt-ridden, and the first estate to have all the claims against it determined by the courts.[130] In August 1757 Baron Maule and Lord Prestongrange were set up as a committee by the commission — the only others at the meeting were Milton, Tudor and Lord President Glendoick — to look into the settling of the debts on the estate of Perth; the next spring Maule was in London personally waiting upon Newcastle and Hardwicke in an attempt to get the money. Dundas, he reported to Milton, took little or no lead in the matter, and seemed 'diffident'.[131] Maule, presumably with Argyll's help, was successful in his solicitations; the next year's Act of Supply included the huge sum of £69,910.15.9¼ towards settling the debts on the Perth estates, with the disposal of the money entrusted to the Scottish Barons of Exchequer.[132] This represented a substantial injection of capital into the Scottish economy and provided the precedent required for future appeals to Parliament. It was another result of Argyll's increased power within the ministry after 1756.

Obtaining the money marked some progress by the board, but much else remained outstanding, including claims on the other estates in its care. At least these were being processed, however slowly, by the courts; five estates and parts of two others were still administered by the Barons of Exchequer pending a settlement with their Subjects Superior, or those from whom the land had been held by individuals involved in the rebellion, most notably the Dukes of Atholl, Argyll and Gordon. The Court of Session had no jurisdiction over the claims to these estates until the Treasury had reached an agreement with the Subjects Superior as to the value of their superiorities. In an attempt to hasten settlement, Dundas managed to get an Act through Parliament which authorised the Court of Session to settle the claims on the estates, giving the creditors higher priority than the Subjects Superior in regard to payment. This was negotiated only after several delays and much suspicion between Dundas and Lord Milton, who was intent on safeguarding the Duke of Argyll's interests as a Subject Superior.[133] There the matter stood for the rest of the reign as the claims on the annexed estates were paraded before the Court of Session. The Treasury had appointed its Secretaries, West and Hardinge, to negotiate with the Subjects Superior in 1755, but had so lost interest by 1757 that it neglected to make out a new commission to renew the Secretaries' authority after one had been replaced.

The status of the claims on the estates and the energy required to administer this aspect of the commission's business must have affected its performance in the first five years of its existence, which everyone agreed was bad. The expense of running the estates also left little room for grandiose plans for civilising the highlands. According to Lord Milton, a rent of about £5494 net had to meet annual expenses which in the late 1750s were sometimes as high as £3000 a year.[134] In addition there was the lamentable record of attendance by the commissioners and their secretary; many did not live near Edinburgh and so could only attend infrequently, others withdrew on account of political differences, and the supposed workhorse of the commission, its secretary, spent his time in London seeking another post. The failure of the commission, therefore, cannot be blamed completely on neglect in London, although that was a factor too. Four or five active but unpaid commissioners, most with other occupations, could do little more than run the estates like any eighteenth-century laird who dabbled in improvement. The commission was a victim of events; its initial identification with Argyll's political enemies, ministerial hostility, and the commencement of the war all diverted attention and encouraged apathy on the part of the commissioners and their agents, with the result that little was done in the first years of its existence.

There is an air of shadow play about the political activities of Argyll and Newcastle in the 1750s, particularly after Newcastle's own ministry came to grief over his inability to manage the war. Argyll, Newcastle and Hardwicke were all old men preoccupied with the issues of the 1730s and 1740s: Jacobitism, barbarity in the highlands, the old Tory party and the Whig state. Politics were shifting beneath their feet and they barely knew it, preferring to fight their old wars in the way they knew best.

Newcastle was determined to stamp out Jacobitism in Scotland by reducing Argyll's political power, by directly extending his own, by placing competent English officers in the Treasury boards there, by encouraging trade and manufactures, and by improving (or destroying) the old order in the highlands. He attempted to make Hopetoun, Deskford and Dundas his own representatives in Scotland in order to reduce his dependence on Argyll for information and advice on Scottish affairs. He appointed Dundas Lord Advocate and Robert Craigie Lord President to increase the independence of the law. He persuaded Deskford to take a place at the Board of Customs, put Dauber in the Excise, Brooksbank at the Commission of Annexed Estates, and tried to get another English Baron of Exchequer in Scotland. He helped pass a bounty on the export of linen and he attempted to implement the highland annexation act in a manner that can only be termed ambitious.

Yet the same flaw emerges in all of Newcastle's actions. He would not support his friends and ventures once he had encouraged them to start. His legal appointments did not continue to follow a consistent pattern; only Dundas proved exceptional and only Dundas did well out of his association with Newcastle. Deskford was destroyed by putting too much faith in Newcastle, and English officers such as General Bland, Richard Dauber and Stamp Brooksbank all found themselves stranded in Edinburgh without the support that Newcastle had led them to expect. In regard to the law, the revenue and the annexed estates, Newcastle's determination to uproot 'highland power' or Argathelian influence proved short-lived, though liable to sporadic resurgence at various times during the coalition ministry. Dundas had the wisdom to seek an accommodation with Argyll; the revenue remained an Argathelian strongpoint; and the Commission of Annexed Estates was allowed to stagnate.

How much of this was owing to the well-known contradictions and inconsistencies of Newcastle's character and how much to the balance of political power in London? It is tempting to dismiss Newcastle's actions as eccentric and episodic, but this would allow the man to obscure the events in which he participated. He, Hardwicke and Dupplin were well on their way to creating a system of governing Scotland reminiscent of Harley's attempt at direct control from 1710-1713, with genuine change as their goal. They failed because Newcastle's ministry failed. If they had not blundered into war, if Pitt and Fox had not been able to humiliate them in the House of Commons, etc., Scottish government would have been assimilated into English government, perhaps before most Scots were prepared for such an eventuality. Deskford and Dundas were the political ancestors of Jeffrey, Cockburn and Brougham: Dundas had to retreat to the bench; Deskford, tragically, was driven to suicide in 1770 by the failure of his public career; but they were the first of the new-style Scots Whigs. If they failed and Newcastle failed, at least there were some accomplishments: Dundas was a good Lord Advocate who did yeoman service in clearing away many of the claims on the annexed estates; the foundation of the Court of Session was broadened; and the window tax was finally collected. It was not much, but it was something.

The Duke of Argyll, as usual, acted from motives which can only be dimly perceived. He had a faction to protect and he did not enjoy the humiliation of being proved publicly to lack the status with which he was credited in Scotland. He was quite capable of perpetuating political jobs, but his general stance of Scots jobs for Scots, no matter how self-interested politically, worked in the Scots' interest. It kept English customs laws from strangling the development of Scottish trade, particularly the tobacco trade; and his influence helped to keep the army from interfering too much with civil authority in Scotland. He and his followers, as they had done since the rebellion, served as a healthy check on the excesses of the anglophiles. In London, Argyll was able to use his parliamentary strength to the utmost advantage in the unstable years of the Newcastle ministry to extract every possible advantage for his followers and for his country. His actions in regaining the bounty on coarse linen illustrate this perfectly; only he had the political power to achieve renewal. One must keep this in mind when considering the rights and wrongs of the terms he accepted from the English and the Irish to secure the renewal of the bounty. The acquisition of very nearly £70,000 for Scotland to pay the creditors of the Perth estate is another example of Argyll's influence leading to substantial results of very real economic significance.

Argyll had managed to maintain his position and eventually see it revive by swallowing his pride and waiting his chance; astutely taking advantage of divisions amongst English politicians to improve his own fortunes. His actions illustrate the advantages of a national spokesman in London and a group of M.P.s who were capable of acting as a coherent national group. The other side of this situation was that Argyll and his lieutenants acquired an unofficial position and authority which ambitious Scots who did not agree with his views found obnoxious. Walpole's way and Argyll's way had been to leave the Scots to themselves and avoid trouble. This had been successful partially; but the rebellions had shown its shortcomings, and much time had passed. As Lord Elibank wrote in 1760: 'It was natural, and perhaps prudent, to leave that Country to the direction of those who had governed it before the Union, but now that that set of men is gone, and the removal of the seat of government has made it impossible that others should rise up in their stead, the case is widely altered.'[135]

Argyll's skill at making life difficult for Newcastle, and the erosion of Newcastle's own power, had defeated another attempt to extend the powers of central government to Scotland. This time Argyll had only the help of Fox, who after all was no Walpole or Pelham in terms of power. During the last years of his life, however, Argyll had to contend with new figures who represented political forces which were just emerging in Scotland as well as in England. It so happened that one of these figures was his nephew, the Earl of Bute, whose influence increased with each passing day as the old King drew closer to the grave and Bute's young friend the Prince of Wales approached the throne.

4

The Duke of Argyll and Lord Bute, 1759-1761

JOHN STUART, third Earl of Bute, was one of the early Anglo-Scots; educated in England at Eton and in Holland at Leyden, he did not live in Scotland until 1739, and left again, for good, in 1745. His character in some ways resembled that of his uncle John, second Duke of Argyll. They were both proud, assured of their own virtue, and contemptuous of other politicians. Bute yearned to play a noble part in public life, which may have created that 'theatrical air of the greatest importance' noted by the Earl of Waldegrave.[1] He was a sensitive, honourable, pompous, elegant and unimaginative man, well-educated but hopelessly deficient in common sense. Much that was negative in his character would not become apparent until the new reign, however; in the meantime his increasing influence over the Princess Dowager and the young Prince of Wales at Leicester House made him the rising sun of British politics. In reality it was George III whose star would shine, but at the time his mentor was seen as the new force which would cause new adjustments to the political scales. Bute looked and acted the part; helping to bring Pitt and Newcastle together in 1757, attempting to influence government policy, continuing to prepare his pupil for his destiny. The promise of power suited him much better than power itself.

Bute's relationship with the third Duke of Argyll was cool but not openly hostile. Neither left a specific record of the differences between them, though the differences in their temperaments were self-evident. Whereas Argyll had stood by Walpole in 1739, Bute had joined the Patriot opposition. After Bute's return to London before the 1747 general election, Argyll wrote to Lord Milton that he would rather not depend on Bute's help in the election for the Ayr district of burghs (which included Rothesay on the Isle of Bute), even though he had just helped him obtain a pension of £800 a year.[2] Argyll was not specific, but the inference was that their relationship was strained. Later Argyll became identified with Henry Fox, while Bute was an admirer of William Pitt, which inevitably led to some friction. When Bute became disenchanted with Pitt, Argyll's continued association with the ministry could not have been agreeable to him. Yet as long as the coalition ministry continued, contact between them was minimal. Bute took little interest in Scottish patronage, at least partially because he found it obnoxious to apply to Argyll for patronage.[3]

85

Argyll was almost as old as George II. Any politician who knew his sums could not help but come to the conclusion that provision had to be made for the future. Bute was Scottish only by birth, not by sympathy, upbringing, or manner, but this was still enough to lead many to expect that he would take an interest in Scottish as well as British affairs. From the 1755/56 session of Parliament onwards, a small group of Scottish M.P.s led by Gilbert Elliot and Bute's brother James Stuart Mackenzie had already detached themselves from the Argathelian group and looked to Bute for leadership. This development was bound to lead to some conflict at the next general election. It is well known that Argyll and Bute quarrelled in 1758 over the representation of the Ayr district of burghs; recently it has even been suggested that this quarrel was part of a concerted election campaign by the Leicester House group;[4] but the exact nature of the political relationship between Argyll and Bute in 1759 and 1760 is still not known. It remains unclear whether their quarrel was a local affair or a battle for political influence in Scotland.

In the spring of 1759 Lord Bute decided to put up his own candidate for the Ayr district of burghs. This was an understandable decision, as one of the five royal burghs which made up the district, Rothesay, virtually belonged to him. The other four burghs were Campbeltown, Inveraray, Ayr and Irvine. Campbeltown and Inveraray were part of the Argyll estate and voted as the Duke directed; Irvine and Ayr were prosperous Ayrshire ports dominated by a more independent merchant oligarchy. Argyll and Bute together could dictate the choice of an M.P. for the district, as they did in 1754 when they arranged the return of Bute's younger brother James Stuart Mackenzie; but if the two peers did not agree, the merchants of Ayr and Irvine found themselves in a position of some influence. By 1759 uncle and nephew were again in political disagreement; if Bute was not in opposition to the ministry, he was certainly estranged from it. This time another character had entered the fray, for the young Earl of Eglinton had written Bute that their friendship had persuaded him 'to part with all my horses and turn politician'. Eglinton's estates were in north Ayrshire, very close to the port of Irvine, and the young lord began to cultivate the friendship of the more influential merchants in the town. In 1757 he wrote Bute to assure him of his interest in the burgh, pointing out that this alliance would place Bute on a level with Argyll in determining the choice of the burghs' M.P.[5]

The Earl of Eglinton's character was an important element in the series of events which followed his attachment to Bute. He was a charming, if somewhat bizarre, man; a likeable, lazy soul with an endearing sense of humour; but he was not the stuff of which politicians were made. The following three comments, made over the span of a decade, illustrate his problem and the impression it made on others. 'Eglinton had done quite in character,' wrote William Mure in 1759, 'he promised to you to write, but he has catched hold of some Italian air, and whistled the whole thing out of his memory, for we have never heard of him.' 'I believe you intend to do what you say,' James Boswell once told him, 'but perhaps the song of *three blind mice* comes across you and prevents you from thinking of it.' 'Just the same as always,' the Duchess of Hamilton wrote in 1769, 'whistling to himself for want of thought.' 'I have a thousand projects in my head,' Eglinton himself once wrote, 'not one of which in all human probability will ever suceed; — no matter; they amuse in the meantime, which is always realising something.'[6]

By 1759 Bute's brother had made it clear that he was not going to stand for the Ayr district at the next general election. Bute's friend William Mure, Member of Parliament for the neighbouring county of Renfrew, recommended Patrick Craufurd of Auchenames as an appropriate candidate: an old country Whig who had represented Ayrshire before the Earl of Loudoun and the Duke of Argyll had turned him out in 1754. He was an earnest, if at times foolish, character. Eglinton and he would make an unusual pair in the campaign to come, as one of Eglinton's descriptions of their activities makes clear:

> all this is but a joke to Peter Craufurd [.] he is drinking, hunting, and whoring *com un possede*. I am an eye witness to the drinking, an ear witness to the whoring, and as he has just brought a terrier from a tailor in Ayr I can make no doubt he intends to commence foxhunter. Lord have mercy upon us what a figure Peter will cut flying over a five bar gate, with his flowing bob, jackboot, holster, bit, and housing. Perhaps this may not strike you for I know you like a big bit and a dancing horse but Peter Craufurd a foxhunting is to me like the Chancellor at Court with a bob wig and buckskin breeches, playing at romps with the Duchess of Somerset for kisses.[7]

Mure would not always find it easy to manage two such colourful personalities.

Mure departed for Scotland in May 1759 to persuade Craufurd to stand and to secure the support of the burgh councils of Irvine and Ayr. 'I own, I'm very doubtful of our success in this,' he wrote Bute when he had arrived in Scotland, 'nothing strikes these bodies but a visible and immediate interest, though there is no harm in the trial, even if we fail.' His next comment in the letter reveals more of Bute's motives: 'if we succeed, it may render your application to a near relation either unnecessary, or irresistable.'[8] Mure's efforts ran into difficulties when Eglinton forgot to forward a letter recommending Craufurd to his friends in Irvine, making it impossible to take any action in the affair until August. By the time the letter did arrive, both Mure and Craufurd were having second thoughts about proceeding with the plan. Mure advised Bute to inform 'a certain near relation' of his activity 'in order to save appearances': 'He might take it in better part to be informed by yourself rather than by information from hence.'[9] Nevertheless Mure and Craufurd set off to visit Irvine and Ayr, where they met with a certain amount of success, though the respective magistrates of each burgh demanded additional proof of Bute's involvement before committing themselves to the scheme.[10]

Bute was not the only one of Argyll's relations dabbling in Scottish politics that summer. Charles Townshend, an ambitious and talented English M.P., had married Argyll's niece, the Countess of Dalkeith, and through his marriage had become the guardian of the young Duke of Buccleuch. Townshend and the Countess had travelled north to Scotland in July to inspect the vast Buccleuch estates in the county of Edinburgh and the borders. Their levees at Dalkeith Palace soon attracted all of Edinburgh society. Townshend charmed, flattered and talked his way to popularity; and ambitious thoughts began to assert themselves.

His moment of triumph came on 18 July, when he was presented with the freedom of the city of Edinburgh, and made an address to the notables of the city. His speech had a tremendous effect on his listeners. The war was going well abroad, but there were rumours of an invasion from France that would include a descent on Scotland. Pitt had called out the militia in the south to defend the country, but Scotland had no militia, because the 1757 Act which established it in England had excluded Scotland. Townshend called on the Scots to join in the efforts at national defence and take their place in the nation. 'History can hardly produce so strong an instance of the force of persuasion,' Lord Elibank later wrote to Townshend, 'and though you had only the opportunity of exerting it among a few of us, the spirit you infused on that occasion, had been able to get the better of the servility of some, the envious selfishness of others, and the timidity of all.' Other Scottish correspondents of Townshend later recalled 'your dinner in the restoration room when heart of oak took fire and kept it' (John Dalrymple) and 'your endeavours to rouze the benumbed genius of this country' (William Robertson).[11]

The success of this speech made Townshend the man of the moment in Edinburgh, and caused him to hit upon a plan of further nurturing his popularity by beginning a campaign to become M.P. for Edinburgh in the 1761 general election. He was encouraged in this ambition by Lord Milton who, according to Carlyle of Inveresk, was that summer 'Dazzld at first with Charles' Shining Talents and Elegant Flattery'.[12] Milton was thinking of the future as well, for he had three grown sons whose careers had just started in politics and the army. The militia issue was a perfect vehicle for this; Townshend, the Englishman who sympathised with the Scots, could lead them to their rightful place as equals and colleagues in the empire of the English: 'indeed I can hardly conceive, how a man of genius can think of a more certain means of gratifying his ambition and humanity, than by giving some attention to us —,' Lord Elibank advised the Englishman.[13] 'With all the principles of Mankind in us we have hitherto, as a Country, made a Sneaking figure,' Carlyle of Inveresk wrote after Townshend had returned to London, 'because our leaders have almost always been vile tools & slaves, Come & compleatt the Union, & teach us to talk and act like Freemen & Britons.'[14]

Carlyle obviously meant Argyll when he wrote about leaders who were 'vile tools & Slaves'. The Duke himself arrived in Edinburgh on 10 September 1759, about a month after Townshend had returned to England.[15] He surveyed the excitement over Townshend's militia idea with a singular lack of enthusiasm, while Lord Milton held his tongue and watched for the Duke's reaction. Argyll flatly refused to consider a Scottish militia bill, much to the disappointment of Townshend's new friends: 'Aged pulses dont beat high enough for the many things this country needs,' Sir Alexander Dick of Prestonfield wrote to Townshend.[16] Instead, Argyll had proposed the appointment of Lords Lieutenant in several Scottish counties to raise 'fencible' regiments under seventeenth-century legislation passed by the old Scottish Parliament; already that summer he had persuaded the ministry to allow the Earl of Sutherland and himself to raise regiments in their home counties as Lord Lieutenants.[17] The different approaches to the problem of defence well illustrate the difference in attitude between the old generation and the new. Argyll wanted to use the old Scottish laws and institutions to meet the problem when nothing but the same law and the same militia that operated in England would satisfy the younger members of the ruling class.

From Edinburgh, where he found one younger relation tampering with his interest, Argyll moved to Glasgow, where he found Mure and Craufurd well advanced in their scheme to take the Ayr burghs. Bute and Argyll had already come to an open disagreement in London over Argyll's failure to consult Bute in regard to raising a regiment in Argyll as well as over the Ayr burghs. 'Since my speaking to the D—,' Bute wrote to Mure at the end of August, 'I hear he talks of me in a manner that would tho'rily fix my determination if that had been to do. My temper is not overly patient, and I am very well content to stand by the award.'[18] Argyll had already taken steps to frustrate Bute's plans. He had intended to secure the district for Frederick Campbell, a mutual relation of Bute and himself, but faced with opposition, he decided that his best chance of defeating Craufurd was to find a candidate with influence in the town of Ayr, the most independent burgh of the five and thus the key to the situation. Sir Adam Fergusson of Kilkerran, a young, wealthy lawyer with an estate near Ayr, seemed to be the best available candidate to oppose Craufurd. Argyll's friend the Earl of Loudoun served as Argyll's agent in securing the services of Fergusson as well as other local merchants and gentlemen with influence on the burgh council. Loudoun was already involved in a contest with Eglinton in the county of Ayr, where Loudoun's cousin was seeking re-election to Parliament against Eglinton's brother. The idea was to undermine the efforts of Mure and Craufurd in Ayr by bringing new uncommitted members on to the council at the Michaelmas election.[19]

Bute, however, wanted to avoid an open conflict, suggesting to Mure that Craufurd should wait upon Argyll at Glasgow and politely ask his interest. This Craufurd did, writing to Lord Milton in praise of Argyll's 'great abilities and moderation', and proposing a meeting with the Duke.[20] Their meeting, from Craufurd's point of view, was a disaster, serving only to make the disagreement between Bute and Argyll public knowledge in Scotland and the subject of much gossip. Bute, Argyll claimed, was even more arrogant than the second Duke of Argyll had been, and he pointedly reminded Craufurd that the election was still a full eighteen months away. In fact the Duke had already taken steps to encourage an opposition to Mure in his constituency of Renfrew, where the Earl of Glencairn had been making interest for the son of Mure's predecessor as county M.P. This forced Mure to journey to Inveraray to attempt to mollify Argyll, with only limited success. The Duke made plain his displeasure over Bute's attempt on the Ayr burghs. 'He is excessively hurt with that thing,' Mure reported to Bute, 'more than one could imagine, though on the other hand he dreads an open rupture with your Lordship.'[21]

Mure was now forced to look to his own county and leave Craufurd to his own devices. 'I fancy by this time Lord Bute is satisfied he has made a confounded *faux pas*,' John Dalrymple of Cranstoun wrote to Charles Townshend.[22] Bute found himself drawn into the 'election business' he so disliked. 'All the counties in the kingdom shan't make me ask another favour,' he finally wrote to Mure.[23] Patrick Craufurd followed Bute's example by retiring to his country seat at Auchenames, declaring that Ayr had promised him its vote and that he would be doubting the council's word if he continued to solicit them. Meantime the Earl of Loudoun and his allies succeeded in bringing in a new, uncommitted, but essentially Argathelian Provost of Ayr, William Ferguson, at the Michaelmas town council elections, and so achieved a good start to Sir Adam Fergusson's campaign. As the irrepressible John Dalrymple again commented, Craufurd's retreat and trust were 'weak enough bulwark against the presence and money of Sir Adam Fergusson, the industry of Lord Loudoun and the promises of the Duke of Argyll!'[24]

Yet the campaign in Ayr, and even that in Irvine, was not all about flattering councillors, or obtaining military commissions and customs offices for their relatives. In this sense one can begin to perceive similarities between the sentiments Charles Townshend had capitalised upon in Edinburgh, and those Mure and Craufurd had encouraged during their jaunt to Irvine and Ayr. Loudoun's principal associate in his efforts to influence Ayr, Charles Dalrymple of Orangefield, wrote the following just after Mure and Craufurd had left Ayr (the queries indicate words of doubtful legibility):

> I perused P[atrick] C[raufurd]'s credentialls from Ld: B[ute] and Ld: E[glinton] which were strong & narrated between him and me in a letter by last post to Baron Erskine. So believe it will be needless to Repeat the particulars here only must take notice of one thing that is Greatly made use of by him & friends in this Corner & Seems to have Influence. That his G: of A[rgyll] is strongly blamed Above for standing by & Supporting Mr F[ox] and his partie. Who are Supposed the worst Enemys of our Constitution & that his best friends are Disobliged & leaving him on that account. Your Lop can Easily see their drift in this, as it exposes the - - -? and meaness of their addresses and only Calculated? for the low Rable of a Burrow.[25]

Craufurd represented himself as the candidate of Bute and Pitt, despite the coolness that had arisen between the two, 'as Mr. Pitt's great character and exertions are justly admired by all honest and disinterested men and particularly regarded by all the trading towns'. Loudoun's response in September was to emphasise the differences between Bute and Pitt, which Craufurd attempted to counteract by appealing to Bute for some token of Pitt's support for himself and his friendship with Bute. Later he even wrote directly to Pitt, who still maintained his general stance of refusing to interfere in election affairs.[26]

Craufurd did manage to gain an indirect association with Pitt in the autumn of 1759; curiously enough, he got it through the Scottish militia issue which Charles Townshend had so encouraged during his time in Edinburgh. The news of a planned French descent on the Clyde with an army of 20,000 men, complementary to an invasion of England, naturally caused great consternation in Ayrshire. At the same time Argyll was dampening the efforts of Townshend's friends in Edinburgh; Lord Auchinleck of the Court of Session travelled back to his home county and arranged a county meeting to petition the Crown on the subject. Auchinleck had been influenced by Townshend, but his loyalty had usually been directed to Argyll, who must have spoken with him before he left

Edinburgh, because his proposals followed Argyll's plan in requesting a Lord Lieutenant for Ayrshire to call out a fencible regiment under the old Scottish laws. Loudoun spoke in support of Auchinleck's proposals at the county meeting while the Earl of Eglinton opposed them.[27] There was an obvious political connection.

Ayr and Irvine followed the county's example by drawing up their own addresses to the King for arms and troops for protection. It is particularly interesting that the new council at Ayr sent their address to the Duke of Argyll while Eglinton's friends on the council at Irvine sent their address to Lord Bute, on the grounds that Bute's brother was then the sitting M.P. for the district. Argyll forwarded Ayr's address to the proper Secretary of State, the Earl of Holderness; who, on orders from Newcastle, delayed dealing with it until Argyll had returned to London.[28] Bute forwarded Irvine's address to Pitt, who as Secretary of State for the Southern Department should have had nothing to do with it, but who nevertheless went ahead and promptly presented it to the King, and had it printed in the government *Gazette*. As a result Loudoun and Sir Adam Fergusson suffered considerable embarrassment. 'Your opponents say that now their assertions concerning the political views of your patron are plainly justified by Mr. Pitt's interesting himself so clearly on the other side,' the Provost of Ayr wrote to Sir Adam Fergusson:

> ... I must at the same time with the sincerity and frankness of an honest man declare to you that however much I love and esteem you; as I heartily do, yet no consideration shall ever make me subservient to the interest of those whose aim shall plainly appear directed to oppose or overturn an administration in which Mr. Pitt's great talents have been so conspicuous and procured so much glory and substantial advantages to Great Britain.

The Provost repeated his warning to Loudoun: 'The present administration being so universally and justly approved of, that any person who was thought to have views of joining an opposition to it, would lose all his influence in this place.'[29]

Both Townshend's appeal to Edinburgh and Bute's to Ayr represented an appeal to a newly emergent 'Britishness' in Scotland which had come about through the war. The gentry and the merchants of the country had made substantial sacrifices for the war effort, which they saw as a means of wiping away the stain of the 1745 rebellion. Argyll's standing in London had benefited from Scotland's contribution to the war, but it was very possible that Argyll on his summer visits did not completely grasp the political transition which was taking place amongst the ruling class in Scotland. Pitt had become a hero north of the Tweed as well as south of it. An English politician had at last emerged who scorned to seek political advantage in England by attacking the Scots. Scotland's nobility and gentry were eager to prove that they could equal and better their peers in England in support of the state. One outlet for their zeal was their recruiting activity, where they were so successful in finding men for the army that there was a scarcity of fighting men in Scotland as early as 1759.[30] The success of the highland regiments raised in 1757 became a kind of British badge which the Scottish gentry could wear with pride. Townshend's call for a militia offered a similar outlet, only in this instance they were prevented by law from demonstrating their patriotism.[31]

Politics in London, as a consequence, were no longer remote and of little interest, as the gentry and merchants of Scotland, eager to follow the progress of the war, avidly consumed the London newspapers and supported the expansion of Scotland's fledgling national press at Edinburgh — the *Edinburgh Evening Courant*, the *Caledonian Mercury*, and the *Scots Magazine*.

Argyll's problem was to maintain his influence in Scotland by demonstrating his own influence with the ministry, which meant forcing Newcastle to stage some kind of demonstration of ministerial favour. On the other hand, Bute, and perhaps Townshend, wished to do the same thing. Thus an application by the Earl of Eglinton to become Governor of Dumbarton Castle (a sinecure), which Argyll had not opposed when it was first broached in early August 1759, became an object of some importance once Bute and Argyll were clearly at odds. Newcastle was astonished to receive another application for the post, after Argyll had departed for Scotland, from Argyll's cousin and eventual successor, Lieutenant General John Campbell of Mamore. Attempts to clarify the situation by writing to Argyll naturally failed to elicit more than a vague reply, designed to give Argyll time to take account of the situation in Scotland.[32]

On his return to London in December, Argyll took steps to counter the efforts of Bute's friends. He arranged for Holderness to reply to the address of the county of Ayr with a promise to send arms to Ayr and Irvine for the defence of the towns by their citizens. Copies of Holderness's letter were sent to the Provosts of Ayr and Irvine by the Secretaries' office at Argyll's request.[33] At the same time Newcastle was informed of his opposition to giving Eglinton a place, much to Newcastle's disgust, for the English Duke now found himself caught between the two relations. By the end of February 1760, Argyll was threatening to go to the King in order to prevent the appointment, telling Newcastle that Bute and Eglinton were attacking his interest and that Eglinton's appointment would give the appearance of government support to that attack. Argyll threatened to tell the King (and here Newcastle's account has been much quoted) 'that Lord Bute had set up the Prince of Wales' standard in Scotland against the King'. A desperate Newcastle, frightened of offending Bute, tried everything he could to dissuade Argyll, who he knew was crucial to the success of the ministry in Scotland at the next general election. Lord Mansfield reported to Newcastle that there was no moving Argyll from his purpose: 'he acts so differently upon this from what he has done upon former occasions that I believe you will find him immovable.'[34]

Having put a stop to Bute's pretensions for the moment, Argyll still had to deal with Townshend. The militia issue in Scotland continued to excite interest, particularly after a French squadron of frigates appeared off the north-east coast in October.[35] On 30 November 1759 Lord Elibank and Lord Milton held a militia meeting in Edinburgh which appointed a committee of four peers, six Lords of Session, a merchant banker, Edinburgh's Lord Provost, and four advocates (including Sir Adam Fergusson) to draw up proposals for a Scottish militia bill.[36] Milton appears to have dominated this committee, who drafted a bill which they sent down to Argyll, along with letters to Speaker Onslow, George Townshend, Charles Townshend, Mansfield, Hardwicke and Newcastle. Argyll supervised the distribution of the plan, although he stopped the delivery of Milton's letter to Charles Townshend.[37]

Townshend had been spending quite a bit of time with Argyll in January of 1760, but his ardour for a militia had cooled since his return to London; as early as the previous November one of Carlyle's letters to him expressed regret 'that you think our applications for a Militia will be in vain'.[38] Unfortunately, some letters by one of Milton's colleagues on the committee, Lord Coalstoun of the Court of Session, were made public in the middle of January 1760, and possibly affected Argyll's relationship with Townshend, for the letters put 'the scheme in a pitiful and partial light, as tending to advance Mr. Townshend's interests in Scotland'.[39] Later, when Gilbert Elliot introduced a Scottish militia bill on his own initiative, Townshend sided with Pitt and other English M.P.s identified with the militia movement in seeking a compromise with the Newcastle Whigs that would exclude the highland counties. This probably finished any inclination Milton might have had to persist in getting Argyll to agree to allow Townshend to become Edinburgh's M.P. 'The attempt to make an odious and disgraceful distinction betwixt the south and north parts of Scotland I cannot make sense of unless it was a design formed to overturn the whole system,' he wrote to Townshend:

> as for my part I would rather give up the whole than submit to fix such a lasting mark of Infamy upon those who during this present heavy war have signalised themselves in the service of our King and Country so as to be the dread of our enemy and to have gained the love and esteem of his Majesty's dominions and allies.[40]

There was no break or outright hostility between Milton and Townshend, just a mutual realisation that the 'schemes' of the previous summer would remain just that. The militia issue, however, was by no means dead in certain influential Scottish circles, as Bute himself would later discover in 1762.

Townshend had expressed the aspirations of a new kind of Scotsman, the self-anointed stay-at-home Briton; but Townshend instinctively thought of acquiring power in Scottish politics by ingratiating himself with those who were influential there. Bute was beginning to come close to the idea of rejecting them outright, not by offering opposition, but by renouncing any connection with Scotland. He constantly refused reconciliation with Argyll. He refused to allow Patrick Craufurd to stand down when the latter offered to do so to resolve the conflict over the Ayr burghs. Gilbert Elliot, reporting to his father in April 1760 the failure of these attempts at reconciliation, remarked that 'the one least suspected by you is by no means the least violent.'[41]

As the time for his yearly departure for Scotland drew closer, Argyll became more interested in settling his disagreement with Bute, and made more determined efforts to resolve their quarrel. First he sent Samuel Martin (one of the secretaries of the Treasury) to his nephew with a conciliatory message, but Bute rejected this as 'letting the English into their dispute'. Then in August he tried his personal secretary, Andrew Fletcher, who had inspected Bute's Scottish estate the previous autumn, but again no progress was made.[42] Argyll finally gave up and, much to Newcastle's horror, went to the King to ask for his support. Newcastle found the King 'most violent for supporting the Duke of Argyll against my Lord Bute' after his interview with Argyll, and even determined to prevent Bute from becoming one of the sixteen Scottish Representative Peers. The King also pointedly informed Newcastle that he had assured Argyll of the government's support 'if his servants did not cheat him', a remark which the sensitive Newcastle did not fail to feel.[43] Having secured the King, and through him the unwilling Newcastle, Argyll set out for Scotland in September 1760.

The open breach between Bute and Argyll had led to a great many rumours and much unfounded suspicion. For example, both Gilbert Elliot and James Stuart Mackenzie were suspicious of Argathelian opposition in the counties of Selkirk and Ross, and Argyll had suspected that Bute was intending to set up his own candidate for the county of Aberdeen, but in all three cases no such project materialised. In fact Argyll refused to countenance a plot by the Earl of Galloway to oppose Bute's follower, John Mackay Ross, on the grounds that he had supported him in 1754 and would again.[44] Dr. McKelvey has argued recently that Lord Bute was involved in the election of thirteen Scottish Members of Parliament in 1761, but fails to distinguish between the period before the death of George II and the period immediately preceding the general election. Before the death of the old King, Bute was involved in only one contest apart from those of Craufurd, Eglinton and Mure; this was Alexander Wedderburn's attempt on the Stirling burghs, but even here his involvement was, to say the least, marginal. The mere fact that someone wrote a letter to Lord Bute asking his support does not indicate that they had become allies of Bute in outright opposition to the ministry.[45] There was no Prince of Wales standard in Scotland in the summer and autumn of 1760. The quarrel between Bute and Argyll was a local, almost a family, affair; the Duke of Argyll felt sufficiently threatened to try to make it more than it was in order to gain the King's support and thus frustrate Bute's attempt on the burghs. It had become a battle of pride, a clash between two different kinds of vanity.

In September 1760 it looked as if Argyll had won: the death of George II on 25 October 1760 transformed the situation. Argyll's trump card had been the King's support; now it was Bute who had the support of the King. As he had done several times before in times of political change, Argyll remained in Scotland until he could 'see the candles lighted up a little', as he wrote to the Earl of Loudoun.[46] He did not return to London until 15 December, even then remaining at home in 'the Library', claiming to suffer from a bad, and suspiciously fortuitous, cold.[47] Newcastle and Hardwicke entertained fond hopes of a change in the system of Scottish government by the forcible retirement of Argyll and his replacement by a more amenable Scottish peer, but Bute had evidently decided that Argyll should be retained, just as the other old ministers had been continued in the other areas of government. Gilbert Elliot was sent to call upon Argyll to arrange a reconciliation, Bute apparently feeling more inclined to forgiveness now that he had arrived at a position of real power through his influence over the King. Elliot reported that Argyll seems mighty well disposed to be the instrument to execute your Lordship's commands in Scotland, provided you are inclined to employ him, to treat him gently, and to protect him from the oppression of the Duke of Newcastle, which though he has struggled with in former times, yet he is now much too old and too unambitious any longer to endure.[48]

Bute himself visited the Duke the next day to complete their treaty and persuade Argyll to end his self-imposed convalescence.

Argyll appeared at Court to kiss hands on his re-appointment as Keeper of the Great Seal in Scotland, meeting a reception he described to Lord Milton as 'very gracious', but which his old enemy the Earl of Marchmont described as 'a dry reception, more was said to me who have been there often. He looks red but old and feeble and surly.'[49] The Duke was not slow to grasp the implications of the new distribution of power, as his first conference with Newcastle demonstrated, for Newcastle reported it to Hardwicke in the following terms:

He told me in general, that he had had a conversation with the King; and I scarce know by his own report, which of them commended my Lord Bute the most. He said, the King's attachment to, and affection for My Lord Bute, was the strongest he ever saw; and that his Majesty made use of this expression to His Grace — 'Whoever speaks against My Lord Bute I shall think speaks against me.' And I can assure you, My Lord Duke gave the King no occasion to apply that to him.[50]

Argyll also made use of the occasion to inform Newcastle 'that Lord Bute would expect the power of Scotland', or in other words that Newcastle would be excluded from influence in Scottish affairs. Scottish affairs became the exclusive preserve of Argyll working under the general supervision of Bute, a situation which had become clear to outside observers by February 1761. 'I take it for granted,' the Earl of Kinnoull (formerly Lord Dupplin) wrote to the isolated Lord Deskford, 'that everything relating to the King's service in Scotland will be entirely under the management of the Duke of Argyll and Lord Bute, and that no other of the ministers will interfere at all with them in that department.' 'It is universally allowed that the Duke of Argyll is more the minister for Scotland just now than ever he was in his life,' Adam Drummond of Megginch informed the Duke of Atholl.[51]

Thus George II's death, which had seemed to ensure the forcible retirement of Argyll, led to a new relationship between Bute and Argyll once the former had genuine power to influence Scottish affairs. Argyll's expertise and experience were simply too valuable for his inexperienced nephew abruptly to cast away; for his part Argyll proved willing to work 'in perfect subordination', while Bute ensured that the other ministers, Newcastle in particular, were excluded from Scottish affairs.[52]

This arrangement was reflected in the compromise which settled the quarrel Bute and Argyll had pursued the year before. Almost as soon as they were reconciled, it was agreed that William Mure would be made Baron of Exchequer in Edinburgh, thus allowing him to arrange to have Patrick Craufurd stand for his seat in the county of Renfrew and free Bute and Argyll to arrive at a compromise in the Ayr burghs. It was this plan which was the major topic of Argyll's interview with the Duke of Newcastle in January. Baron Edlin had died in December and left a vacancy which Mure could fill, but Newcastle adamantly opposed this plan on the grounds that Edlin had been an Englishman and must be replaced by an Englishman. 'The question with me,' he wrote to Hardwicke,

> is how far the English interest is concerned, and the Crown, in this question? The Court of Exchequer is a revenue court, and has an immediate connection with the Treasury of England; and the moment it is, as upon the next vacancy of a Chief Baron, it will be, solely in Scotch hands, the King of England will never get a farthing from thence.[53]

The affair was the first test of the new arrangement between Argyll and Bute. The latter made it clear that he supported Argyll, and later the King gave Argyll permission to put Mure on the bench in spite of Newcastle's objections. Newcastle was still of some importance to Bute's plans for the ministry, however, and some concessions had to be made. An attempt was made to create another vacancy in the Court of Exchequer by reshuffling the Scottish bench, although this was done over Argyll's protests. Patrick Boyle, Lord Shualton of the Court of Session, was persuaded to resign from the bench in return for a pension for his nephew the Earl of Glasgow; James Erskine of the Court of Exchequer was to be given Shualton's gown, thus allowing Newcastle to obtain a place on the court for a George Winn. The arrangements were completed in March 1761, although for various reasons the necessary appointments were not made until May.[54]

Another part of the compromise between Argyll and Bute related to the candidate for the Ayr burghs, where Bute insisted that Sir Adam Fergusson stand down. He attempted to sweeten this bitter pill for Argyll by suggesting that the candidate Argyll had originally intended, their mutual cousin Frederick Campbell, be chosen for the district. This Argyll, or 'old Buckram' as Sir Henry Bellenden called him, would only accept if Fergusson could be persuaded to stand down of his own accord, as otherwise the measure would 'wear so strong an appearance of double dealing and partiality to a near relation'.[55] Mure was dispatched to Scotland to deal with Sir Adam, but both he and the subtle Lord Milton found it impossible to resolve the situation. As Mure reported to Milton from Ayr, he had been told 'that Lord Loudoun had tied a knot twice which nobody but himself was likely to unloose; . . . his Lordship [is] the only person, to free us of our difficulties, either by dealing with one obstinate person, or a Corporation of fickle ones.'[56]

Fergusson refused to stand down until the burgh council of Ayr had released him; and the council, stung by accusations that Argyll would abandon the town and that they had hurt its interest by doing his bidding, refused to release Fergusson from his commitment. In fact, they recorded their support of his candidacy in their council minutes as a token of their determination. Loudoun had to return to Ayr to undo his own work, only to find, when he did return, that the council was still 'too mad at present to be managed'. Indeed, the council demanded letters from both Bute and Argyll 'to take off the imputation of neglect shown to the town'; demands which Loudoun had to forward to his masters in London.[57]

Loudoun was more successful with Sir Adam himself, who realised that he could not force Argyll to adhere to his commitment: 'what really weighed strongest with me,' he wrote to a friend, 'was the ridicule that would necessarily attend my forcing myself into Parliament by keeping the Duke of Argyle to his word against his will, if it was not followed by better behaviour in Parliament than I know myself capable of.'[58] He wrote to both Bute and Argyll on 28 March, just after joining Loudoun in Ayr from Edinburgh, intimating his willingness to stand down if the council agreed, but insisting on his pride in the council's loyalty as 'it was obtained entirely without any of those means, which though I have been told they are common in other burghs, would neither have been accepted by them nor used by me.'[59] Eventually the burgh's councillors were mollified, and agreed to support Frederick Campbell at the general election.

These arrangements reflected the new balance of power in high politics between Bute, Argyll and Newcastle in the first months of the new reign. Bute had most of the power through his influence over the King, Scottish affairs were delegated to Argyll, and Newcastle was excluded, although the appointment of George Winn demonstrated that as long as he was at the Treasury he could not be completely without influence. Newcastle was also able to protect two Englishmen in the subordinate boards of the Treasury at Edinburgh when Argyll supervised a reshuffle in March 1761. Lord Deskford finally received a pension, still against Argyll's wishes, and retired from the Board of Customs to be replaced by the Board's former secretary, Corbyn Morris. This was part of a settlement negotiated by Newcastle and Argyll in 1758 but never implemented because of the disagreement over a pension for Deskford. The other part of the settlement gave Brooksbank, Secretary of the Commission of Annexed Estates, the additional place of secretary to the Board of Customs.[60] At the Board of Excise, Commissioner Rhodes (an Englishman) was retired on a pension and replaced by the Board's secretary, George Burgess. Burgess was English but related by marriage to Argyll's friend Lord Somerville; he was replaced by a Scot, universally described as a very competent General Supervisor of Excise, who was connected with George Drummond and the Earl of Loudoun. Newcastle's *protégé* Richard Dauber, on the other hand, received a letter from his patron asking him to moderate his conduct at the board.[61]

Of course the area most obviously affected by the changes which took place with the beginning of the new reign was the conduct of the general election in Scotland. Newcastle had been planning for an election in consultation with Argyll, but a new King changed everything, as Argyll's own experience in the west of Scotland illustrated. Just as Argyll had been obliged to give way to Bute on most points regarding Ayrshire and Renfrew, so Newcastle had to yield some points to Argyll once it became apparent that Bute would generally support him in Scottish affairs.

There had been six seats in Scotland where Argyll had made some concessions to Newcastle. Newcastle had made Argyll promise to support the Earl of

Hopetoun's brother in Linlithgowshire (West Lothian), despite his opposition to the Scottish militia bill the previous winter; but in the new reign Lord Milton began actively encouraging an opposition to Charles Hope Weir that in the end came within a single vote of taking the seat.[62] In the Perth district of burghs, where Newcastle had already forwarded £500 of the Secret Service money to help secure the return of the Earl of Rothes' brother Thomas Leslie, Bute's favourable opinion of Leslie's opponent George Dempster allowed Argyll to persuade the Duke of Atholl to swing the burgh of Perth to Dempster and secure his election.[63] Another candidate whose interest was primarily with Newcastle, Robert Haldane of Gleneagles, withdrew from his attempt to secure re-election for the Stirling district of burghs because Lord Bute wanted the district for Alexander Wedderburn.[64]

There were two elections in highland counties which most certainly were affected by the new relationship between Argyll and Bute. Newcastle had vehemently opposed the Duke of Atholl's plan to set up John Murray of Strowan for the county of Perth because Murray, in addition to being both Atholl's nephew and son-in-law, was the son of the Jacobite Lord George Murray. Hardwicke was related to Atholl's rival in the county, the Earl of Breadalbane, and the outgoing M.P., Lord John Murray (yet another brother of Atholl's), was seeking his support, so there was much scope for intervention. Argyll had obtained George II's permission for Murray of Strowan to stand in the summer of 1760, but Newcastle and Hardwicke continued to intrigue through Breadalbane against Atholl's plan. It was only when the new alliance between Bute and Argyll became obvious, in February 1761, that they gave up their opposition.[65]

A similar situation existed in the county of Inverness, except that Newcastle and Hardwicke were even more alarmed by the affair. The incumbent M.P. was Pryse Campbell, an anglicised Scot whose return had been arranged by Newcastle (through Argyll) in 1754 but who had since become attached to Pitt. He had little rapport with his constituents, and had voted to allow the importation of Irish cattle into Britain in 1759, an action not calculated to please the freeholders of the leading centre of black cattle stockfarming in Scotland. Even before the death of George II, Argyll expressed the freeholders' dissatisfaction in London; in 1761 he absolutely refused to countenance Campbell's candidacy. Newcastle was not so much keen on Pryse Campbell as opposed to the alternative, Lord Lovat's son Simon Fraser, who had raised a regiment of highlanders during the war but had not yet been fully pardoned for his youthful involvement in the 1745 rebellion. It is possible Argyll encouraged plans to return Fraser as M.P.; certainly he never discouraged them. Despite Newcastle's frequent attempts to get Bute to intervene, the project of bringing Fraser in for Campbell was allowed to continue without any check from the ministry.[66]

Argyll's part in the election of Scottish Representative Peers can also serve as an example of his new role. In contrast to 1754, when there were almost no changes to be made from those who had served in the previous Parliament, a substantial number of changes had to be made in 1761 to accommodate Lord Bute and his friends. The process by which these changes were made illustrated the new scheme perfectly: Bute chose the new peers but Argyll determined who they would replace. The five who were left out were the Marquess of Lothian, who was connected with Lord Holderness; Lord Deskford's father the Earl of Findlater; the debt-ridden Earl of Lauderdale, one of Newcastle's connections; the Earl of Aberdeen, another of the peers chosen by Cumberland in 1747; and the leader of the rival interest to the Argathelians in the Lanarkshire election, the Earl of Hyndford. Those who came in were Bute, the Earl of Eglinton, the Earl of Abercorn, the Earl of Dunmore, and the Earl of March. 'I believe some of Bute's low friends may thrive at the expense of some I have no reason to support,' Argyll commented when he forwarded a list of the new sixteen to Lord Milton in Edinburgh.[67]

Argyll had settled into a comfortably subordinate role which for the first time since 1741 somewhat mirrored his place within the Walpolean system. He suffered much less interference from others in Scottish affairs, but he took his orders when they were given to him. It is against the background of the information given above that Newcastle's often quoted description of Argyll as 'absolute governor of one of his Majesty's kingdoms' must be interpreted.[68] As we have seen, even for the short period of co-operation between Bute and himself there were many limitations on his power, not only because Bute's wishes had to be taken into account but because Newcastle could not be too sharply shut out of Scottish affairs. Argyll was not the 'absolute governor of one of his Majesty's kingdoms'; Newcastle himself had seen to that.

The new settlement between Bute and Argyll had no sooner emerged, however, than another became necessary. Argyll died on 15 April, quietly expiring just before he was to leave for Scotland to attend the election of the Scottish Representative Peers. All thoughts, in Scotland at any rate, now turned to Lord Bute. Many considered him Argyll's political heir; all speculated on the direction he would choose to take in dealing with the government of Scotland. In England, Newcastle and Hardwicke entertained fond hopes of change in Scottish government by replacing Argyll with a more amenable Scottish peer, such as the Earl of Marchmont or the Earl of Hopetoun, with Lord President Arniston taking Lord Milton's place in Edinburgh. They did not envisage a change in the system of Scottish government, but a change in its ideology. Hardwicke put it this way:

> My apprehension is, to keep down the Highland Influence, which has always been either Jacobite in itself, or has supported the Jacobites in order to avail itself of their strength. The remains of *the Squadrone* are the true Whig Interest in Scotland, but they have few capable men amongst them . . .

He went on to suggest Hopetoun and Arniston 'as subordinate ministers in Scotland'. Newcastle was not as optimistic, but he shared Hardwicke's hope that the Lord President might replace Milton as the ministry's correspondent in Edinburgh, 'but I fear we shall not be able to bring it about'.[69] His interview with Bute two days after Argyll's death confirmed his doubts. Bute merely expressed the wish that Newcastle would support Argyll's friends, as they would now be dependent upon himself. He told the Duke that Gilbert Elliot would be too busy with his new post as a Lord of Treasury to administer Scottish affairs, remarking that Lord Milton was 'a clever fellow', and astounding Newcastle by speaking of himself 'as having little to do in Scotland; or at least, as being in no degree, particularly concerned about it'. Scotland should be considered as 'any other part of the United Kingdom', Bute told Newcastle.[70]

Bute did not want to assume his uncle's mantle as a Scottish politician; he gloried in the name of Briton as much as the young King, and felt that the divisions between Englishmen and Scots had existed for too long and should cease, just as he abhorred the older generation's use of the labels Whig and Tory. Bute looked to the great stage of state, the Peace which would have to be made, and the reign of a Patriot King. Scotland was a tangent, a distraction — even an inconvenience.

Yet Bute would no longer allow Newcastle to meddle in Scottish affairs. Newcastle proposed that the distribution of Argyll's Privy Council offices should benefit the Earl of Morton and the Earl of Marchmont, both associates of his if not exactly friends. Instead Bute advised the King to make his close friend the Duke of Queensberry Keeper of the Great Seal, and the Marquess of Tweeddale Lord Justice General, neither of whom could sit in the House of Lords. Queensberry claimed the right to sit in the Lords as the Duke of Dover, and refused to stand as a Representative Peer while the Lords refused to admit him as a British peer. Tweeddale had become a cripple, barely able to stand; he had been appointed because the Earl of Granville claimed it his right as the last Extraordinary Lord of the Court of Session. Newcastle was deeply offended, complaining to the Duke of Devonshire that the appointments had been made without 'concert or consultation with any of us', although he later allowed himself to be persuaded that Morton and Marchmont would receive favour in the future.[71]

Like Newcastle, Bute assumed that Argyll would have to be replaced, that there had to be a minister for Scotland, but he was not thinking of Morton or Marchmont, or even Queensberry. He did not want to be bothered with Scottish affairs, yet he felt obliged to take up the Argathelian interest, partly because he had in a sense inherited it and partly because Argyll's followers were eager to transfer their loyalty to him. The only person he felt he could trust to relieve him of the burden of Scotland without forcing him to relinquish it was his own brother, James Stuart Mackenzie, at that time British minister in Turin. Two days after Argyll died, Bute wrote to Mackenzie to inform him of their uncle's death, and complained of the problems caused by the event:

> See my brother the perverseness of human fate; I have been these five months carefully avoiding all Scotch affairs; and now they are thrust upon me in a manner not to be resisted; the patronage alone I could despise; and give the power to another without the least regret, but to deliver my uncle's friends, my friends, into the hands of their enemies when they implore my protection is not honourable, judge then what a load of business comes upon me; sinking under the former load.[72]

A second letter asked Mackenzie to return to Britain to manage Scottish affairs and stand by his brother in his time of need. This Mackenzie, who had been urging Bute to appoint him Ambassador to Venice, reluctantly agreed to do. Until he reached London, Bute turned to Gilbert Elliot to undertake Scottish affairs on a temporary basis. Elliot's new place at the Treasury put him in a good position to look after Scottish affairs in that department while at the same time working through Bute's secretary Charles Jenkinson in the Secretary of State's office, for Bute had just become Secretary of State for the Northern Department.

It was also decided to continue to use Lord Milton as the government's sub-minister in Edinburgh. Within a few days of Argyll's death Bute had sent a letter to Lord Milton[73] assuring him of his willingness to support Argyll's friends, which gave Milton a token of support to quash the inevitable rumours that were circulating in Edinburgh. At the same time Gilbert Elliot began corresponding with Milton on Scottish affairs, particularly the mass of business which had to be transacted at the beginning of a reign when so many commissions and appointments had to be renewed, and which Argyll had only partially completed before his untimely death. Lord Milton, who had one son in Parliament and two in the army, was pleased to have the chance to establish their careers under Bute by continuing to serve himself.[74]

Thus the return of Argyll's body to Edinburgh from London on 15 May became a ritual demonstration of the continued influence and importance of the Argathelian party. Milton took charge of the ceremonies, which were given all the trappings of a state occasion. As the body was taken down the High Street and the Canongate to lie in state at Holyrood Palace, it was followed by a procession of mourners that included several Scottish peers who were then in Edinburgh, the Judges of the Court of Session, the Barons of Exchequer, the Commissioners of Customs and Excise, the Magistrates of Edinburgh, the Professors of the University, the leading clergy in Edinburgh, and many gentlemen of substance who also happened to be in the city at the time.[75] And to ensure that the point was driven home to one and all, Milton wrote the following account of the ceremony for the Edinburgh newspapers and the *Scots Magazine*:

Last night the corpse of the late most noble Archibald Duke of Argyle was brought to the apartments of his Grace's family, in the Palace of Holyrood House, and there laid in state, in the presence of a numerous company of nobility and gentry, together with the magistrates of this city, and members of other respectable bodies here, who by their attendance on that occasion, testified their regard to the memory of this illustrious person. The crowds, which filled every avenue through which the hearse was to pass, and the silent appreciation which preceded its appearance, gave proof that that singluar importance and consideration which this great man had acquired, more by his abilities, and the lustre of his public conduct, than even by the nobility of his birth, or the eminence of his station, without any badges of honour, even without affecting to possess the favour of courts; those abilities drew upon him the attention and confidence of his fellow subjects; and without the advantages of a minister, bestowed upon him a very high degree of ministerial power. His strength lay in depth of judgement, the talents of conversation, and graceful elocution, discernment, moderation and caution. The part which he took in the divisions of his country during the course of a long and active life, whilst it threw him in the way of opposition, never drew upon him the personal and bitter enmities which too often attend the contentions of party. Nor did his firm attachment to the interests of the protestant succession, for which in his youth he distinguished himself in the field, ever appear in that invidious scrutiny of party distinction, by which the divisions of a people are unhappily fomented; and personal importance acquired by exasperating the misfortunes of a country. On these foundations were built his extensive influence, the sincere regret with which his death is lamented by his numerous friends, and the view of importance in which that event has been considered by the public.[76]

The reference to 'personal importance acquired by exasperating the misfortunes of a country' was not lost on several interested observers. 'Your Lordship may perceive to what quarter the discourse is directed,' the Earl of Morton wrote to Hardwicke in a letter which was accompanied by a copy of the *Edinburgh Evening Courant*, and added, after identifying the author, 'would he have spoke this plain without a hope of support.'[77] 'I observed the printed Character & political Conduct of the late Duke of Argyll,' wrote the Earl of Breadalbane to Hardwicke. 'It seemed a pretty extraordinary performance and I believe the same observation occurred to me as to your Lordship upon it.'[78] In short, it had been made clear to all concerned that Lord Bute did not intend to dismantle his uncle's political system.

The chief instrument of this policy, Lord Milton, spent the next few months supervising the completion of the elections in Scotland and helping Gilbert Elliot see to the completion of such tasks as drawing up a new Commission of the Peace for Scotland. Most of this was routine administration involving much drudgery and a little politics, as in the distribution of some sinecures and Customs posts which had not been filled. Elliot proved diligent, but noticeably lacking in enthusiasm. 'I hope in time to be relieved from a task which I am in general neither fond of, nor indeed very fit to engage in, as my business and application here rather lie in different channels,' he wrote in his first letter to Milton after Argyll's death. Later he remarked that 'I protest I do my part in it from a mere sense of duty, for this detail is to me no amusement, and hardly comes within the pale of what is called ambition.'[79]

Elliot's one major influence on Scottish policy concerned the annexed estates. He had been on the old commission, although he had attended only a few times in 1755, but he had renewed his interest in 1760 when looking for material to justify the inclusion of the highland counties in his militia bill. Perhaps he was influenced by a letter he received in December 1760 from John Swinton, Sheriff-depute of Perthshire, which called Elliot's attention to the renewal of the commission which would have to take place after the accession of a new king, expounding:

> The state of the highlands is far from being understood. I observe these have not turned to any great account to the public or that much has really been done for the inhabitants. I except those who have gone to Canada. I mean there is really a Canada at home *si sua bona NORUNT*. There is a noble field for any man of attention, and I own I would wish to be in the Trust that I might be entitled and enabled.[80]

Argyll had prepared a draft of a new commission in early 1761 that had left out two old enemies of his, William Alexander and Lord Deskford, and included some of Lord Bute's friends. It was stopped at the Treasury by Newcastle, as soon as he heard of Argyll's death, in the hope of significantly changing it by the exclusion of Lord Milton and other friends of Argyll. He was unsuccessful in his attempt to choose a new commission, but Bute did decide to revise Argyll's draft after consulting Elliot on the matter.[81] Elliot was able to turn his attention to the business in the summer of 1761, when he got Bute to arrange the appointment of new Treasury representatives to negotiate with the Subject Superiors of those estates still administered by the Barons of Exchequer, to appropriate £30,000 to settle the debts on the Lovat estate, and to appoint a new commission. Both the new Commission of Annexed Estates and the new Board of Trustees were appointed almost completely on the basis of suggestions from Lord Milton; Newcastle could only ensure that Stamp Brooksbank continued as the commission's secretary, and delay Treasury approval for several of its projects.[82] Despite Newcastle's resistance, Elliot had been successful in finally getting the Treasury to pay some heed to the almost moribund commission, providing a basis for the attempt to expand its activities in the next few years. It was his one real accomplishment during the brief time he served as Scottish minister.

Elliot gave up Scottish affairs in favour of Treasury finance and parliamentary debates at the end of August 1761. James Stuart Mackenzie had arrived in London and was ready to take his place, the King having provided him with a pension of £2000 a year on the understanding that he would be given the first vacancy among the Scottish offices of state. George II was dead, Argyll was dead, and soon Newcastle would be out of office. In their place was a very young King, Lord Bute and his brother, and new politicians with new attitudes like Gilbert Elliot or Charles Townshend. Something was changing in Britain, and changing more rapidly because of the war. Political opinion in Scotland was shifting, becoming more British, demanding equality, not independence, within the United Kingdom. Perhaps the success of the war had encouraged the growth of this sentiment amongst a generation of gentlemen Scots who had grown to maturity since the 1745 rebellion. The assumptions of Argyll and Newcastle were those of a different world. After 1761 one of this new generation of Scots, raised in England, took Argyll's place. James Stuart Mackenzie was Bute's surrogate in taking Argyll's place; he and Bute together were continuing an arrangement which symbolised a separate Scotland yet were members of a generation that wanted to assimilate to British values. There was a contradiction inherent in the situation which would be unhappily resolved during the first years of the reign of George III.

5

James Stuart Mackenzie and the Government of Scotland, 1761-1765

JAMES STUART MACKENZIE was the younger and only surviving brother of the Earl of Bute, taking his surname from the entailed estate he had inherited from his great grandfather.[1] He shared his brother's conceited attitude to politics, demanding significance as a reward for moral virtue, an attitude in which both of them drew much from the example of Pitt, but without Pitt's passion and vision. Whereas Pitt, the true country Whig, spoke of the people and the state, Bute and Mackenzie's thoughts never strayed beyond the King and the Court. They were rigid and doctrinaire on small issues without ever grasping the larger ones. Namier was right to emphasise that Bute was nothing like the malignant figure that loomed so large in the Whig histories, but John Brewer's recent attempt to show that Bute was still a pernicious influence on the development of the British constitution carries much conviction.[2] The King was entrusting power to a personal favourite who had little or no basis of power in Parliament or in England generally. Bute, essentially, held himself accountable to the King alone.

Mackenzie took his political ideas from his elder brother. By contrast with the constant tension that had existed between Ilay and the second Duke of Argyll, their nephews were devoted to one another. Both were closer to the second Duke than to the third in temperament and outlook. Both took an intensely moral view of the world and both followed the second Duke into opposition against Sir Robert Walpole. Mackenzie, in his youth, was every bit as impetuous as his uncle had been. Shortly after his return to London from the Grand Tour, in 1742, he began to pursue an impassioned love affair with a famous dancer, Barberoni, whom he followed abroad to Venice and Berlin. The third Duke of Argyll felt obliged to end the affair by arranging Mackenzie's deportation back to London, where he suffered something very like a nervous breakdown.[3] Later he rejected his youthful escapades, married a plain but devoted daughter of the second Duke of Argyll, began to attend Parliament regularly, and in 1758 took up an appointment as British envoy to Turin.

Several historians have expressed their admiration for Mackenzie's outbursts of virtuous rhetoric and his undeniable honesty, adopting the accolade published by his personal secretary, Louis Dutens.[4] While there is no need to quarrel with the fact that Mackenzie was upright, honourable and scrupulously honest, it is possible to regard his insistence on proclaiming the fact at every opportunity, his pride and his lack of sensitivity, as negative characteristics that affected his fortunes as minister for Scotland. Perhaps the emotional catharsis of his youthful love affair may have had some effect. 'The conclusion I draw is, that in this uncle of mine there existed two separate, different men,' Bute's youngest daughter, Lady Louisa Stuart, wrote in her memoirs:

> that one soul had at a certain moment quitted his frame, and another of quite distinct properties entered it, and taken peaceable possession. For surely there are extraordinary mental commotions which (once thoroughly experienced) do in general leave as indelible marks behind them as those violent bodily diseases which change the whole mass of our blood . . .

His niece remembered him as 'the best humoured mortal alive — always in good spirits, always happy, fond of society and from his lively, amusing conversation formed to delight it'.[5] This agrees with a brief aside in a draft letter by Lord Milton which describes Mackenzie's 'lively sweet tempered gentleness, judicious *life* & *spirits*'. Yet Lady Louisa also noted that Mackenzie's temper had been 'once impetuous', and Mackenzie himself once admitted that 'I . . . have not so much stoical virtue allotted me.' By 1761 his passionate nature had mellowed, at the age of forty-two, to a joking affability which enabled this highly strung man to cope with life. 'Though I sometimes deal in roguish *double entendres*,' he wrote to Lord Milton, 'I have not wit enough to deal in *knavish* one[s].'[6] Lady Louisa qualified her affectionate account of her uncle by recalling:

> only with us, his relations, he had a trick teasing to all except absolute simpletons. You never grew up for him: at eighteen you were five years old; at thirty — nay — forty, not above twelve; assailed with jokes and nursery stories . . . Girl or woman, you found this annoying; but for men! I have seen my elder brothers ready to knock him down.[7]

One wonders if the trait his niece noted was visible to those outside his family circle as well. Alexander Carlyle's memoirs contain the following acerbic account of his meeting with Mackenzie in 1754, and their subsequent relationship:

> Mr. Mackenzie was very agreeable, his vanity having carried it so far above his family pride as to make him wish to please his inferiors. I was simple enough then to think that my conversation and manners had not been disagreeable to him, so that when I was at London four years after, I attempted to avail myself of his acquaintance; but it would not do, for I was chilled to death on my first approach, so that all my intimacy vanished in a few jokes, which sometimes he condescended to make when he met me on the streets, and which I received with the coldness they were entitled to.[8]

Even with so close an associate and aide as Baron William Mure, Mackenzie employed a banter that contrasted with the respectful tone of his letters to Lord Milton. He was even prepared to scold Mure outright: 'if you could find for love or money a good writing master I should be very glad to contribute largely to his upkeep,' or again, 'I beg you'll make this matter a little plainer, that the unlearned may comprehend it,' or yet again, 'these half words of information, at 400 miles distance in a pressing affair, are intolerable.'[9]

This attitude did not matter so much in dealing with his relations, a parish minister like Carlyle, or even the patient Mure, but it did matter very much in dealing with those who applied to him for patronage and help with the government. Though Mackenzie himself was an exceedingly sensitive man, he was insensitive to the feelings of others. A minister could not always obtain what was asked of him, but the first rule of such an office, particularly one primarily concerned with patronage, was to pay attention and marks of respect to those who did ask. Mackenzie saw this as empty show, or even insincerity; as he explained to Lord Rollo:

> Let me assure you, that my not answering your former letters did not proceed from the smallest indifference towards you, or neglect of your interests; but I wished to have it in my power, when I did write, to tell you, that my endeavours to serve you, had been attended with success . . .[10]

The freeholders, Members of Parliament and peers who needed his help, however, found this tone unsettling, or even offensive. Expressions of dissatisfaction by those attached to Bute indicate that Mackenzie's later troubles under Grenville may have been at least partly of his own making. The Earl of Erroll, for one, complained to Mure in 1761 that a memorial he had sent to Mackenzie had met with no response, and 'if there has been no mention made to you of this affair, I must directly apply to superior powers, where I hope I shall at least be used with civility.'[11] James Coutts, Member of Parliament for Edinburgh, complained in 1763 that 'notwithstanding I was so much obliged to Mr. M[ackenzie] for bringing me into Parliament, I do not think (but from what reason I know not) that he has that opinion and confidence in me he ought; and, allow me to say, even that I deserve.'[12] Lord Milton broached the matter to Mackenzie in 1763, informing him that Lord Frederick Campbell had expressed the 'high obligations' he owed to Bute and Mackenzie, but felt he was never consulted or kept informed by Bute and Mackenzie, 'and this is a common complaint from all your best friends'.[13] As long as Bute continued to hold office, Mackenzie's personality caused no problems, but after the arrival of Grenville, Mackenzie's lack of political instinct and tact weakened an already tenuous position within the ministry.

The Scottish ministry was a political post designed to maintain the government's grip on the forty-five Scottish M.P.s and sixteen Representative Peers. Mackenzie, however, viewed the office as a department of state like the War Office or a Secretary of State's office, and so set out to learn the Scottish 'business'. He complained to Lord Milton that he could not find any information in London, that 'there does not appear even a vestige of the business carried on, previous to this time.' 'I expected to have met with a variety of papers relative to the political and commercial state of that country, none of which, I have yet set eyes on.' Milton replied that Scottish affairs had not previously 'been reduced to any proper useful science, but things were considered as they occurred, and executed according to the former precedents'.[14] Argyll had not needed papers on

Scottish administration because he had been an integral part of its evolution since the Union; but now a man of the post-Union generation was undertaking the task. Mackenzie had not previously been involved in any aspect of Scottish government; like the Marquess of Tweeddale in 1742, he was faced with a task for which he had little experience. He was a born bureaucrat, or perhaps he had become one while he had been a diplomat at Turin; and many of his subsequent difficulties were those of a talented administrator forced to work through a structure which had evolved out of political pressures rather than administrative ones.

Lord Milton became Mackenzie's principal tutor in his study of Scottish government. Milton continued the series of memorials he had begun to write for Gilbert Elliot's benefit: material based on his own knowledge, what others in Edinburgh could tell him, and what he could find in the Laigh Parliament House. In addition, Mackenzie began to correspond with Baron William Mure once he had taken his place on the Scottish Court of Exchequer, as well as Commissioner Corbyn Morris at the Board of Customs, on revenue problems in Scotland. He also took a great deal of care in obtaining accurate information on the salaries and fees of offices, and Scottish pensions.[15]

Mackenzie's interest in the particulars of his office and information concerning Scotland and Scottish government was not confined to the first few months that he was learning his job. The man had an almost obsessive taste for book-keeping, indicated by the mass of tables, lists and abstracts in the remnant of his papers which survives today at Mount Stuart on the Isle of Bute. He was a man who wanted the facts at his fingertips, as his comments to Baron Mure on the proposals for a Forth/Clyde canal show:

> You know how very vaguely the people the most conversant in those matters will talk to you on such a subject. We see this every day in committees of Parliament, when witnesses are examined concerning facts that one would think the most stupid of them could not fail to know with precision; and yet no two of them will give anything like the same account of the matter.[16]

Throughout 1762 and 1763 Mackenzie continued to ask Milton and Mure for more information on Scottish revenue and offices; from a copy of the current Establishment at the Court of Exchequer to a table of military offices connected with Scotland; from the amount of tax paid on salaries in Scotland to lists of officers employed by the Commission of Annexed Estates and the Board of Trustees. He also took an interest in Alexander Webster's work on Scottish demography, obtaining several of Webster's papers which he used in having one of Dorret's maps of Scotland marked 'in such a manner as to distinguish on the map clearly the highlands and the lowlands'.[17]

Bute placed everything regarding 'our country and our friends' under Mackenzie's direction: all Scottish offices nominally at the disposal of the Secretary of State for the Northern Department or the Board of Treasury and all exclusively Scottish concerns of the government. Final decisions, as under Bute's arrangement with Argyll, were left to Bute when he had the time to discuss

Scottish affairs. Newcastle generally accepted this arrangement while he remained at the Treasury; after Bute had moved to that department his clerk Charles Jenkinson generally helped Mackenzie's patronage requests through both the Secretary's department and the Treasury.[18] Jenkinson was particularly useful because he had served in both offices and so had a thorough knowledge of the bureaucratic procedure involved. There were attempts to circumvent Mackenzie; but Bute was usually conscientious in referring all such attempts back to his brother, who saw him almost daily: 'in truth as I have more than once wrote to you,' Gilbert Elliot reminded his father, 'Mr. Mackenzie is the Minister for Scotland and going anywhere else is only giving offense without any chance of success.'[19] Indeed, when Bute was ill in the spring of 1762, Mackenzie postponed all but the most pressing appointments until he was well.[20]

Lord Milton served Mackenzie and his brother as their chief correspondent and spokesman in Scotland as long as Bute held office. When Mackenzie was ready to take up Scottish affairs, Elliot wrote to Milton that he would 'enter upon this scene with your Lordship under his brother's auspices'.[21] Even after Bute had left the government, Mackenzie continued to depend on Milton, and stayed with him when he visited Edinburgh in the summers of 1763 and 1764, much as Argyll had done during his annual jaunts north in the 1740s and 1750s. Milton's health had not been good for years, but he decided to press on, as we have seen, because he hoped to safeguard the military careers of his two younger sons. His hopes were amply repaid by Bute and Mackenzie. In 1764 they persuaded George III to give Milton's second son, Henry Fletcher, the colonelcy of a regiment of foot at a time when numerous officers were being reduced to half pay; they also obtained a captaincy, and then a majority, for Milton's youngest son Jack, although the majority cost Milton £3000 in purchase money.[22]

Milton's tasks extended beyond forwarding information on Scottish administration to London. In the autumn of 1761, for instance, Mackenzie had asked him to revise the proposed lists of Justices of the Peace in Scotland which had been submitted by the various M.P.s and ineptly revised by the Lord Justice Clerk, or at least, not revised to the Lord Chancellor's satisfaction.[23] Milton served as the channel of communication between Bute and Mackenzie and the old Argathelian party, or others, like Lord Advocate Miller, who had accepted Milton's help in the past. Milton also acted as a kind of parliamentary whip for Mackenzie, taking some measure of responsibility for getting Scottish M.P.s to attend Parliament in 1761, 1762 and 1763, in which last year George Grenville's circular letters were sent to Milton for distribution. 'I thought Mr. Fox's famous letter had put them [circular letters] out of fashion,' Sir James Carnegie wrote to Milton in 1762, 'but since this method is renewed, though by second hand, and that your Lordship has undertaken for me, I shall endeavour to kiss your hands at Edinburgh about the end of the month.'[24]

Milton was an old man, however, and could not live forever. 'Lord Milton continues to be our minister here,' the Earl of Breadalbane wrote to Hardwicke after Argyll's death, 'but the bad state of his health makes it impossible for his power to last a great while.'[25] Bute and Mackenzie realised this as well, and looked to Baron William Mure as Milton's eventual successor. 'Though his [Mure's] Manner was Blunt and unattractive,' Alexander Carlyle recalled, 'Yet at the same time he was unassuming, of excellent understanding, and Great Ability for Business.'[26] When Mure first went north to take his place in the Court of Exchequer, Bute expected him to serve as an aide and link with Milton. He corresponded with Mackenzie and with those who had adhered to Bute in the 1750s while Milton attended to the former Argathelians. He kept Mackenzie informed of affairs at the Scottish Court of Exchequer, helped gather information on Scottish administration and, like Milton and Corbyn Morris, was asked to send his recommendations for Customs posts to London. Eventually he began to assume more of Milton's responsibilities. By the autumn of 1764 he had completely replaced Milton as sub-minister,[27] although Mackenzie's loss of office the following May ended his tenure. He afterwards continued for some years as the chief representative of the Bute interest in Scotland.

Mackenzie, Milton and Mure enjoyed a particularly peaceful political situation in Scotland in the early 1760s. The old aristocratic interests which had held sway in Scotland at the time of the Union had almost completely faded away. There had never been very many of them, but by 1761 they were in a particularly depleted state. The great ducal houses of Gordon, Buccleuch, and Hamilton were represented by minors; the new Duke of Argyll was old and stupid, the Duke of Atholl infirm, the Duke of Montrose blind, and the Marquess of Tweeddale a cripple. Of the sixteen Representative Peers, Bute had personally chosen five, and he chose two more at by-elections in 1761 and 1762; the rest were too old or too cautious to cause trouble. The Scots in the House of Commons were notorious for their slavish support of the government of the day, as they still showed little interest in English domestic issues. Bute inherited the Argathelians, and most of the others had already been associated with him one way or another, with four exceptions, whom Mackenzie once referred to as 'the scabby sheep': Daniel Campbell of Shawfield, George Dempster, James Murray of Broughton and Sir Alexander Gilmour. Campbell had chosen opposition because he had been disappointed in seeking a favour from the Crown; the others could be termed, with varying degrees of accuracy, opposition Whigs.[28]

There were some Scots, like Dempster and Gilmour, who opposed Bute in Scotland on much the same grounds as the Old Corps Whigs opposed him in England. In February 1762 there was some dissatisfaction expressed in Edinburgh when Bute recommended a new Member of Parliament to the Town Council, and the following year he was attacked for being involved in the Town Council's attempt to choose the town's ministers without consulting the kirk sessions.[29] The Duke of Atholl refused to allow Mackenzie to browbeat him into supporting the Queen's secretary in a by-election in Perthshire on the grounds that 'Ministry shall always find me their friend whilst I think the measures they pursue are good, but never their SLAVE.'[30] Sir Alexander Gilmour wrote of the need to make a stand in Scotland 'against those who I am sure govern this part of the World with a rod of Iron, and whose whole conduct is applied to suppress the least Idea of a spirit of Liberty'.[31] Yet such opposition seems to have been scattered and weak, as even Newcastle's friends, the Earl of Hopetoun, Lord President Arniston and the Earl of Kinnoull, refused to become involved in formal opposition.

When Bute and Mackenzie's grip on Scotland weakened, however, it was not because they could not contain their enemies, but because they could not control their friends. The trouble started when Bute left office after concluding the Peace of Paris in 1763. One of the measures he took to safeguard the position of those who were identified with him was the appointment of Mackenzie as Lord Privy Seal of Scotland. Bute's successor at the Treasury, George Grenville, was to be a cipher in Scottish affairs while Mackenzie was to become what Argyll had been. 'The Scotch affairs will go on under the care of my brother, as they did under my late uncle,' Bute wrote to Baron Mure.[32] He and the King took some trouble to impress on Grenville 'that Mr. Mackenzie must be the recommender in the Scotch affairs', and Grenville wrote to Mackenzie that he had 'directed Mr. Jenkinson to pay an implicit obedience to Mr. Mackenzie's orders . . . in the same manner as when he was under Lord Bute'.[33] When Lord Milton, the voice of experience, expressed his doubts about the arrangement to Mackenzie, he was met with the emphatic reply

> that when I am no longer supported, I will no longer have anything to do with the Scotch business; I know well what my uncle went through, at times, in that department, and sure I am, that ten times the power he ever had, would not tempt me to submit to the same . . .[34]

Bute's attempt to make Grenville consign Scotland to Mackenzie appears wildly impracticable in retrospect. 'No first Commissioner of the Treasury ever gave way to the recommendations of any one man in Scotland to the degree which I have always done,' Grenville complained in 1764;[35] and he was right. The quick tempered Mackenzie could not summon the diplomatic resources one would expect of a former minister to Turin in dealing with the stiff, stubborn Mr. Grenville.

The great problem in Bute's arrangement, of course, was that Mackenzie had been set up as the King's minister for Scotland, not as Grenville's colleague; yet Scottish patronage passed through offices which Mackenzie did not control. If Mackenzie had continued to reside at London and if he had kept in close communication with Grenville, he might have avoided difficulty. Instead, he had closer relations with the King and with Charles Jenkinson at the Treasury than with Grenville. He also began to go north for the summer as his uncle had done, which brought him much closer to the realities, traditions and needs of the country he purported to manage. Soon he began to adopt an Edinburgh (and Perthshire, where he had an estate) perspective rather than a London one, a development which came to contribute much to his estrangement from Grenville. Like his brother, Mackenzie suffered from the ever-mounting cry in England against the Scots in general and Bute in particular, but unlike his brother he returned to his native land each summer, and sympathised with the spirit of improvement amongst the Scottish aristocrats and landed gentlemen who were determined to counter English prejudice by the rapid economic and cultural development of their country to reach and better English standards.

One must remember that John Wilkes published No. 45 of the *North Briton* just after the ministerial changes which had followed the Peace of Paris. The explosion which followed the arrest of Wilkes for seditious libel, the dispute over the use of a general warrant to do so, Wilkes's appeal in the Court of Common Pleas, and the other measures associated with this sensation not only preoccupied the Grenville ministry during most of its period in office, they encouraged the anti-Scottish feeling prevalent in England since Bute had acquired political power to reach new heights of abuse. Bute was the minister behind the curtain, went the cry, his retirement had been nothing but a sham. The Scots continued to act as servile servants of the Crown, acquiring offices and pensions through Bute's influence: the fact that the ministry followed the success of Wilkes's appeal in the Court of Common Pleas by starting a prosecution for seditious libel in the Court of King's Bench did not help matters, as the head of that Court, Lord Mansfield, was Scotch in addition to being more sympathetic to the Crown than Charles Pratt in the Court of Common Pleas. Here was an issue on which Pitt and Newcastle, who had both left the ministry before the conclusion of the Peace of Paris, could unite in opposition to the government. They never did so completely, but they did so often enough to give Grenville a rough ride in the House of Commons. Wilkes stood for opposition to Bute and protest at preferment for the Scots. Mackenzie was Bute's brother, a Scot, and responsible for Scottish patronage. These were not easy years for him.

While political difficulties in London encouraged Mackenzie to become re-acquainted with the country of his birth, George Grenville was as incapable of grasping the different context of Scottish affairs as he was incapable of grasping the different context of affairs in the North American colonies. Unlike Mackenzie, he was not concerned with the needs of the Scottish aristocracy at large, a group which he considered an unnecessary drain on the pension funds. Grenville believed that a man deserved patronage if he was a government supporter in Parliament. All other projects were frivolous. Nor was this attitude limited to patronage. Grenville's response to requests from Scotland for funds to build a Register House is a good case in point. The Duke of Queensberry reported to Lord President Arniston that Grenville had told him

> that an application there [to Parliament] would prove ineffectual because that in England the repositaries of the records of the several counties are provided at the expense of the counties themselves, and our records in Scotland would be considered in the same local view; but I think there is a great difference between the records of particular counties and those of a whole nation now happily united in England.[36]

Similarly, it was Grenville who actually began the long process of making the Customs system work in Scotland, most spectacularly by his purchase of the Isle of Man from the Duke of Atholl in 1764, a project long dearly desired by the Treasury. He also tightened up Customs appointments in Scotland and encouraged the Scottish commissioners, led by new appointment George Clerk, to inspect the outports and to dismiss any officers they suspected of dishonesty.[37] Grenville's attitude to Scotland was the same as his attitude toward America: each would have to pay its way.

Mackenzie did not quarrel with Grenville's attempt to reform the Scottish Customs, in fact he actively aided him in the attempt. He came to be obnoxious to Grenville because he represented Bute's interests, and Grenville soon wanted to forget Bute and sever any connection that remained between him and his ministry. The outcry in England against Bute's Peace of Paris and his supposed influence with the King had turned him into the political bogeyman of the decade. Mackenzie's independence in Scottish affairs was an affront to his authority, particularly as Mackenzie was on good terms with the King and Grenville was not. Their understanding began to disintegrate after Bute's involvement in an abortive attempt, without consulting Grenville, to get Pitt to form a ministry in the summer of 1763; in the aftermath of the failure of that initiative Grenville brought the Duke of Bedford and his adherents into the ministry to strengthen it before the new session of Parliament. Bedford had already begun to attract the allegiance of a number of important Scots in Parliament, including Sir Lawrence Dundas, the Earl of Panmure, Lord Frederick Campbell, and the Earl of Galloway's son, Lord Garlies. Through Bedford, they soon expressed an alternative view of Scottish affairs within the ministry. A projected plan to pension off the Duke of Atholl from his office as Keeper of the Great Seal in Scotland in favour of the Earl of Marchmont proved a harbinger of things to come. 'I am much convinced from some circumstances in the way I heard it that it has not been communicated to My Lord Privy Seal,' wrote one of Atholl's relations, 'and if so it shows in what new train they think of changing in part the management of Scotland, if not altogether.'[38] Ambitious Scots were again refusing to accept the authority of a Scottish minister.

Shortly afterwards Mackenzie's troubles began in earnest when the Earl of Galloway's son, Lord Garlies, began to make interest with the Duke of Bedford in an attempt to secure a lucrative office for his father. Garlies had entered Parliament in 1761 as M.P. for Morpeth in Northumberland. As the eldest son of a Scottish peer he was not able to sit for one of his father's seats in Galloway; nevertheless he continued to look on himself as a guardian of his father's interest and took an active role in the compromise over a Galloway election dispute in 1762. Bute and Newcastle (then still at the Treasury) agreed that the Argathelian candidate, John Hamilton of Bargany, would sit for the Galloway (or Wigtown) burghs in place of Garlies' brother, Keith Stewart, while Garlies' brother-in-law, James Murray of Broughton, took the county seat. Within months of this compromise Murray of Broughton had followed his friend the Marquess of Rockingham into opposition, and Mackenzie accordingly favoured Hamilton of Bargany's requests for vacant Customs offices in the county. Garlies, however, still supported the ministry as a follower of Bedford, and claimed that Mackenzie's treatment was unfair to his father and himself and was destroying their electoral interest. He and Mackenzie apparently quarrelled over the issue, and Garlies began to voice his complaints to Bedford, who passed them on to Grenville. Garlies claimed that his father and he had a right to government patronage for the county and burghs in which they held influence, even if the M.P. they had supported had turned against the ministry.[39]

Bedford took up the affair with Grenville, writing that 'I find not only in Lord Garlies, but in every Scotch nobleman or gentleman I speak with, a repugnance to have anything to do with Mr. Mackenzie, who has not the good fortune to be much liked by his countrymen.'[40] Grenville was anxious to prevent Garlies joining his brother-in-law in opposition. 'I see with concern every symptom of discontent and jealousy which your Grace observes amongst the Scotch noblemen and gentlemen,' he replied to Bedford, 'and should hope for the public benefit that harmony and good will might be conciliated, as far as possible, at such a conjuncture as this is.' He flatly refused to be browbeaten into any hasty action by Garlies, but he did offer to mediate with Hamilton and Mackenzie in order to obtain some consideration for Galloway and Garlies in Customs patronage in Wigtown. Garlies, however, soon had another grievance, claiming the office of First Lord of Police for his father on the grounds that he was the senior ordinary lord. He again sent a strong letter to Bedford demanding action, as Mackenzie's recommendation, Lord Cathcart, had nothing to recommend him but his interest with Bute, 'for I am sure he has no Parliamentary'.[41] Bedford complained to Grenville 'of want of participation in the distribution of offices', when he was so important a figure in the ministry. Grenville, trying to keep peace, promised to mention Galloway to the King, but explained 'that the Scotch promotions were made upon a former destination long before his Grace came into the office of President [of the Board of Trade]'. This Bedford seemed to accept.[42]

A few months later Bedford again became involved in Scottish patronage, this time on behalf of Sir Lawrence Dundas, another Scot who sat in Parliament for an English borough. Dundas had attended the winter session of Parliament to support the Government despite a severe fit of gout. As a reward, he wanted his brother-in-law and Stirlingshire elections manager, Robert Bruce of Kennet, named to a vacancy on the Scottish Court of Session that had arisen in April 1764.[43] Mackenzie, on the other hand, planned to name the Dean of the Faculty of Advocates in Scotland, James Ferguson of Pitfour, a very prominent figure at the Scots Bar who had not previously been considered for a gown because of his Jacobite connections. Mackenzie was supported by Lord Mansfield, and together they persuaded the King to appoint Ferguson, despite contrary applications from Grenville and Bedford. 'I am glad there has been this struggle of the Ministers,' the King wrote to Bute,

> for I will show them who recommends Scotch offices. I have ever declared Mr. Mackenzie for that department; I will settle that matter instantly and if they have not understood my orders on this occasion it is not for want of explaining the thing clearly, my words were that Mr. Grenville should see Mr. Mackenzie and desire him to name the person whose character would best supply the vacant gown.[44]

Shortly after this Mackenzie departed for Scotland, only to find, on his arrival at Edinburgh, that another judge had died. Along with the Edinburgh legal community, he wanted to name one of the joint Solicitors General, Francis Garden, and so restore that office to its normal state of being held by only one advocate. However, on finding that Bruce had a good character, 'though perhaps not the *properest* of any at the Bar', he decided to try to keep up good relations with Grenville and Bedford by recommending Bruce. Mackenzie knew that there was a strong possibility of yet another vacancy by the death of Garden's uncle, Lord Prestongrange, which actually did occur shortly afterwards, so Garden was also able to take his place on the bench (as Lord Gardenstone) later that year.[45]

Bruce of Kennet's promotion soon provided more trouble. He left a vacancy as Sheriff-depute of Stirlingshire, a county then in dispute between Bute's friend James Campbell of Ardkinglass, the sitting M.P., and Sir Lawrence Dundas, who was expanding his interest in the county. At first Mackenzie decided to solve this problem by appointing a friend of Lord Milton's who had been very useful in the 1764 Perthshire by-election,[46] but he soon received a request from the Sheriff-depute of Banff, George Cockburn of Ormiston, who had also helped in the Perthshire by-election. Mackenzie thought he could satisfy both requests by recommending Cockburn for the Sheriffdom of Stirling, shifting Milton's man to Banff. In so doing he stepped on a political landmine in the form of the interest of Lord Fife, Member of Parliament for the county of Banff.

Fife had recently succeeded his father as an Earl in the Irish peerage, a title that Newcastle, as a favour to the Grenville brothers, had upgraded in 1758 from the barony they had originally obtained from Walpole.[47] He had represented Banff since 1754, and though at one time associated with Pitt through the Grenvilles, he had chosen to attach himself to George Grenville when Pitt and Lord Temple went into opposition in 1763. When Fife heard that there was to be a new Sheriff for his county, he immediately wrote to Grenville complaining that such an action was a personal affront to an M.P. who supported the ministry, and he put forward the name of his brother-in-law, Keith Urquhart, as an alternative to Milton's man.

Grenville immediately wrote back promising to do all in his power to correct any attack on Fife's interest, although at the same time he confessed that he did not know which office at London handled the appointment.[48] He wrote to his two secretaries at the Treasury, Charles Jenkinson and Thomas Whately, to attend to the affair. They reported that the appointment had already passed through the Secretary of State for the Northern Department's office. They also, however, found that the same office had previously been in dispute between Fife's family and the Earl of Findlater in 1754-56, and from that assumed that the appointment Fife had complained about had been made in favour of the Earl of Findlater; Whately even claimed that Findlater was still hereditary Sheriff of the county. On the basis of this, Grenville assumed that Mackenzie was allied with Findlater in an effort to attack Fife's electoral interest, and despite Jenkinson's efforts to prevent any hasty action, he wrote a very bitter letter to Mackenzie:

> Can Lord Findlater's wish be urged as a good reason for attacking a Member of Parliament of Lord Fife's rank and fortune in the county for which he serves and could I believe that this would be done against one who is known to be personally attached to me without giving me the least notice of it [?][49]

Table IX: *Legal Appointments, 1761-1765*

date	office	appointee	interest	predecessor
May 1761	Lord of Session	J. Erskine of Barjarg	Lord Justice Clerk	P. Boyle, Lord Shualton, deceased
May	Baron of Exchequer	W. Mure	Lord Bute	J. Erskine, promoted
May	Baron of Exchequer	G. Winn	Duke of Newcastle	E. Edlin, deceased
Feb. 1762	Sheriff-depute of Haddington-shire	W. Law of Elvingston	Lord Milton?	J. Hamilton, resigned
June 1763	Lord Justice Clerk	Sir G. Elliot of Minto, Lord Minto, S.C.J.	G. Elliot, younger	C. Erskine, formerly Lord Tinwald, Lord Alva, S.C.J., deceased
June	Lord of Justiciary	H. Home, Lord Kames, S.C.J.	Lord Bute?	Lord Minto, promoted
June	Lord of Session	J. Campbell, younger, of Stonefield	Lord Bute	Lord Alva, deceased
June	Sheriff-depute of Angus	G. Ramsay	Earl of Pan-mure, M.P., Baron Maule	J. Campbell of Stonefield
Feb. 1764	Stewart-depute of Kirkcud-bright	A. Gordon	Earl of Aberdeen, Duke of Queensberry, Lord Advocate	D. Ross of Inverchassly, promoted Clerk of Session

The People Above

Table IX: *Legal Appointments, 1761-1765, cont.*

date	office	appointee	interest	predecessor
June 1764	Lord of Session	J. Ferguson of Pitfour	J. Stuart Mackenzie, Lord Mansfield	R. Pringle, Lord Edgefield, deceased
June	Lord of Justiciary	J. Ferguson of Pitfour	J. Stuart Mackenzie, Lord Mansfield	W. Grant, Lord Prestongrange, deceased
July 1764	Lord of Session	R. Bruce of Kennet	Sir L. Dundas, Duke of Bedford	G. Sinclair, Lord Woodhall, deceased
July	Lord of Session	F. Garden of Gardenstone	Lord Milton, Stuart Mackenzie	W. Grant, Lord Prestongrange, deceased
July	Sheriff-depute of Stirling-shire	G. Cockburn of Ormiston	R. Oliphant of Rossie	R. Bruce, promoted
July	Sheriff-depute of Banff	J. Erskine of Balgownie	Lord Milton	G. Cockburn, resigned
Aug. 1764	Sheriff-depute of Orkney & Shetland	W. Nairn	Earl of Morton, David Graeme, M.P.	Sir A. Mitchell, bart., deceased
Nov. 1764	Sheriff-depute of Banff	K. Urquhart	Earl Fife, M.P.	J. Erskine of Balgownie, resigned
Dec. 1764	Lord of Justiciary	G. Brown, Lord Coalstoun, S.C.J.	Lord Milton, Stuart Mackenzie	A. Fraser, Lord Strichen, resigned

Table X: *Appointments to Sinecures, 1762-1765*

date	office	appointee	interest	predecessor
Feb. 1762	Conservator of Scots Privileges at Campvere	G. Lind, Lord Provost of Edinburgh	Lord Milton	C. Stuart, deceased
March 1763	Gentleman of Police	Sir R. Menzies, bart.	Lord Bute	Sir R. Stuart, resigned to take a pension
March	Gentleman of Police	A. Fraser, younger, of Strichen	Lord Bute	N. Macleod of Macleod, resigned
April 1763	Conservator of Scots Privileges at Campvere	John Home	Lord Bute	G. Lind, resigned
April	Lord Justice General	Duke of Queensberry	Lord Bute	Marquess of Tweeddale, deceased
April	Keeper of the Great Seal in Scotland	Duke of Atholl	Lord Bute	Duke of Queensberry
April	Keeper of the Privy Seal in Scotland	J. Stuart Mackenzie	Lord Bute	Duke of Atholl
May 1763	Governor of Stirling Castle	Isaac Barré, M.P.	Lord Bute	Earl of Cassillis, deceased
May	Governor of Edinburgh Castle	Earl of Loudon	Lord Bute	General H. Bland, deceased

Table X: *Appointments to Sinecures, 1762–1765, cont.*

date	office	appointee	interest	predecessor
Dec. 1763	Governor of Stirling Castle	J. Campbell of Ardkinglass, M.P.	Lord Bute	Isaac Barré, dismissed
Jan. 1764	Deputy Postmaster General of Scotland	R. Oliphant of Rossie	J. Stuart Mackenzie	A. Hamilton of Innerwick, deceased
Jan.	Keeper of the Great Seal in Scotland	Earl of Marchmont	Lord Bute	Duke of Atholl, deceased
Jan.	First Lord of Police	Lord Cathcart	Lord Bute	Earl of Marchmont
March 1764	Governor of Dumbarton Castle	Archibald Montgomery, M.P.	Earl of Eglinton	Lord Cathcart
April 1764	H.M.'s High Commissioner to the General Assembly	Earl of Glasgow	Baron Mure	Lord Cathcart
June 1764	Master of H.M.'s Works in Scotland	J. Hamilton of Bargany, M.P.	Stuart Mackenzie?	W. Stewart of Hartwood, deceased
Dec. 1764	Clerk to the Admission of Notaries in Scotland	J. Erskine of Balgownie	Lord Milton	R. Nasmyth, deceased
Jan. 1765	Vice Admiral of Scotland	Earl of Hyndford	Stuart Mackenzie	fifth Earl of Findlater, deceased

Table X: *Appointments to Sinecures, 1762-1765, cont.*

Jan.	General of the Scottish Mint	A. Fraser, Lord Strichen, S.C.J.	Stuart Mackenzie	Lord Belhaven
Feb. 1765	Lord of Police	sixth Earl of Findlater	Stuart Mackenzie	Earl of Hyndford
April 1765	Secretary to the Order of the Thistle	Sir H. Erskine, M.P.	George III	G. Drummond of Blair Drummond, deceased

Grenville's testy letter elicited a terse response from Mackenzie by the next post, explaining why Erskine had been named to Banff, and absolutely denying the 'unfavourable insinuations' in Grenville's letter.[50] At the same time he wrote to his brother about Grenville's 'most high imperious angry letter', noting the ill-founded nature of the attack and commenting bitterly that:

> as the appointment of a Sheriff has nothing to do with the Treasury, but goes through the Secretary of State's office, Mr. Grenville has come a great deal out of his way to attack me with so much violence, and if the King pleases that Grenville should intermeddle in that manner with the affairs of this part of the Kingdom; all I would humbly beg is that I may be allowed to retire from them; for tis impossible for me to go through all the variety of plagues that I have, and at the same time be liable to the mortification of being thwarted and controlled and teized to death by such a man as he is.[51]

Grenville eventually apologised for his mistake, and wrote a long letter to Fife explaining the transaction, informing him that in the circumstances the appointment would stand and that it was not an attack on Fife.

Fife had already written to Grenville that he was not at odds with Findlater; indeed, that Findlater had first informed him of the vacancy. He insisted that the point was that Mackenzie had seen fit to appoint a Sheriff without even consulting, let alone taking a recommendation from, the Member of Parliament for the county:

> Mr. Mackenzie may put it on any footing he pleases to you, the truth is Mr. Cockburn the former Sheriff was put in here by the Duke of Newcastle, at a time when my conduct in Parliament and my *friends* [including Grenville] was in opposition to his Grace. I did not *then* complain, it was rather doing me an honour, for his Grace to mark me out in so particular a manner; Mr. Erskine's appointment is just in the same style without ever acquainting me . . .[52]

Fife got his way in the end. In September a good sinecure, Clerk of the Admission of Notaries, fell vacant, and Milton was able to secure it for his friend. As soon as Fife heard of this he renewed his applications to Grenville, who wrote to Mackenzie asking that no one be appointed to the Sheriffdom of Banff until he could meet with him in London. Charles Jenkinson later recalled that Mackenzie did not feel Urquhart, writing to Baron Mure that 'the fact between you and I, is really this: it intended to appoint a brother of the Earl of Aberdeen, but when Mackenzie returned to London in November, he granted Grenville's request to appoint Urquhart, writing to Baron Mure that 'The fact between you and I, is really this: it was not a thing of moment enough to differ about, and thereby to delay or prevent other matters of much greater consequence.'[53]

Most of these 'matters of much greater consequence' involved the disposal of more valuable offices. Fife's supposed rival, Findlater (the former Lord Deskford), was becoming quite friendly with Mackenzie, who proposed giving him a place on the Board of Police.[54] A project even closer to Mackenzie's heart concerned the provision of some sinecure for his step-father, Alexander Fraser of Strichen, a Lord of Session and Justiciary, who was now too old to fulfil his circuit duties as a Lord of Justiciary. Mackenzie wished to provide him with an income to make up for the loss of his Justiciary gown. Knowing Grenville to be vehemently opposed to pensions of any kind, Mackenzie hit upon the idea of making Strichen General of the non-existent Scottish Mint, a sinecure left vacant in the summer of 1764 by the death of Lord Belhaven. This, he claimed, would provide for Strichen and ensure that the office of Lord Justice Clerk would be open to a younger man when Lord Minto died, specifically, Lord Advocate Miller.[55]

Again Mackenzie fell foul of a Member of Parliament. This time it was John Dickson, M.P. for the county of Peebles, who had been angling for an office for years. Mackenzie was attempting to find something for Dickson, who had quarrelled with him because he had not yet received an office, but Mackenzie felt:

> Were he (from his character and turn and the idea people here [Edinburgh] have of him) to be made General of the Mint it would raise the laugh everywhere against me, for it would be placed to my account let who will have brought it about.[56]

Instead, he proposed that Strichen resign his Justiciary gown and that George Brown (Lord Coalstoun, S.C.J.) be appointed to it; Strichen would become General of the Mint at £250 per annum. He wrote to Milton for advice on how Strichen should resign, and received it, but also a caution against 'diverting offices which have always been held by the nobility into a different channel which . . . may create a general dissatisfaction among them'. Mackenzie replied

> that if [not] a reverend Judge of a worthy character, it might possibly have fallen to the lot of a Captain of an Indiaman, or to one, perhaps the least illustrious, of our representatives here; and such would have been the case I believe, if I had not strongly objected to it. With respect to any Peer obtaining it, I never found in any conversation I had on the subject with Mr. Grenville, that any one of them all *Out of Parliament* would have been acquiesced in, by him; and no one *in Parliament* had ever made the most distant application to me for it.[57]

Strichen got the Generalship of the Mint, despite 'Mr. Grenville's most unnecessary delays',[58] and Coalstoun got his Justiciary gown, but yet again Grenville was convinced that Mackenzie was unnecessarily antagonising Members of Parliament. By January 1765 relations between Grenville and Mackenzie were very cool indeed. 'Whatever office you have to solicite for your friend that I am unacquainted with,' Mackenzie wrote Mure at the time, 'for God's sake keep off your town of Glasgow from writing to their member, for that involves me in difficulties.'[59]

Even Gilbert Elliot began to come into conflict with Mackenzie in the winter of 1765. He was trying to become M.P. for the county of Roxburgh, where his family had some political interest, and to give up the county of Selkirk, where he was dependent upon the goodwill of the Buccleuch family. The Member of Parliament for Roxburgh, Walter Scott of Harden, was willing to resign if a place could be found for a relation of his, which would in turn allow Scott to take his relation's place as Cashier of the Scottish Board of Excise. Elliot soon became impatient with Mackenzie's efforts to fulfil Scott's requests, and began to solicit Grenville's help. When the sinecure office of Secretary to the Order of the Thistle fell vacant in March 1765, Elliot applied to Mackenzie for it in favour of Scott's relation, commenting to Scott that 'the whimsical situation of things between a Scotch and English Minister makes it the most difficult thing in the world to come to an issue upon any application whatever.'[60]

The appointment of a new Secretary to the Order of the Thistle provided the spark which made the 'whimsical situation' between Mackenzie and Grenville explode into something even worse. Grenville was determined to secure the office for Lord Fife's brother as a test of the King's confidence in him. Mackenzie claimed to have twelve applicants for the office and decided to submit a list to the King in order to allow him to choose for himself; Grenville took Mackenzie's refusal to recommend Lord Fife's brother to the King as a personal affront. The King had chosen an M.P., Sir Harry Erskine, who was of course much more closely identified with Bute than with Grenville. From that point onward Grenville and the King himself were embroiled in a battle over ministerial power which left Mackenzie a mere bystander of the contest, and ultimately its principal victim.

The breaking point came with the ministry's Regency Bill, which excluded the King's mother from any regency council in the event of another royal minority. George III was furious, and retaliated by renewing negotiations with Pitt for a new ministry with a view to ridding himself of Grenville.[61] The failure of these negotiations gave Grenville the opportunity to impose his will on the King, with Bedford's support, in the form of conditions for his continuing in office. The condition the King found most difficult to accept was the demand that Mackenzie lose his office so that he could no longer 'hold up the standard of ministry for Lord Bute in Scotland'.[62] George III agreed that Mackenzie should give up Scottish affairs but asked that he keep his office, as he had promised never to dismiss him; Grenville, however, insisted on replacing Mackenzie with Lord Frederick Campbell. As Horace Walpole later observed, it was impossible at that time to dismiss a ministry simply because it had no use for Lord Bute's brother.[63]

Grenville's wish to assert his authority and to mollify Bedford had both contributed to his quarrels with Mackenzie, but the specific issue of most of their disagreements concerned Grenville's insistence that Members of Parliament be favoured in the distribution of government patronage. He was not alone in this. Lord Milton had advised Mackenzie in 1761 that to preserve power, one had to make 'a proper use of it':

> There is one great object of a minister's attention [which] should be the establishing and preserving a Parliamentary Interest in the country which is indeed necessary for carrying on the public service by adding a proper weight to the power and influence of the Crown — the sinecure employments may be dedicated for those purposes with as few deviations as possible.[64]

This advice was seldom heeded by Mackenzie, who seemed to take everything but parliamentary interest into account in the distribution of patronage. The preceding narrative of his disagreements with Grenville reflects both his personal integrity and his lack of understanding of the political system.

The same dichotomy existed during the Grenville ministry that had existed in the Duke of Argyll's day: the ruling elite in Scotland was by and large quite happy to accept Mackenzie as a minister but the Scottish politicians in London, eager to attach themselves to English ministers, found his existence obnoxious and obstructive. Mackenzie was fated to be a victim of the constitutional struggle of the 1760s from the day Bute had left the Treasury. He was too closely identified with his brother, and Bute was too closely identified, justly or unjustly, with expanding the prerogative of the Crown at the expense of Parliament. Argyll had survived because of his close association with Walpole, not the King; but Walpole had held power for twenty years whereas Bute had lasted only two. Any hopes of establishing Mackenzie as a royal minister for Scotland, separate from the rest of the ministry, were illusory and naive, to say the least. They were hopes that belonged to the days of King William rather than King George. One could argue in theory that the King could pursue such an arrangement, but this argument ignored mid-eighteenth-century political reality, which dictated, quite bluntly, that a minister's power was founded on his influence on the House of Commons, despite the fact that he was appointed by the King.

Mackenzie might have survived if he had reached some sort of accommodation with Grenville, but neither he nor Grenville were very accommodating people. Grenville wanted his own minister for Scotland, not Lord Bute's brother. It is important to note that Grenville apparently did not intend to dispense with having a Scottish minister. When he imposed his terms on the King in May 1765, he sent for the Marquess of Lorne (the fourth Duke of Argyll's eldest son, later to become fifth Duke) and offered him Mackenzie's place as Lord Privy Seal of Scotland. It was hardly a break with tradition for an English minister to look to the Campbells for help in managing the Scots. Though Lorne refused to become involved, he persuaded Grenville to appoint his younger brother, Lord Frederick Campbell.[65] The plan probably was for Campbell to make recommendations on the distribution of Crown appointments in Scotland to Grenville, but that Grenville would have sole access to the King to obtain royal approval for these appointments. The only reason that this arrangement never came into effect was that the King was successful in persuading the Marquess of Rockingham to undertake the formation of a ministry to replace Grenville and his associates in June 1765. Thus, if we wish to discover the reason for the absence of a Scottish minister for more than a decade after Mackenzie's departure from office, we must look beyond the Grenville ministry to the ministries which followed it.

6

English Ministers and Scotch Politicians, 1765-1784

THE important point about eighteenth-century governments' attitudes towards Scotland was that they very seldom took the trouble to have one. Whereas the adjustments attendant on the Union several times forced the government to deal with Scottish problems in the first half of the century, by mid-century the Scottish ruling elite were beginning to consider the exploitation of the possibilities of participation in a British state rather than the preservation of the old Scottish social order. At the same time, they chose to eschew politics, largely because they could not afford the luxury of opposition while they were seeking acceptance as equals by the English elite. The national effort required by the Seven Years War and the heroic role adopted by Pitt attracted the support of most of the Scottish gentry for the first time since the Union. The war and Pitt seemed to offer Scotland a chance to win back its rightful place in the Union and thus erase the discrimination it had suffered since the 1745 rebellion.

In the postwar period improvement ceased to be the concern of a small, largely Whig, coterie, and became the object of the gentry's attention all across Scotland. 'At no period surely did there ever appear a more general, or a better directed zeal for the improvement and prosperity of this country,' Lord Minto wrote in his proposals for the improvement of the city of Edinburgh in 1752, 'persons of every rank and denomination seem at length to be actuated by a truly public and national spirit.'[1] This trend in public thinking continued with additional force after the Peace of Paris in 1763, though it was not to the liking of everyone. Many of those who supported the agitation for a Scottish militia from 1759 to 1762 did so from a conviction that Scotland was sacrificing its public virtue in its eagerness to ingratiate itself in the good graces of government. One militia proponent, in a letter to the press in 1762, urged 'that my countrymen would reflect on the fatal error which they commit in throwing all their attention on the side of commerce and wealth . . .'[2] But the pro-militia Scots, although their proposals were revived at the beginning of the American war, were fighting a losing battle. Public energy was put into the building of bridges and roads, the construction of a Forth/Clyde canal, the construction of a new town and public buildings in Edinburgh, the deepening of the Clyde, and the maintenance of an independent Scottish financial system. Historians seem doomed to eternal disagreement over the pace of economic change in the second half of the eighteenth century, but none of them denies its existence, and no one can deny that the elite of the country, whether it was successful or not, was trying to lead the country into a period of rapid economic development.

At the same time the state of politics in London, particularly the intensity of anti-Scottish sentiment aroused during the years Lord Bute was a public figure, did not encourage Scottish peers and gentlemen to take up public life. The third Duke of Atholl's response to contemporary politics was a perfect example of this. 'I would think it my Duty to Sacrifice my Private Satisfaction [to public service],' he wrote in 1766,

> but the more I see of the ways of the World at present, the more I am Convinced that the Post of Virtue & Happiness as well as of Honour is a Private Station — With Pleasure and Satisfaction amongst our peaceable Roks and mountains I view the distant Voice of Faction and Licentiousness.[3]

Two years later, after service as a Representative Peer, he wrote: 'Every days experience Convinces me that Planting trees is a more agreable & more Honest business than either supporting or opposing Ministers.'[4] The attitude of Bute and Mackenzie towards politics was similar; indeed both of them behaved very much as Atholl did in the years following 1765, by drawing back from public life. This did not affect the ministry because Scottish opinion was basically committed to the government. There were small mistakes and upsets in the decade which followed 1765, but nothing which would convince a ministry that Scotland required attention. Wilkes, the Americans, the Irish, and the East India Company were more pressing concerns.

This explains why none of the ministers who followed George Grenville employed a Scottish minister again until 1780. There no longer seemed to be a need for the 'semi-independent' system which had evolved after the Union, efficiently organised by Walpole and Ilay. When Scotland again acquired a minister in the person of Henry Dundas, the system which evolved would be on a very different basis from its predecessor. A description of that new system cannot be attempted here, but some account of the establishment of Henry Dundas's position as Scottish minister is offered by way of an epilogue to the demise of the old Argathelian system in 1765.

Grenville had intended to appoint his own Scottish minister, and Rockingham had tried to appoint one, but neither ministry lasted long enough to implement their plans. It is surely significant that only Newcastle pressed for the designation of a Scottish minister in the first Rockingham ministry.[5] The ministry which the elder Pitt, now Earl of Chatham, constructed to replace Rockingham's government in 1766 at no stage included a Scottish minister, and the thought of designating one does not seem to have crossed Chatham's mind. Perhaps he felt such an arrangement was not in keeping with the spirit of the Union; he never recorded his thoughts on the subject. Scottish affairs became the province of the Secretary of State for the Northern Department and Scottish patronage largely the responsibility of the Duke of Grafton as First Lord of the Treasury. Both took decisions on Scottish affairs, usually appointments, only when it was absolutely necessary for them to do so. Otherwise Scotland was ignored. After 1770 Lord North followed Grafton's approach in regard to Scotland until Henry Dundas's value as a government speaker in the House of Commons forced him to change. There were so many Secretaries of State for the Northern Department from 1765 to 1780 that few had time to exploit the potential influence of their office; most allowed Lord Mansfield to guide them in making the Scottish legal appointments that were part of their departmental responsibilities.[6]

In the meantime a succession of prominent Scottish public figures were credited with being Scottish minister in Scotland itself. Having dealt with central government via a minister or manager for so long, a sizeable proportion of Scotland's elite could not accept that the government expected Scots to pursue their claims on its services in the same manner as the nobility, gentry and clergy of England and Wales. Thus James Stuart Mackenzie (who had regained his place as Lord Privy Seal when Chatham formed his ministry in 1766), the Earl of Marchmont (Keeper of the Great Seal), the Duke of Queensberry (Lord Justice General), and Sir Alexander Gilmour (a friend of Grafton's), all received a steady stream of requests for favours and patronage. All of them had some influence with various ministries, but none of them was a minister. 'I am now so happy . . .,' Mackenzie wrote in 1767, 'as to have no sort of Concern in the Disposal of Offices in Scotland, nor in the Elections of Members of either House of Parliament.'[7] Queensberry answered an approach from the city of Edinburgh to become its political patron by pointing out that

> It is a Misfortune, at least a great inconvenience to our Country that no man who has knowledge of it is now in a ministerial Situation, So that any Service I can be of must depend upon the degree of weight the persons in the Administration may allow me as an individual, without any official authority.[8]

Of all these politicians the most influential in the House of Commons after 1768 was Sir Lawrence Dundas. Ramsay of Ochtertyre, his memory confused, speaks of Sir Lawrence in 1764 as a man 'who without the name of Minister, had at that time the disposal of almost everything in Scotland'.[9] Lord Garlies complained to the Secretary of State for the Northern Department in 1769 that he had 'as good political interest as either the Duke of Queensberry or Lord Marchmont, who generally ask and get everything to be disposed of in Scotland except what is given to Sir Lawrence Dundas'.[10] Dundas's influence was directly related to the group of M.P.s he had established in the House of Commons, which varied in strength from four to eight votes, and to his connection with the Duke of Bedford, which helped him obtain patronage from the administration. His influence waxed to its fullest extent after the election of 1768; when Sir Lawrence himself was successful in obtaining the representation of Edinburgh, his brother was brought in for Orkney and Shetland (the superiority of which he had bought from the Earl of Morton in 1766), his son came in for the county of Stirling, his electoral manager, Colonel James Masterton, for the Stirling district of burghs, and two friends (including Alexander Wedderburn) for his borough of Richmond in Yorkshire.[11]

Sir Lawrence had started life as the son of an impoverished Edinburgh draper. He made his fortune as a commissary for the army during the 1745 rebellion, during which he had secured the patronage and friendship of the Duke of Cumberland, who helped him obtain contracts to supply the army in Germany during the Seven Years War. Through this activity Dundas became a very wealthy man. It could easily have been Dundas that Ramsay of Ochtertyre had in mind when he wrote that during the Seven Years War 'princely fortunes were acquired with great rapidity by some of our countrymen', whom Ramsay called 'blazing stars, which eclipsed our first nobility'.[12] Dundas bought extensive estates in Yorkshire, town houses in London, and much land in the central lowlands of Scotland where his family had originated. In 1764 he became the Governor of the Royal Bank of Scotland. During the Chatham ministry he became very active in Parliament on behalf of Scottish projects such as the Forth/Clyde canal and the Edinburgh Town Council's private bill to extend the royalty of the city as part of its project for a New Town.[13] Dundas was ambitious for his family; above all else, he wanted a British peerage to cap his riches. By making himself significant in Scotland and in Parliament he thought he could accomplish this ambition. Over the winter of 1768/69 he prevaricated over whether to join Bedford and the Court or Grenville and the opposition; but in the end, without a British peerage, he supported the ministry.

From that time until about 1772 Sir Lawrence secured much from the ministry, including a place on the Commission of Excise for former Lord Provost Gilbert Laurie of Edinburgh, and a coveted place as Gentleman of Police for his brother.[14] His friendship with the Earl of Sandwich and his importance in East India affairs increased his influence.[15] The trouble was that Sir Lawrence, having made himself important in Scotland, became involved in other things. When Parliament was dissolved in 1774, the baronet found himself beset by considerable electoral problems in Scotland. 'The handle or argument used against you,' his brother wrote to him from Stirling,

> is your indifference & no [sic] residence in the Country, The Voters are not noticed, when they are wanted they know their value & the combination of great families, encreases your difficulties, with uncertain friends.[16]

The 'combination of great families' which Dundas's brother referred to was led by the fifth Duke of Argyll, infuriated by Sir Lawrence's support for a rival of the Argyll interest in Dumbartonshire. Argyll carried his resentment over into opposition to Dundas's son in Stirlingshire, and opposition to their interest in the Linlithgow district of burghs. In retaliation, Sir Lawrence made the Glasgow and Clyde navigation bill, which was the first of Glasgow's attempts to organise itself to make the Clyde navigable, into a test of strength between Argyll and himself, delaying the bill for some time.[17] Dundas was also challenged in the Stirling burghs by a Colonel Campbell (no relation to Argyll), a wealthy nabob just returned from India; while in Edinburgh Dundas was attacked for ignoring the city's interests in Parliament and charged with corruption by his opponents. Sir Lawrence's attempts to get Lord North to support him came to naught, as North insisted that he wished to remain neutral in election disputes, though he categorically denied ever encouraging any opposition to Dundas.[18]

Sir Lawrence managed to hold on to his interest in Edinburgh and Stirlingshire in 1774, although he lost the Stirling district and failed to expand his influence anywhere else in Scotland. From that time onwards his relationship with the North ministry was an uneasy one, particularly after Henry Dundas became Lord Advocate in 1775 and, with the support of the wealthy Duke of Buccleuch, began an enthusiastic assault on Sir Lawrence's interest in the city of Edinburgh. There were strenuous contests over the Town Council elections of 1776 and 1777; at the same time Henry Dundas and Buccleuch succeeded in ousting Sir Lawrence from the Governorship of the Royal Bank of Scotland.[19] It became increasingly difficult for Sir Lawrence to support a ministry which permitted the Lord Advocate to engage in a systematic campaign against him. His son, Thomas Dundas of Castlecary, reported from Edinburgh in 1777 that

> If Lord North does not chuse to stop the Lord Advocate in opposing you and making use of the Crown's servants here as agents against you, I would have you put it at once upon the footing of his preferring the Advocate's interest in this country, I can give you twenty instances of his interfering, of his offering pensions to the wives and children of different people, of his attempting to attack the private credit of merchants because they came into Council avowedly to support your interest . . .[20]

Lord North continued his policy of neutrality in this dispute, despite Sir Lawrence's protests. Partly because of this attitude on the part of Lord North, Sir Lawrence ceased to support the ministry on the American issue by the autumn of 1779, his family connection with Rockingham — his son had married Rockingham's niece a decade before — making his transition to the opposition all the easier. The general election of 1780 saw Sir Lawrence and Henry Dundas battling for Edinburgh; and though Sir Lawrence won the battle over the election petition to the House of Commons, his death in 1781 ensured the ultimate victory of the Lord Advocate.

Henry Dundas re-established strong executive government in Scotland by attaching himself to the younger Pitt and unifying the ruling elite of Scotland in his interest. He started his career, as Solicitor General, under the patronage of his half-brother, Lord President Arniston. Later, when he began an attempt to secure election as Member of Parliament for the county of Edinburgh, he came into contact with the young Duke of Buccleuch, a wealthy Scottish peer (stepson of Charles Townshend) with extensive estates south of Edinburgh. Though Buccleuch had been brought up in England, he returned to Scotland to live upon his estates in 1767 and aspired to a place in Scottish public life. By 1773 he had come under the influence of Henry Dundas and Lord President Arniston. They helped Buccleuch to manage his electoral influence and he ensured their continued influence in Edinburgh county politics. And they seemed to think of more ambitious projects. Boswell's journal for 6 April 1775 recounts the current gossip in Edinburgh 'of the Duke of Buccleuch's imagining that he should be Prime Minister for Scotland, and that Harry Dundas was to act along with him'.[21] A month later Henry Dundas became Lord Advocate.

Henry Dundas used the authority of the Lord Advocate's office with a confidence that recalled the days of Duncan Forbes's tenure of the place earlier in the century. He actively sought the prevention of emigration from Scotland to America once it became apparent that war was imminent, acting in an executive capacity by writing to the Commissioners of the Customs and all the Sheriff-deputes of Scotland directing them to ensure that Customs officers prevented emigration from the outports and Justices of the Peace discouraged potential emigrants before they reached the ports.[22] Dundas went on to associate himself with criticisms of the Scottish electoral system, to introduce a Scottish militia bill in Parliament, to obtain the passage of a Corn Act which benefited the gentry in 1778, and to attempt an extension of Catholic Emancipation to Scotland in 1779.[23] He used the office of Lord Advocate to appeal to a national constituency, to set himself up as a representative of the landed interest of Scotland.

His ambition was manifest. Though he maintained an independent stance in regard to North's ministry, which he nevertheless generally supported,[24] he, his half-brother and Buccleuch were simultaneously propagating an altogether different image in Scotland, clearly displayed in their vendetta against the influence of Sir Lawrence Dundas. The centre of this conflict, with all the atmosphere of an eighteenth-century cockpit, was the city of Edinburgh, and the pamphlet literature of the time reflects Dundas's activity. Two examples will suffice. *A Dream*, published in 1777, depicts the extension of his influence over all areas of Scottish public life:

> From his right waistcoat-pocket depended this label, *Member for the County*; from the left, *Would be for the City*; from his right fob, *Attorney-General*; from his left, *Dean of the Faculty*; on his cravat, *Embargo on Shipping, Additional tolls*, 1775. On a feather, which waved from his hat, these words, *President of the Court of Session*; in his hand he held a Great Seal, which, however, some other person jointly grasped. And from his mouth these words: *Virtue its own Reward*. He muttered also something about Moderation, Modesty, and Meekness of Spirit, which I did not distinctly hear. At his back was a picture of the Temple of Liberty; on the pillars which supported it, on one side was written *Placemen*; on the other, *Pensioners*; over the capitals, *Plurality of Benefices*. In the centre of the pediment, was a medal, bearing a cheveaux de frise or Isle of Man coat-of-arms; on the one limb was written, Legislative; and the other, Judicative; on the third, Executive; round the margin this motto, *Tria juncta in uno*.[25]

Other writers opposed to Dundas contented themselves with mocking his pretensions:

> ... yet, as he has the disposal of some offices which are naturally bestowed at his recommendation, as member for the county, and Lord Advocate; by the help of this circumstance, that arrogant presumption, and those blustering airs, which are natural to his family, he has most artfully impressed upon his brethren, and many others in this country, a most ridiculous notion concerning the importance of his power; and to that effect, will tell twenty different stories to twenty different people, just as they will best suit his purpose. For instance, he tells to one set of people, That he is to make the Solicitor-General of England

[Alexander Wedderburn] member of parliament for Edinburgh: That Lord Suffolk, [Secretary of State], the said Solicitor-General, and himself, are hand and glove: That, through them, he has the disposal of *all offices in Scotland: And That Lord North has nothing to say in the matter*! — Again, he tells others, that he himself is to be member for Edinburgh; and to a third class, he will say, he is to make a *certain banker* the member. All of which, I am fully persuaded, *are equally true*. Nay, he had lately the presumption to send a clergyman, the most impudent of his order, to a person of high literary reputation, with a thundering message and declaration, 'That no person could pretend to rise in Scotland without the patronage of his Lordship and the Duke of Buccleuch'.[26]

There was more to Dundas's success than ambition; the landed interest of Scotland needed a political leader, as John Mackenzie of Delvine had commented in 1770 (see page 15): Dundas made himself the most obvious candidate for that leadership. His influence over areas remote from Edinburgh was still limited in 1780, but Sir Lawrence Dundas's death in 1781 ensured the ascendancy of his rival and namesake over the city of Edinburgh. Henry Dundas's and the Duke of Buccleuch's dominance over the Scottish metropolis implied political influence and power in Scotland which was perhaps more apparent than real.

Dundas did not fail to make use of this in London, where his abilities and confidence in parliamentary debate were making his support increasingly important to a ministry which was weakening year by year. Against the King's inclinations, Lord North made Dundas sole Keeper of the Signet in 1779 to help encourage him to act as North's principal lieutenant in the House of Commons.[27] This accession of influence in Parliament, and over North, gave Dundas the benefit of the ministry's influence in Scotland. With the outbreak of war with France and later Spain in 1778 and 1779, Dundas as Lord Advocate again took unprecedented initiatives for an occupant of his office in directing recruitment in Scotland.[28] In ecclesiastical affairs, it has been argued by Dr. Clark that Principal Robertson gave up his leadership of the so-called Moderate party in the Church of Scotland because of his distaste for Dundas's increasing influence in the affairs of the Kirk.[29] Dundas in 1781 saw himself 'in possession of the Confidence of Scotland, much great Influence there, and the avowed favourite of the Minister'.[30]

Dundas continued as Lord Advocate after the fall of the North ministry in 1782, probably because his disillusion with the war and support for peace had become well-known and because he had been the man who had forced the resignation of Lord George Germain as Secretary of State for the colonies, despite opposition from the King. North urged Dundas to continue in office, arguing that the various factions which made up the new ministry would soon be competing for his support. This proved to be the case, with the Earl of Shelburne especially keen to come to some terms with the Lord Advocate. After Rockingham's death he gave Dundas the entire patronage of Scotland, in addition to a sinecure for life and the Treasurership of the Navy. His friendship with North kept him his places when the Fox-North coalition took power, but Dundas eventually broke with his former leader over the coalition with Fox, siding with the younger Pitt and the King.[31]

As a result, Fox and the Home Secretary, the Duke of Portland, arranged the dismissal of Dundas in the summer of 1783, and his replacement by Henry

Erskine, who was not in Parliament. Apparently Scottish patronage was referred to Sir Thomas Dundas, Sir Lawrence Dundas's son. Boswell made an interesting observation of Whig intentions and of what actually happened: 'There was to be no go-between,' he claimed,

> nobody to keep back the individuals of that distant part of the island [Scotland] from fairly asserting their pretensions, whether from birth, wealth or merit. But alas! we soon found there was only *a change of Dundases*. Instead of Mr. *Henry Dundas*, we got Sir *Thomas Dundas*; now we have *Henry Dundas* again.[32]

Boswell was writing in 1785. Henry Dundas had become as important to the younger Pitt as he had been to Lord North in the last years of the American war. He had met and become friends with Pitt while serving under Shelburne. When the King dismissed the coalition and set up Pitt as his minister in December 1783, Dundas emerged as Pitt's lieutenant during the war of words which followed in the House of Commons over the next few months. Pitt made him Treasurer of the Navy again, as well as a Lord of Trade and a Commissioner of the Board of Control, which gave him a special authority in Indian affairs. His *protégé*, Ilay Campbell, became Lord Advocate, but Dundas kept control of Scottish patronage and exercised general authority over Scottish affairs; a role made possible by his close relationship with Pitt. Although Dundas had only limited success as an election manager for Pitt in Scotland during the general election of 1784,[33] his personal connection with the minister and his parliamentary importance established a new basis for Scottish government. Dundas had not yet become 'King Harry' in 1784, but he was certainly Crown Prince. The 'Dundas despotism' had arrived.

Conclusion

THE research which began this book was first undertaken with three goals in mind: to examine the nature of Scottish government in the eighteenth century, to study the political activity of the third Duke of Argyll in the last decade or so of his life, and to chart the decline of the Argathelian system of politics. All three of these goals were related to the question of why there was no Scottish 'manager' between 1765 and 1780. It seemed odd that a system which was often portrayed as one which prevailed from 1707 right through to 1832 should break down for such a length of time. The question clearly involved a period of transition from one system, the Argathelian, to another, that created by Henry Dundas, but there were many additional questions which remained unanswered.

As work progressed, it became apparent that the political fortunes of the third Duke of Argyll had to be set in the context of the 1745 rebellion and the Seven Years War. The distinction between Argyll's managerial capacity and his ministerial, or representative, capacity, is important here. Final assessment of Ilay's activity under Walpole must await the appearance of further research, but certainly after the 1745 rebellion and the repression which followed it in Scotland, Argyll acted as a guardian of national interests within the Union. Mild as English reaction was when compared with similar situations on the continent, reaction there was, and Scotland suffered accordingly. Argyll's political clout and instinctive diplomacy prevented some excesses and modified others.

The pressures of the Seven Years War provided a common crisis and a common enemy to unite the Scottish and English ruling elite, with Pitt as the symbol of a new British, and imperial, patriotism. The practical aspect of this was the disproportionate burden Scotland bore in providing manpower to fight the war. This is a subject which has never received the extensive study it deserves, though even the slightest familiarity with the source material available establishes Scotland's extensive contribution to the war effort. This activity made Argyll necessary to the government and put paid to any projects the Newcastle Whigs might still have harboured regarding his place in Scottish affairs. Thus Argyll's position in relation to central government was at its strongest in the last four years of his life.

The Earl of Bute and his brother James Stuart Mackenzie unwittingly presided over the demise of the Argathelian system. Bute's conception of Scottish politics betrayed his lack of understanding of both Scotland and politics. His attempt to set up his brother as an independent minister crashed to the ground after he left government and Lord Milton left politics. Mackenzie was a charming individual, but his ministry was merely an epilogue to the Duke of Argyll's career. The

132

vacuum which resulted eventually was filled by Henry Dundas after his appointment as Lord Advocate in 1775. The difference between the old way and the new was that Dundas went on to become a British politician in a way that was never possible for Argyll; ultimately his suzerainty of Scotland became a mere sideline to his career as an imperial minister. At the heart of this distinction lies an historical problem which dwarfs the subject of this book: the growth of an imperial consciousness amongst the ruling elite of Britain. The nature of the British state was changing from a national basis to an imperial one, and this development had to affect the political conduct of the elite which maintained the state. Like Argyll, Dundas saw to the management of the Scots for the government, but whereas Argyll had protected the Scots from English interference, Dundas won them a piece of the imperial pie.

This grand theme must be developed in another book. The subject of this book is the nature of Scottish government in the eighteenth century. Administratively, it is possible to use the term 'semi-independent' in relation to Scottish government, not in reference to a viceroy or manager, but in reference to the subordinate boards and officers of state in Edinburgh. Government in London never retained sufficient interest in Scotland to pursue a coherent Scottish policy. Administrative devolution made the Union work by providing a buffer between the English-dominated parliament and ministry and the Scots. The system was only broken up with the growth of parliamentary power in the nineteenth century and the progress of assimilation amongst the middle and upper classes who were represented in Parliament. Thus the policy of executive devolution which has been pursued since the Gilmour report of 1937 and the Reorganisation of Offices (Scotland) Act of 1939[1] has not been a new departure at all, but a return to the method of governing Scotland adopted in the eighteenth century.

There was another theme in the political aspect of Scottish government in the eighteenth century. It is summed up in the words of Duncan Forbes, written in 1725: '. . . if any one Scotsman has absolute power, we are in the same slavery as ever, whether that person be a fair man or a black man, a peer or a commoner, 6 foot or 5 foot high, and the dependence of the country will be on that man, and not on those that made him.'[2] This tension is inherent in the Union situation and remains with Scotland today.[3] Forbes was a Unionist, and wanted Scotland to get its government from London, but his comment raises another point about a Scots 'manager'. If a minority can unite behind one party or one leader, it can by its unity force concessions from a majority; but that unity stifles criticism and prevents initiative from those of the minority outside the leadership. The Dukes of Argyll and Henry Dundas provided strong leadership for the Scottish political nation, at the cost of preventing effective political debate in Scotland.

There is no doubt that the high road south offered the best opportunities for an ambitious Scot; but the Scottish community as a whole could not solve its problems by preferment in London. Some had to, and have to, remain in Scotland: 'fair man or black man', they require government. Government exists to act: in what areas and to what extent depends on the proclivities of those involved in the government and the demands of their political constituency. Areas remote from the centre of government face the problem of securing government action when the locality cannot act, or cannot act effectively. After 1707 Scottish affairs that required parliamentary or ministerial attention had to be considered by a largely English parliament and a largely English ministry hundreds of miles to the south. The Scottish M.P.s could unite in voting on Scottish legislation, but initiative rested with the ministry, and that ministry seldom took an interest in Scottish affairs. Government acted only when action was forced upon it, as in the Porteous affair or the 1745 rebellion. The rest of the time those Scots who wanted something from the government had to find a method of attracting its attention. The only means of doing this was through the mediation of the Scottish representatives in London. Counties and towns could go to their Member of Parliament; but the problem of dealing with Scottish affairs remained. The Scottish M.P.s very seldom met as a group to discuss a national issue, and, as we have noted, there was seldom a separate Secretary of State to administer Scottish affairs. Officially, there was no single Scot in London who could represent Scotland at the decision-making level of government.

The government, in turn, had the problem of distributing offices in the gift of the Crown in Scotland. There were a substantial number of offices involved (see Appendix II), and there was no one in the government with enough knowledge of Scotland to supervise their distribution. There was nothing to stop the government from using several advisers, but those Scots who wanted patronage wanted to know where to apply for it, which led to pressure for a single manager of patronage. It was much easier for the government to consign Scottish patronage to someone who was prepared to ensure that it caused no one else aggravation. It was convenient for the government to have a Scottish manager and it was convenient for most Scots to have a minister in London who could attract the attention of the government and influence its policy. Argyll and Dundas were more managers than ministers, though I have tried to point out that they were not exclusively managers. They represented Scotland; but they kept it manageable. One cannot separate the two. One also cannot avoid the analogy with the twentieth-century Secretary of State for Scotland.

Political Chronology

1713-15	Peace of Utrecht
1714	Accession of George I
1715	Jacobite Rebellion in Scotland
1721	Sir Robert Walpole becomes First Lord of the Treasury and Chancellor of Exchequer
1725	Shawfield Riots in Scotland over the introduction of a Malt Tax to Scotland. Duke of Roxburghe dismissed as Secretary of State
1727	Accession of George II
1733	Crisis over Walpole's Excise Act
1737	Porteous Riots in Edinburgh
1739	Britain declares war on Spain
1741	Opposition gains in the general election force the resignation of Walpole in Feb. 1742
1741	Britain declares war on France
1743	Henry Pelham becomes First Lord of the Treasury and Chancellor of Exchequer; death of John, second Duke of Argyll
1745-46	Jacobite rebellion in Scotland
1748	Peace of Aix-la-Chapelle
1754	Death of Henry Pelham; Duke of Newcastle becomes First Lord of the Treasury
1756	Britain declares war on France; defeat of Braddock in America; fall of Minorca
1757	Ministry of the elder Pitt; (June) coalition ministry takes office with Pitt as Secretary of State and the Duke of Newcastle at the Treasury
1757	Convention of Klosterseven and disgrace of the Duke of Cumberland
1759	Wolfe takes Quebec; Amherst takes Ticonderoga; Barrington takes

135

	Guadeloupe; Relief of Madras
1760	(Nov.) Accession of George III
1761	(March) Lord Bute takes office as Secretary of State; (April) death of Archibald, third Duke of Argyll; (Oct.) resignation of Pitt
1762	(Jan.) War with Spain
1762	(May) Resignation of Newcastle; Lord Bute becomes First Lord of the Treasury
1763	(10 Feb.) Peace of Paris
1763	(April) George Grenville becomes First Lord of the Treasury and Chancellor of the Exchequer; (May) arrest of John Wilkes, suppression of *North Briton*, no.45; (Dec.) Wilkes flees to France
1765	(May) James Stuart Mackenzie relieved of the patronage of Scotland; (June) Marquess of Rockingham becomes First Lord of the Treasury
1766	(March) Repeal of the American Stamp Tax
1766	(June) Pitt becomes Secretary of State; Duke of Grafton becomes First Lord of the Treasury
1768	General Election; return of Wilkes from France and his candidacy for Middlesex; (Oct.) Pitt resigns
1769	Middlesex by-elections and expulsion of Wilkes from Parliament
1770	Lord North appointed First Lord of the Treasury, continues as Chancellor of Exchequer
1774	(March) Boston Port Act as punishment for the Boston Tea Party
1774	(Nov.) General Election
1776	American Declaration of Independence
1777	Surrender of Burgoyne's army at Saratoga, New York
1778	Britain declares war on France
1779	Britain declares war on Spain
1780	General Election
1781	Surrender of Cornwallis's army at Yorktown, Virginia
1782	(March) Marquess of Rockingham becomes First Lord of the Treasury; (August) Earl of Shelburne becomes First Lord of the Treasury with the younger Pitt as Chancellor of the Exchequer; Henry Dundas given the patronage of Scotland

1783	(Feb.) Fox-North coalition, with the Duke of Portland as First Lord of the Treasury
1783	Peace of Paris
1783	(Dec.) The younger Pitt appointed First Lord of the Treasury and Chancellor of Exchequer
1784	General Election; triumph of the younger Pitt; (March) Henry Dundas appointed a Lord of Trade; (Sept.) Henry Dundas appointed a commissioner of the Board of Control for India
1789	Revolution in France
1790	General Election
1791	(June) Henry Dundas appointed Secretary of State for Home Affairs, an office he holds until July 1794
1793	War with France
1793	(June) Henry Dundas made President of the Board of Control, an office he holds until 1801
1794	(July) Henry Dundas made Secretary for War, an office he holds until 1801

Appendix I

Saltoun Papers, SB 364 (Chancery, Police, etc.), folder 2, 'Memorandum', almost certainly by Lord Milton (1761-62)

THE most certain way of preserving power is certainly by making a proper use of it — And as there never occurred an Era in Britain wherein his majesty and his servants were more desireous of doing good, The following hints are thrown out with that view.

There is one great object of a Ministers Attention should be [sic] the establishing and preserving a Parliamentary Interest in the Country which is indeed necessary for carrying on the Public Service by adding a proper weight to the power and Influence of the Crown — The Sinecure Employments may be Dedicated for those purposes with as few Deviations as possible.

A particular list of these offices and of the persons who now hold them shall be made up.

The judges of the Court of Session Justiciary and Exchequer should always be filled up with persons Eminent for their Probity and knowledge in the Law and of Estimation in private Life; For nothing contributes more to satisfy the people than when they see their lives and properties Committed to the Care of such Judges.

A List of Lawyers fit for such promotions may be made up.

Care should also be taken in naming the Sheriff Deputes as a Seminary from which in time the judges may be taken.

A List of young Lawyers fit for Sheriff Deputes shall be made up.

When the English Revenue Laws were Introduced into Scotland at the Union it became absolutely necessary to send down some English Judges and officers to the Court of Exchequer with some Commissioners and Officers to the Boards of Customs & Excise. But now except as to the Chief Baron of the Court of Exchequer whose knowledge in the English Law is still requisite has ceased as to all the rest. Because this Country there are to be found Gentlemen every way well Qualified for discharging the Duty of these offices; and yet the Custom of giving these offices to Englishmen still prevails: These English Gentlemen taken all together have not the least Influence in Scotland, so that bestowing Scots Offices upon them is really curtailing the means by which the King and his Servants ought to preserve their Influence in Scotland.

This should be done gradually as proceeding from sound Policy not from national prejudice:

The Disposal of the military commands in Scotland such as Governours of Castles, and Forts &c. is another mean of Supporting Parliamentary Interest.

A List of such Military Commands shall be made out.

In order to know what Families and persons have the natural and best Influence in the several Counties and Districts of Burrows in Scotland and are most likely to be friends a State of their present situation can be made out.

Appendix II

List of Government Offices in Scotland, based on the *Edinburgh Almanack* of 1755; and the Scottish Civil List for 1761

THE following list and transcription of the Civil Establishment of 1761 are printed to give an indication of the extent of Crown patronage in Scotland, and to indicate the size of the administrative community in mid-eighteenth-century Edinburgh. One note of caution. The following do not list all offices of government in Scotland, or all offices in the gift of the Crown; they establish a general point of some significance in this book, that there was an administrative community in Edinburgh. The Scottish manager was involved in the distribution of these offices; and in addition, some 500 customs and salt offices in the outports, ranging in value from £14 per annum for a boatman to the place of Collector at Port Glasgow, worth about £500 a year. Thus the importance of the Treasury, which approved all the appointments to these 500 places. The Crown was also patron in a third of the parishes of the Church of Scotland. It must be emphasised, however, that the political potential of this patronage was exploited sporadically and with variable effect. Ilay and Henry Dundas came closest to determining their distribution, but even they cannot be portrayed as monopolising patronage, even at the height of their influence.

List of Government Offices in Scotland, based on the *Edinburgh Almanack* **of 1755**

OFFICERS OF STATE IN SCOTLAND

Archibald, Duke of Argyll, Keeper of the Great Seal, 3000£
James, Duke of Athol, Lord Privy Seal, 3000£
William, Marquess of Lothian, Lord Register, 1200£
James, Earl of Findlater and Seafield, Ld. Vice Admiral, 1000£
Archibald, Duke of Argyll, Lord Justice General, 2000£
Robert Craigie, Esq; Lord President of the Session, 1000£
John Idle, Esq; Lord Chief Baron of Exchequer, 1000£
Robert Dundas of Arniston, Esq; Lord Advocate, 1000£
Charles Areskine of Tinwald, Lord Justice Clerk, 500£

List of Government Offices in Scotland, based on the *Edinburgh Almanack* **of 1755, cont.**

COURT OF SESSION

Lords of Session:
Robert Craigie of Glendoick, Esq; Lord President
Andrew Fletcher of Milton, Patrick Boyle of Shewalton, Sir Gilbert Elliot of Minto, Bt., George
Sinclair of Woodhall, Hugh Dalrymple of Drumore, Alex. Boswell of Auchinleck, Alex. Fraser of
Strichen, Wm. Grant of Prestongrange, J. Sinclair of Murkle, R. Pringle of Edgefield, Charles Erskine
of Tinwald, T. Hay of Huntington, Sir James Fergusson of Kilkerran, Bt., Henry Home of Kames

Principal Clerks:
John Murray, William Kirkpatrick, Hugh Forbes, Thomas Gibson, James Justice, James Pringle

Depute Clerks:
Alex. Keith, Alex. Gray, Thos. Bruce, Alex. Ross, John White, Robt. Leith

Principal Clerks to the Bills:
Sir Philip Anstruther and James Burns of Dorater

Depute Clerks to the Bills:
Charles Inglis, William Scot, and Laurence Inglis

Clerk to the Register of Seizures: Baron John Maule
Depute Clerk of Seizures: John Foulis
Clerk to the Register of Hornings: Sir Arch. Grant of Monimusk
Clerk to the Commission of Teinds: Joseph Williamson
Depute Clerk of Hornings and Teinds: George Buchan
Keeper of the Minute-Book: John Murray
Clerk to the Admission of Notaries: John Nasmyth

COURT OF JUSTICIARY

Archibald, Duke of Argyll, Lord Justice General
Charles Areskine of Tinwald, Esq; Lord Justice Clerk

Commissioners: Sir Gilbert Elliot of Minto, Sir James Fergusson of Kilkerran, Hugh Dalrymple of
Drumore, William Grant of Prestongrange, Alexander Fraser of Strichen

Principal Clerk: John Davidson
Depute Clerk: Robt. Leith

COURT OF EXCHEQUER

Rt. Hon. John Idle, Esq; Lord Chief Baron
Barons: Sir John Clerk, John Maule, Edward Edlin, James Erskine
King's Remembrancer: William Stewart
Deputy King's Remembrancer: David Moncrief
Lord Treasurer's Remembrancers: Wyvel Boteler, George Clerk
Auditor of Exchequer: Andrew Fletcher
Deputy Auditor: John Philp
Clerk of the Pipe: John Stewart of Castlestewart
Presenter of Signatures: John Dundas
Examiner: Sir James Holburn, Bt.
Heretable Usher of Exchequer: Rt. Hon. Lord Bellenden
Deputy Usher: Archibald Tod

List of Government Offices in Scotland, based on the *Edinburgh Almanack* of 1755, cont.

COURT OF ADMIRALTY

James, Earl of Findlater, Lord Vice-Admiral
Judge-Admiral: James Philp
Judge Depute: John Gordon
Clerk: William Ruthven

COMMISSARY COURT

Commissaries: Hon. James Leslie, James Smollet, Archibald Murray, Robert Clark
Commissary Clerk: Alexander Nairn
Depute Clerk: William Russell

SHERIFF-DEPUTES

Edinburgh: Walter, Lord Torphichen
Haddington: James Hamilton
Berwick: George Carre (or Ker)
Roxburgh: Walter Pringle
Selkirk: Andrew Pringle
Peebles: James Montgomery
Lanark: William Crosse
Dumfries: William Kirkpatrick
Wigton and Galloway: Thomas Dundas
Ayr: William Duff
Dumbarton: James Smollet
Renfrew: Charles MacDoual
Stirlingshire and Clackmannan: David Walker
Linlithgow and Bathgate: John Gillon
Perth: John Swinton
Kincardine: Francis Garden
Aberdeen: David Dalrymple
Inverness: David Scrimzeour
Argyll and Bute: Archibald Campbell of Stonefield
Fife and Kinross: James Leslie
Forfar: John Campbell
Banff: vacant
Caithness and Sutherland: John Sinclair
Elgin and Nairn: James Brodie
Orkney and Zetland: Sir Andrew Mitchell
Ross and Cromarty: Hugh Rose
Steward-depute of Kirkcudbright: Thomas Miller

EXCISE OFFICE

Commissioners: Richard Dowdeswell, Christopher Rhodes, Thomas Cochrane, Alexander Udney, George Drummond
Comptroller: Stephen Penny
Deputy-Comptroller: Walter Cosser
Secretary: Peter Wedderburn
Auditor: William Williams
Deputy Auditor: George Fraser
Cashier: James Nimmo

List of Government Offices in Scotland, based on the *Edinburgh Almanack* of 1755, cont.

Deputy Cashier: Alexander Alison
Solicitor: Patrick Haldane
Assistant Solicitor: James Hamilton
Deputy Solicitor: William Clifton
Agent at London: Milward Rowe
General Accomptants: John Dickie and Alex. Chalmers
General Examiner: Samuel McCormick
Accomptants: Andrew Home, Edward Swift, Richard Marshal, James Menzies, John Blair, William Robinson, Robert Chalmers
Agent and Messenger: David Bruce
Store-Keeper: Robert Rance

CUSTOM HOUSE

Commissioners: Rt. Hon. James Lord Deskford, Colin Campbell, Mansfeldt Cardonnel, Alexander LeGrand, Joseph Tudor

Secretary: Corbyn Morris
Receiver General: James Murray
Comptroller General: William Jones
Solicitor: Richard Swanston
Examiner: Samuel Pleddel
Register of Seizures: William Gray
Register of Shipping: Joseph Douglas
Register of Tobacco: Gideon Shaw
first Clerk to the Secretary: William Nelthorp
first Clerk to the Comptroller General: Richard Gardiner
first Clerk to the Solicitor: Hugh Fraser
Housekeeper: William Rowley

POST OFFICE

deputy Postmaster General: Alex. Hamilton of Innerwick
Secretary: William Jackson
principal Clerk: Walter Foggo
Clerks: David Bennet, William Ker, Charles Malcolm
Clerk to foreign letters: Thomas Mathew

LYON OFFICE

Lord Lyon: John Campbell, younger of Calder
Lyon-depute: Thomas Brodie, WS
Lyon-clerk: David Erskine

STAMP OFFICE

Head Distributor and Collector: William Dempster
Collector's Clerk: George Innes
Comptroller: Patrick Anderson
Comptroller's Clerk: Thomas Skey
Distributor for Edinburgh and Leith: John Pringle
Distributor's Clerk: George Duncan
Solicitor and Secretary: John Young

List of Government Offices in Scotland, based on the *Edinburgh Almanack* of 1755, cont.

CHANCERY

Director: Hon. Robert Ker
Deputy Director: Alex. Campbell
principal Clerk: William Smith
Clerk: John Irvine

OFFICERS OF THE MINT

General of the Mint: Lord Belhaven, 300£
Master: Archibald Bothwell, 200£
Warden: James Hay WS, 150£
Counter Warden: John MacFarlane WS, 60£
Assay master: James Ker, 100£
Engraver: Joseph Cave, 50£

ESTABLISHMENT OF POLICE

President: Hugh, Earl of Marchmont, 2000£
Lords of Police: 800£: John, Earl of Hopetoun, John, Earl of Hyndford, James, Lord Somerville, Alexander, Earl of Galloway, one vacancy
Gentlemen of Police: 400£: Mungo Haldane of Gleneagles, Thomas Grant, Norman MacLeod of MacLeod
Secretary: George Carre (or Ker), 300£

HIS MAJESTY'S FORCES IN NORTH BRITAIN

Commander in Chief: Lieut. Gen. Humphrey Bland
Adjutant General: Lord Cathcart
Deputy Quarter Master General: Lieut. Col. David Watson
Major of Brigade: Major Hardgrave
Baggage Master and Inspector of Roads: Major Caulfield
Muster Master General: Hon. Charles Hope Weir
Barrack Master General: Hon. Thomas Leslie
Commissary: Richard Gardiner
Judge Advocate: James Cochrane

GOVERNORS AND LIEUTENANT GOVERNORS OF GARRISONS IN SCOTLAND

Blackness Castle: Hon. Charles Hope Weir
Dumbarton Castle: Earl of Cassillis
Lieut. Gov. of Dumbarton Castle: Robert Turnbull
Edinburgh Castle: Lieut. Gen. Humphrey Bland
Lieut. Gov. of Edinburgh Castle: Capt. Richard Coran
Inverness: Sir Charles Howard
Lieut. Gov. of Inverness Castle: Major Caulfield
Fort Augustus: Alex. Trapaud
Stirling Castle: John, Earl of Loudoun
Lieut. Gov. Stirling Castle: Colonel Abercrombie
Fort William: Lieut. Gen. Onslow
Lieut. Gov. Fort William: Lt. Col. Leighton

List of Government Offices in Scotland, based on the *Edinburgh Almanack* **of 1755, cont.**

COMMISSIONERS AND TRUSTEES FOR IMPROVING FISHERIES AND MANUFACTURES

James Lord Deskford, James Lord Somerville, John Lord Belhaven, Charles Areskine of Tinwald, Andrew Fletcher of Milton, Alexander Fraser of Strichen, Patrick Boyle of Shewalton, William Grant of Prestongrange, Sir John Clerk of Pennicuik, John Maule of Innerkeilor, Thomas Hope of Rankeilor, George Drummond, Archibald MacAulay, William Alexander, Alexander Arbuthnot, David Kinloch of Gilmerton
5 vacancies

The Scottish Civil List for 1761

George R

AN ESTABLISHMENT or List containing
Payments for Civil Affairs, in that
part of Great Britain called Scotland,
which Our Pleasure is shall Commence
and be Paid from the 5th day of April
last 1761. That is to say

	Per Annum
	£ s d
To the Keeper of Our Seal, Used as the Great Seal of Scotland	3,000: —: —
To the Keeper of Our Privy Seal there	3,000: —: —
To Our Register — of Old Salary	444: —: —
To the Lords of Session, the Allowances which were payable to them before the Union out of Customs	1,666: 13: 4
To the President of Our Session £1100 Per Annum And to Each of the other Fourteen Lords £500 Per Annum, as Augmentations of what was formerly Allowed out of Customs and their Fund of Interest	8,100: —: —
To the Clerk of Our Processes before the Court of Session	40: —:
To the Under Clerk of Our said Processes	10: —: —
To the Extractor of Our said Processes	10: —: —
To the Writer of Hornings	50: —: —
To the Keeper of the Register of Hornings	20: —: —
To the Four Macers of Session Each £10 Per Annum	40: —: —
To the Commissioners of Justiciary, the Allowances which were payable to them before the Union out of Customs	500: —: —
To the Lord Justice General	2,000: —: —
To the Justice Clerk	400: —: —

Scottish Civil List, 1761 (cont.)

To the said Justice Clerk, and Five Commissioners of
    Justiciary, as an Augmentation of what was formerly
    Allowed out of Customs Each £100 Per Annum ....   600: —: —

To the Clerk of the Justiciary...   100: —: —

To the Deputy Clerk thereof ....   40: —: —

To Three Macers of Justiciary Each £20 Per Annum ....   60: —: —

To the Housekeepers of Justiciary ....   8: —: —

To the Dempster ....   5: —: —

> To the Commissioners of Justiciary and
> their Officers, for the Charge of Two
> Circuits Yearly, to be paid to such as
> go the said Circuits Vist.

		Per Annum
	£ s d	

To Our Lord Justice General for going the Circuit
    £200 for Every Circuit... 400: —: —

To Our Justice Clerk, and three other Commissioners
    of Justiciary going the South and Western
    Circuits Each £150 for Every Circuit...1,200: —: —

To Our Justice Clerk, or any two of the
    Commissioners of Justiciary, going the
    Northern Circuit, being more Expensive than
    the others Each £180 for Every Circuit .... 720: —: —

To Three Deputy Advocates Each £50 for Every
    Circuit.. 300: —: —

To Three Clerks of the Circuit Each £30 for Every
    Circuit.. 180: —: —

To Three Macers Each £10 for Every Circuit .... 60: —: —

To Six Trumpets, Each £10 for Every Circuit .... 120: —: —

    in all for Circuits per Annum...   2,980: —: —

To the Chief Baron of Our Court of Exchequer ....1,300: —: —

More to Robert Ord Esqr during his continuance in
    that Office   700:—:—   2,000:—:—

To the Person deputed by him to Keep the Exchequer Seal ....   100: —: —

To the other Four Barons of Old and Augmented
    Salary...2,800: —: —

To George Winn Esqr one of the Barons, during his
    continuance in the Office .... 500: —: —   3,300: —: —

To Our Remembrancer of the Court of Exchequer ....   500: —: —

Scottish Civil List, 1761 (cont.)

To Our Principal Auditor .... 1,200: —: —

To the Treasurers Remembrancer or Remembrancers.................................... 200: —: —

To the Clerk of the Pipe .... 200: —: —

To the Solicitor appointed to Attend Our Court of Exchequer &
    to take care of the Prosecutions for bringing in the
    Debts Owing to the Crown .... 140: —: —

To be paid for defraying the Charge of the said Prosecutions
    and such Petty Expenses, as the Barons of Our Exchequer
    shall think necessary to direct for Our Service, and
    for which an Account is to be passed before them, a
    Sum not Exceeding Five hundred Pounds .... 500: —: —

To the Presenter of Signatures in the Court of Exchequer 52:15: 6

To the Deputy Auditor or Auditors .... 200: —: —

To the Examiner in the Court of Exchequer .... 50: —: —

To Two Attorneys of the said Court at £50 Per Annum Each......................... 100: —: —

To the Clerk of the Port Bonds in Exchequer.. 40: —: —

To the Keeper of the Register of Resignations there...................................... 40: —: —

To the Hereditary Usher of the Exchequer of Old Salary .... 11: 10: —

To John Ker Lord Bellenden Hereditary Usher of Additional
    Salary during Pleasure.. 250: —: —

To the Deputy Usher of the Exchequer during Pleasure .... 50: —: —

To the Marishall of the Exchequer.. 80: —: —

To the Three Macers of the Exchequer Each £50 Per Annum......................... 150: —: —

To the Messenger of the Exchequer... 6: 13: 4

To the Two Doorkeepers of Exchequer, Each £15 Per Annum .... 30: —: —

To the Person appointed for taking care of the Business of the
    Exchequer in Scotland, at the Treasury in England .... 200: —: —

To Our Advocate... 1,000: —: —

To Our Solicitor or Solicitors .... 400: —: —

To Our Clerk and Keeper of the Register of Seisines in the
    Shires of Edinburgh etc... 200: —: —

To the Deputy Keeper of the Signet in Scotland.. 100: —: —

To the Secretarys and Chief Clerks of the Treasury .... 100: —: —

To the Sheriff depute of the Shire of Aberdeen .... 200: —: —

To the Sheriff depute of the Shire of Air .... 200: —: —

To the Sheriff depute of the Shires of Argyll and Bute .... 250: —: —

Scottish Civil List, 1761 (cont.)

To the Sherriff depute of the Shire of Berwick .... 150: —: —

To the Sherriff depute of the Shire of Banff .... 150: —: —

To the Sherriff depute of the Shires of Caithness and
    Sutherland .... 200: —: —

To the Sherriff depute of the Shire of Dumfries .... 200: —: —

To the Sherriff depute of the Shire of Dumbarton .... 150: —: —

To the Sherriff depute of the Shire of Edinburgh .... 200: —: —

To the Sherriff depute of the Shires of Elgin and Nairn .... 150: —: —

To the Sherriff depute of the Shires of Fife and Kinross .... 200: —: —

To the Sherriff depute of the Shire of Forfar .... 150: —: —

To the Sherriff depute of the Shire of Haddington .... 150: —: —

To the Sherriff depute of the Shire of Inverness .... 250: —: —

To the Steward depute of the Stewardry of Kirkcudbright .... 150: —: —

To the Sherriff depute of the Shire of Kincardine .... 150: —: —

To the Sherriff depute of the Shire of Lanerk .... 200: —: —

To the Sherriff depute of the Shire of Linlithgow and Bathgate .... 150: —: —

To the Steward depute of the Stewardry of Orkney and Zetland .... 200: —: —

To the Sherriff depute of the Shire of Peebles .... 150: —: —

To the Sherriff depute of the Shire of Perth .... 250: —: —

To the Sherriff depute of the Shire of Renfrew .... 150: —: —

To the Sherriff depute of the Shire of Roxburgh .... 150: —: —

To the Sherriff depute of the Shires of Ross and Cromertie .... 250: —: —

To the Sherriff depute of the Shire of Selkirk .... 150: —: —

To the Sherriff depute of the Shires of Stirling and
    Clackmannan .... 150: —: —

To the Sherriff depute of the Shire of Wigtown or Galloway .... 150: —: —

To the Receiver General of Our Landrents and Casualties and
    Paymaster of all such Salaries and Allowances to Our
    Officers, Servants and others in Scotland, as are herein
    contained and may hereafter be Established by Us for
    himself and Clerks .... 650: —: —

To the Director of the Chancellary .... 25: —: —

To the Lyon King of Arms .... 300: —: —

To the Heraulds and Persuivants .... 250: —: —

To Six Trumpets .... 100: —: —

To the Knight Marishall .... 400: —: —

Scottish Civil List, 1761 (cont.)

To the Hereditary Usher of the Court of Session etc	250: —: —
To Our Three Chaplains Each £50 Per Annum	150: —: —
To the Almoner for his Salary... £41:13: 4	
More to him for Alms to be distributed to Beadmen and common poor on Our Birthday According to the use and wont................................ 108: 6: 8	150: —: —
To Our Limner	100: —: —
To the Master of Our Wardrobe	55:11: —
To the Under Keeper thereof...	40: —: —
To the Second Under Keeper thereof	20: —: —
To the Clerk thereof	30: —: —
To the Hereditary Keeper of Our Palace of Holyroodhouse in Lieu and Satisfaction of all Allowances formerly made to the said House Keeper, both in Money and Victual..	46: —: —
To the Under Keeper of the Palace of Holyroodhouse................................	50: —: —
To the Porter of the said Palace..	37: 15: —
To Our Under Falconer...	50: —: —
To Our First Physician	100: —: —
To Our Second Physician	50: —: —
To Our Apothecary	40: —: —
To the Keeper of Our Physick Garden...	50: —: —
To the Master of Our Works	400: —: —
To the Clerk of the Stores under him	30: —: —
To the Procurator for the Church, for defraying the Charges of the Church Affairs in Scotland, and the Salaries of their Officers	500: —: —
To our Charitys and Bountys, to such Indigent and necessitous Persons, as shall be approved of by the Barons of Our Exchequer in Scotland, and to be distributed amongst them Quarterly in such proportions, as Our said Barons shall think fit...	2,000: —: —
To the Conservator of the Privileges of Scotland in the Netherlands..	200: —: —
To the Secretary of the Order of the Thistle...	300: —: —
To the University of St. Andrews for their Professors	210: —: —
To the University of Glasgow for their Professors......................................	210: —: —
To the University of Edinburgh for their Professors	210: —: —

L

Scottish Civil List, 1761 (cont.)

To the Professors of Our College in the University of Aberdeen .... 105: —: —

To the Professors of the Marishall College in the said
University .... 105: —: —

To the Professor of Astronomy and Observer in the University
of Glasgow.. 50: —: —

To Mr. William Kirkpatrick Advocate for defraying certain
Expenses Incurred or to be Incurred for Our Service
during Pleasure.. 100: —: —

To Sir John Gordon Baronett Secretary, Chamberlain and
Receiver General of the Rents and Revenues etc. of the
Principality in Scotland, and Paymaster of all Salaries,
which shall be directed to be paid out of the same.............................. 400: —: —

To Katherine Dutchess Dowager of Gordon.. 600: —: —

To William Lord Forrester .... 150: —: —

To John Forbes Esqr .... 400: —: —

To Patrick Haldane Esqr.. 400: —: —

To Lady Margaret MacDonald .... 200: —: —

To Walter Lord Torphichen .... 400: —: —

To Isabella late Countess of Cromertie .... 400: —: —

To James Earl of Lauderdale.. 600: —: —

Pensions To James Hay Writer to the Signet in Trust for the
behoof of the Children of John Hay of Hewhall
Esqr deceased .... 400: —: —

To James Lord Deskfoord .... 500: —: —

To Christopher Rhodes Esqr .... 500: —: —

To David Earl of Glasgow... 400: —: —

To John Lord Viscount Arbuthnot.. 200: —: —

To Lady Anne Ruthven .... 400: —: —

To Lady Jane Leslie .... 100: —: —

To Lady Margaret Leslie .... 100: —: —

To Mrs. Margaret Primrose.. 100: —: —

To Doctor James Lydderdale... 50: —: —

To Captain John Macneal.. 40: —: —

Amounting in the whole to the Sum of Fifty two thousand Eight hundred and thirty pounds two Shillings and fourpence. AND Our further Pleasure is And We do hereby also Establish an Allowance to be made for the four Messengers of the Receipt of Our Exchequer at the Rate of Eighteen Pounds for Each Proclamation and Order of Council direct to be distributed through Scotland. Dated at Our Palace at St. James this 19th day of June 1761, In the First Year of Our Reign.

By His Majestys Command

Notes

Abbreviations and Short Titles

ALL manuscript collections in private hands have been cited in the Notes by their title; their location can be determined by reference to the Bibliography. In the case of the Bute Papers and the Loudoun Papers, which have been divided, references are to the manuscripts at Mount Stuart unless otherwise indicated.

Most secondary works are cited by author, title, date and place of publication in the first instance and by a clear short title afterwards. Place of publication in the Notes and the Bibliography is Edinburgh unless otherwise indicated. The following works have been referred to by short title throughout the book:

Caldwell Papers	*Selections From the Family Papers Preserved at Caldwell, Part II,* ed. W. Mure (Glasgow, the Maitland Club, 1854), two volumes
Calendar of Home Office Papers	*Calendar of Home Office Papers of the Reign of George III* (1760-1775), ed. J. Redington and R. A. Roberts (London, 1878-99), four volumes
Oswald Memorials	*Memorials of the Public Life and Character of the Right Hon. James Oswald of Dunniker,* ed. J. Oswald (1825)
Scotland and Scotsmen	*Scotland and Scotsmen in the Eighteenth Century from the Manuscripts of John Ramsay, Esq. of Ochtertyre,* ed. A. Allardyce (1888), two volumes

The following abbreviations have been used:

Add. MSS.	Additional Manuscript
BL	British Library
HMC	Historical Manuscripts Commission
NLS	National Library of Scotland
SCJ	Senator of the College of Justice
SHR	Scottish Historical Review
SRO	Scottish Record Office

Preface

1. T. C. Smout, *A History of the Scottish People* (paperback edition, Glasgow and London, 1972), p. 201.

2. J. M. Simpson, 'Who Steered the Gravy Train?', in *Scotland in the Age of Improvement,* ed. N. T. Phillipson and R. M. Mitchison (1970), p. 48.

Chapter 1: The Government of Scotland

1. *The Treaty of Union of Scotland and England 1707,* ed. G. S. Pryde (1950). All references to the treaty have been taken from Pryde's edition.

2. Quoted in W. Ferguson, *Scotland's Relations with England: A Survey to 1707* (1977), p. 209.

3. T. C. Smout, *Scottish Trade on the Eve of Union, 1660-1707* (1963), p. 256.

4. P. W. J. Riley, *The English Ministers and Scotland, 1707-1727* (London, 1964), pp. 90-97.

5. The Keepers of the Great and Privy Seals, which were copies of the principal British Seals in the possession of separate keepers in London, usually held their posts as sinecures, with deputies resident in Edinburgh to execute the ordinary business of affixing the seals to state documents, mostly appointments on the Scottish Civil Establishment (see Appendix II). Some idea of their business can be gleaned from the printed *Calendar of Home Office Papers*. The Lord Justice General was titular head of the Scottish Court of Justiciary; in the nineteenth century the office was merged with that of the Lord President of the Court of Session in order to give that judge a role in criminal as well as civil law. The Lord Clerk Register was responsible for the records of Scotland, which were kept by his deputies (A. Murray, 'The Lord Clerk Register', *SHR*, LIII (1974), pp. 124-56).

6. J. P. Mackintosh, *The British Cabinet* (second edition, London, 1968), pp. 50-72.

7. Byron F. Jewell, 'The Legislation Relating to Scotland After the Forty-Five' (University of North Carolina Ph.D., 1975), p. 236. I am very grateful to R. B. Sher for informing me of Dr. Jewell's work.

8. For a list of the clerks in both offices, and capsule biographies, see J. C. Sainty, *Treasury Officials: 1660-1870* (London, 1972) and J. C. Sainty, *Officials of the Secretaries of State* (London, 1973).

9. NLS, Saltoun, SC 216, fo. 58, G. Elliot to Lord Milton, 16 June 1761.

10. See the series of letters in the Saltoun Papers on the proposed appointment of a Regius Professor at Aberdeen in 1760 (NLS, Saltoun, SC 209, fos. 166, 171, 175; SC 211, fo. 170).

11. Bute/Loudoun Papers, 1760, bundle 7, 4 July 1760. Also see SRO, Arniston, RH4/15/4, Lord Dupplin to R. Dundas, 29 July 1755; NLS, Saltoun, SC 17, fo. 190, A. Fletcher to Lord Milton, 2 Dec. 1756.

12. M. A. Thomson, *The Secretaries of State, 1681-1782* (Oxford, 1932), pp. 30-38; M. S. Bricke, 'Management and Administration of Scotland, 1707-1765' (University of Kansas Ph.D., 1972), pp. 13-15. Bricke is inclined to over-emphasise the importance of the Scottish Secretary of State. Again, I am grateful to R. B. Sher for informing me of Dr. Bricke's thesis.

13. Riley, *English Ministers*, pp. 124, 162, 165, 264-6, 271; J. M. Simpson, 'Who Steered the Gravy Train?' in *Scotland in the Age of Improvement*, ed. N. T. Phillipson and R. M. Mitchison (1970), p. 59.

14. Jewell, 'Legislation Relating to Scotland', pp. 34-35; A. S. Foord, *His Majesty's Opposition, 1714-1830* (Oxford, 1964), p. 276.

15. Riley, *English Ministers*, pp. 287-90.

16. H. Roseveare, *The Treasury* (London, 1969), pp. 84-116; D. M. Clark, *The Rise of the British Treasury* (New Haven, 1960), deals with the expansion of Treasury influence in colonial administration.

17. SRO, State Papers, RH2/4, fo. 7, W. Alexander to Newcastle, 24 Feb. 1756.

18. Riley, *English Ministers*, pp. 166-7, 170, 172.

19. *Edinburgh Evening Courant*, 16 May 1761; BL, Hardwicke, Add. MSS. 35449, fo. 312, Earl of Morton to Earl of Hardwicke, 18 May 1761, gives Milton as the author.

20. C. Harvie, *Scotland and Nationalism* (London, 1977), pp. 168-71; H. J. Hanham, 'The Development of the Scottish Office', in *Government and Nationalism in Scotland*, ed. J. N. Wolfe (1969), pp. 68-69.

21. Thus the adverse comments on Argyll's speeches in 1747 on heritable jurisdictions and in 1752 on the annexed estates; see P. Yorke, *The Life and Correspondence of Philip Yorke, Earl of Hardwicke* (Cambridge, 1913), i, pp. 592, 595, 613-14; *More Culloden Papers*, ed. D. Warrand (Inverness, 1930), vii, p. 182, Sir A. Mitchell to Lord President Culloden, 22 May 1747. A letter by Lord Deskford mentions that: 'The house of Lords must tire of seeing nothing in Scotch appeals but by the eyes of a minister', which seems to indicate a position of authority by Ilay (SRO, Abercairny, GD 24/1/552, Deskford to H. Home, n.d.).

22. BL, Newcastle, Add. MSS. 32922, fos. 15-22, Newcastle to Hardwicke (copy), 17 April 1761.

23. See Thomas Kennedy's report of the debate on the dispute between the Earl of March and himself over the Earldom of Cassillis: NLS, Saltoun, SC 221, fo. 60, T. Kennedy (later Earl of Cassillis) to Lord Milton, 23 Jan. 1762.

24. *Scotland and Scotsmen*, i, p. 341. For the effect of these decisions see W. Ferguson, 'Electoral Law and Procedure in Eighteenth and Early Nineteenth Century Scotland' (University of Glasgow Ph.D., 1957), pp. 87-88.

25. *Boswell for the Defence*, ed. W. K. Wimsatt, Jr. and F. A. Pottle (London, 1960), pp. 80-81. According to Lord Campbell, Lord Chancellor Bathurst left all Scottish appeals to Mansfield (John, Lord Campbell, *The Lives of the Lord Chancellors* (London, 1846-47), v, p. 452). There is evidence to support this in *Boswell for the Defence*, pp. 67, 99, 104, 114-16, 162.

26. M. S. Bricke, 'Management and Administration', pp. 81-82.

27. BL, Newcastle, Add. MSS. 32935, fos. 331-3, Newcastle to Hardwicke (copy), 12 March 1762; *ibid.*, fos. 364-5, Hardwicke to Newcastle, 13 March 1762; *ibid.*, fos. 390-3, memorandum marked 'Lord Mansfield'.

28. G. W. T. Omond, *The Lord Advocates of Scotland* (1883), 2 vols. For critiques of this thesis see N. T. Phillipson, 'The Scottish Whigs and the Reform of the Court of Session, 1785-1830' (University of Cambridge Ph.D., 1967), pp. 31-32; Bricke, 'Management and Administration', pp. 87-88. H. J. Hanham, 'The Creation of the Scottish Office, 1881-87', *Juridical Review* (1965), p. 206, gives a view of the role of the Lord Advocate at the time Omond wrote his book.

29. W. Ferguson, 'Electoral Law'; R. M. Sunter, 'Stirlingshire Politics: 1707-1832' (University of Edinburgh Ph.D., 1971).

30. Riley, *English Ministers*, pp. 271-4; HMC, *Polwarth*, v, *passim; A Selection from the Papers of the Earls of Marchmont*, ed. Sir G. Rose (London, 1931), iii, *passim; The Arniston Memoirs*, ed. G. W. T. Omond (1887), pp. 156-68.

31. NLS, Saltoun, SC 17, fo. 11, A. Fletcher to Lord Milton, 15 Jan. 1754.

32. *Ibid.*, SC 216, fo. 54, G. Elliot to Milton, 11 June 1761.

33. Bute/Loudoun Papers, 1768, bundle 2, John Campbell to the Earl of Loudoun, 7 Jan. 1768: 'Do for me your weak Petitioner While you are in London, for their is no wheir to get it Done but in London, with the Lord high treasurer (sic), and if your Lordship Pleases to procure a tidesmans Deputation'; *ibid.*, 1774, bundle 5, Hon. Alexander Gordon to Loudoun, 26 April 1774 (seeking a Session gown): 'I am informed, (but yr. Lop. will know it well) ye proper way is to ask an audience of Ld. North wch he will no doubt appoint, and yt after tabling ye matter a note or Memorandum should be presented His Lop. in order to put it in his book, if he will permit it . . .'

34. Riley, 'The Structure of Scottish Politics and the Union of 1707', in *The Union of 1707*, ed. T. I. Rae (Glasgow, 1974), p. 24.

35. A. Carlyle, *Anecdotes and Characters of the Times*, ed. J. Kinsley (London, 1973), p. 193; *Scotland and Scotsmen*, i, p. 87; T. Somerville, *My Own Life and Times, 1741-1814* (1861), pp. 379-81.

36. HMC, *Polwarth*, v, pp. 215-17, 275-6, 287-8, 308-9.

37. SRO, Scott of Harden, GD 157/2250: no. 5, G. Elliot to W. Scott, 26 June 1764; no. 13, Elliot to Scott, 5 April 1765; no. 14, Elliot to Scott, 13 April 1765; no. 17, Elliot to Scott, 15 May 1765.

38. For the special representatives of the Convention of Royal Burghs see: Riley, *English Ministers*, pp. 120-2; NLS, Saltoun, SC 220, fos. 124-43, Alexander Gray to Lord Milton, 25 March to 20 May 1762.

The London agents were either inclined to the Treasury or to connections in Scotland in the mid-eighteenth-century. Milward Rowe, a Treasury clerk, was London agent for the Commissioners of Annexed Estates, the Boards of Customs and Excise, and the Court of Exchequer. George Ross, a London merchant of Scottish birth, acted as London agent for the Convention of Royal Burghs and the Board of Trustees.

39. Quoted in Simpson, 'Who Steered the Gravy Train?', p. 48.

40. BL, Hardwicke, Add. MSS. 35451, fo. 161, Breadalbane to the second Earl of Hardwicke, 18 Oct. 1765.

41. NLS, Saltoun, SC 218, fo. 11, J. Maule to Lord Milton, 16 April 1761: 'God pity us all who have lost such a friend & ye Country who has lost such a protector'; *ibid.*, SC 215, fo. 193, Sir A. Dick to Milton, 20 April 1761: 'We may really say the Country has lost a father whose place it will not be easy to supply.' Also see *ibid.*, SC 216, fos. 122-3, A. Fairholme to Milton, 30 April 1761; Bute/Loudoun Papers, 1761, bundle 4, W. Ferguson to Lord Loudoun, 20 April 1761: 'Even those who thwarted his Measures may ere long have reason to regrett his death and Scotland in general will feel the loss of a man of such great abilitys and long experience in business.'

42. Atholl Papers, Box 54, section 1, no. 244, J. Mackenzie to Atholl, 24 Dec. 1770.

43. Quoted in *Letters of George Dempster to Sir Adam Ferguson, 1756-1813,* ed. Sir J. Fergusson (London, 1934), p. 169.

44. C. Harvie, *Scotland and Nationalism,* p. 266; W. Ferguson, *Scotland's Relations with England* (1977), pp. 274-6.

45. Used in reference to Lord Milton in *A Biographical Dictionary of Eminent Scotsmen* (Glasgow, 1835), ii, p. 325; and in regard to William Mure in *Reekiana: Minor Antiquities of Edinburgh* (1833), p. 247.

46. (London, 1802), also see *Scotland and Scotsmen,* i, p. 88; A. Carlyle, *Anecdotes and Characters,* p. 210n. *'Sous Ministre'* was taken by Chambers from the anonymous *Printed Recollections Respecting the Family of the Fletchers of Salton* (1803), which was probably written by Lord Buchan, p. 3: 'Mr. John Hume [sic], in his History of the Rebellion, calls Lord Milton a *Sous Ministre* to the Duke of Argyle, an appellation very little known or used at the time.' The term has in turn been adopted by modern historians: N. T. Phillipson, 'The Scottish Whigs and the Reform of the Court of Session', pp. 29-31; J. M. Simpson, 'Who Steered the Gravy Train?', pp. 66-67.

47. M. S. Bricke, 'Management and Administration', pp. 14, 24, 42, 189, 202; also see NLS, Saltoun, SC 104, fos. 174-5, Argyll to Milton, 14 Feb. (1746, misplaced with 1745 correspondence): 'The Scheme is to sink again the office [Secretary of State] as formerly, but to give the Signet to some Scotsman, this I insisted on.' Also see BL, Newcastle, Add. MSS. 32901, fos. 481-2, Argyll to Newcastle, 26 Jan. 1760.

48. *Scotland and Scotsmen,* i, p. 88. There is additional biographical material on Milton in *The Bee, or Literary Weekly Intelligencer,* XI (1792), pp. 1-5; this is probably by Lord Buchan, based on a memoir of the family of Saltoun by Elizabeth Halkett (a granddaughter of Lord Milton) in the Edinburgh University Library, Laing Papers, La. III. 364. It is marked in a contemporary hand as being presented to Lord Buchan in 1785.

49. M. S. Bricke, 'Management and Administration', p. 150.

50. Riley, *English Ministers,* pp. 280-2, 294; E. Hughes, *Studies in Administration and Finance* (Manchester, 1934), pp. 309-11.

51. M. S. Bricke, 'Management and Administration', pp. 19-20, 143-6.

52. Quoted in (Henry Cockburn) review of W. Ritchie, 'Essays on Constitutional Law . . .' in *The Edinburgh Review,* Vol. 39 (Jan. 1824), p. 370. Also see H. Cockburn, *Memorials of His Times* (second edition, 1909), pp. 178, 386-7; and [——] *Original Portraits and Caricature Etchings by the Late John Kay* (second edition, 1877), ii, pp. 248-9.

53. The point is best developed in N. T. Phillipson, 'The Scottish Whigs', pp. 29-32; and picked up in J. M. Simpson, 'Who Steered the Gravy Train?', pp. 66-67.

54. M. S. Bricke, 'Management and Administration', pp. 20, 152.

55. Phillipson, 'The Scottish Whigs', p. 18.

56. Sir J. Clerk and J. Scrope, *Historical View of the forms and powers of the Court of Exchequer in Scotland* (written before 1724, but published in Edinburgh, 1820). Clerk and Scrope do not mention the deputes, but examples are William Alston, Lord Milton's legal agent, who acted as deputy Auditor of Exchequer for Milton's son Andrew Fletcher; and Dundas of Arniston's friend David Moncrieff (later Stewart Moncrieff) who was deputy King's Remembrancer before he became principal King's Remembrancer. For more information on the deputy King's Remembrancer (or Secretary to the Barons of Exchequer), see Bedford Papers, Vol. LIX, fo. 16, A. Stuart to Bedford, 11 March 1770.

57. For example, Alexander Macmillan, deputy keeper of the Signet (appointed by Milton), Alexander Gray, one of the principal Clerks of Session; and Robert Montgomery, Commissioner of Customs. For evidence of these men's attachment to Milton see the Saltoun Papers, which are now indexed by individual correspondent. William Jackson at the Post Office may serve as a more specific example: William L. Clements Library, Townshend Papers, J. Dalrymple to C. Townshend, 5 Oct. 1759: 'I know *de source* that Letters are opened. Milton has one of his own clerks who is Secretary to the post office, & you may easily imagine how the Secrets are kept.' Also see NLS, Advocates MS. 31.5.3., 'List of offices in Scotland in the gift of the Crown in 1747', in John Maule's hand.

58. M. S. Bricke, 'Management and Administration', pp. 58-59, 192-212.

59. NLS, Aerskine Murray Papers, MSS. 5076-5130; BL, Leeds, Egerton MSS. 3433-4; SRO, State Papers Scotland, RH2/4/380-2.

60. See Glenlee's letters in the *Calendar of Home Office Papers, 1773-1775*. Ramsay of Ochtertyre remarks that even in Tinwald's last years the Lord Justice Clerk's role in affairs of state 'had become almost a sinecure' *(Scotland and Scotsmen,* i, pp. 89, 105).

61. For the Commander-in-Chief, compare the correspondence in *The Albemarle Papers,* ed. C. S. Terry (Aberdeen, New Spalding Club, 1911), 2 vols., with the correspondence in the *Calendar of Home Office Papers, 1773-1775*. For the Lord High Commissioner's correspondence, see SRO, State Papers Scotland, RH2/4.

62. H. W. Meikle, *Scotland and the French Revolution* (1912), p. 285.

63. HMC, *Polwarth,* v. p. 285, Marchmont to Corbyn Morris (draft), 17 Oct. 1754.

64. Riley, *English Ministers,* p. 83; *Oswald Memorials,* pp. 277-81, R. Ord to J. Oswald (late 1760, early 1761). For the Equivalent, see Riley, *English Ministers,* pp. 203-29.

65. Riley, *English Ministers,* pp. 78-79; BL, Newcastle, Add. MSS. 32917, fos. 90-92, Newcastle to Hardwicke (copy), 3 Jan. 1761.

66. A. Murray, 'Administration and Law', in *The Union of 1707,* ed. Rae, p. 78n; BL, Hardwicke, Add. MSS. 35448, fos. 92-93, E. Edlin to Hardwicke, 29 April 1754; NLS, Letterbook of John Maule, MS. 10781, fos. 100-1, J. Maule to J. West, 25 Nov. 1754.

67. The best treatment of the Receivers of the revenue is W. R. Ward, 'The Land Tax in Scotland, 1707-1798', *Bulletin of the John Rylands Library,* XXXVII (1954-55), pp. 288-308.

68. *Ibid.,* p. 305; Bute Papers, no. 20/1757, J. Campbell of Stonefield to Lord Bute, 12 March 1757.

69. NLS, Saltoun, SC 196, fos. 223-4, 'Memorandum STAMPS pr. Mr. Jones 1757'; Ward, 'Land Tax', p. 298.

70. Riley, *English Ministers,* pp. 41, 60, 65.

71. See NLS, Saltoun, SB 368 (Excise & Army), folder 3 (G. Burgess? to Lord Milton?, Oct. 1761?), a letter discussing the abuses in the Excise; *ibid.,* SC 224, fo. 200, Milton to J. Stuart Mackenzie (draft), 19 Dec. 1763.

72. Atholl Papers, Box 47, section 13, no. 160, memorial by J. Drummond (1761). Also see NLS, Saltoun, SC 199, fo. 174, Argyll to Milton, May 1758, in which Argyll claims that Walpole never allowed the practice.

73. Bute/Loudoun Papers, 1761, bundle 5, J. Campbell to Loudoun, 22 April 1761; *Oswald Memorials,* pp. 50-53, Henry Kames (Lord Kames) to J. Oswald, 22 Nov. 1762; NLS, Saltoun, SC 217, fo. 23, Kames to Milton, 21 March 1761.

74. BL, Newcastle, Add. MSS. 32919, fos. 295-6, R. Dauber to (H. V. Jones?), 26 Feb. 1761, which includes a useful, but biased, potted history of English Excise commissioners in Scotland.

75. NLS, Saltoun, SC 19, fo. 56, A. Fletcher to Milton, 19 Feb. 1757. Argyll apparently disapproved of the Magistrates' action.

76. *Ibid.,* SC 215, fo. 217, G. Drummond to Milton, 30 June 1761.

77. Atholl Papers, Box 47, section 11, no. 22, A. Stuart to J. Murray of Strowan, 15 Feb. 1759.

78. BL, Newcastle, Add. MSS. 32893, fos. 297-9, R. Dauber to (J. West?), 26 July 1759.

79. *Ibid.,* Add. MSS. 32919, fos. 295-6, R. Dauber to (H. V. Jones?), 26 Feb. 1761.

80. Bute/Loudoun Papers, 1759, bundle 7, G. Drummond to Loudoun, 19 April 1759.

81. NLS, Saltoun, SB 370, folder 3, memorial on the customs by Lord Milton; Edinburgh, Signet Library, MS.106:54, 'An Account of the Officers of the Customs & Salt Duty at the Out Ports in Scotland, their Salaries, the supposed Value of each Office; their Character, & by whose Interest they held their Employments, as they stood on the Establishment at the 5th of January 1755', a remarkable manuscript which gives all the information its title promises.

82. NLS, Saltoun, SC 217, fos. 173-6, Milton to J. Stuart Mackenzie (copy), 26 Sept. 1761.

83. SRO, Seafield, GD 248/562/55, Dupplin to Deskford, 19 June 1755. Also see NLS, SB 370, folder 2, which contains many lists of recommendations and comments on customs appointments.

84. Bedford Papers, Vol. XLVIII, fo. 214, Lord Garlies to G. Grenville (copy), 19 Dec. 1763.

85. Riley, *English Ministers,* pp. 135-7; T. C. Barker, 'Smuggling in the eighteenth century: the evidence of the Scottish Tobacco Trade', *The Virginia Magazine of History and Biography,* LXII (1954), pp. 387-99; W. A. J. Prevost, 'The Solway Smugglers and the Customs Port at Dumfries', *Transactions of the Dumfriesshire and Galloway Natural History and Antiquarian Society,* third series, LI (1975), pp. 59-67.

86. B. R. Leftwich, 'Selections from the Customs Records Preserved at Dumfries', *Transactions of the Dumfriesshire . . . Antiquarian Society,* third series, XVII (1928), p. 112, letter of 1 June 1761.

87. Riley, *English Ministers,* pp. 190-1, 276-83.

88. *Ibid.,* pp. 177-85.

89. *Calendar of Home Office Papers, 1763-1765,* no. 1586, the warrant of Lord Cathcart as First Lord of Police, 27 Jan. 1764.

90. NLS, Yester, Box 19, folder 3, J. Hamilton to Lord G. Hay, 27 May 1766; the papers in this folder all concern the Board of Police, and demonstrate just how little the Commissioners did.

91. R. H. Campbell, 'Introduction', to *States of the Annual Progress of the Linen Manufacture, 1727-1754,* ed. R. H. Campbell (1964); C. Gulvin, 'The Union and the Scottish Woollen Industry, 1707-1760', *SHR,* L (1971), pp. 124-5.

92. A. J. Durie, *The Scottish Linen Industry in the Eighteenth Century* (1979), p. 29.

93. NLS, Saltoun, SC 216, fo. 45, Lord Milton to G. Elliot (draft), May 1761. Also see BL, Newcastle, Add. MSS. 33049, fo. 289, Deskford to Dupplin (copy), 7 Dec. 1754.

94. NLS, Saltoun, SC 201, fo. 65, D. Flint to Milton, 27 March 1758. Also see *ibid.,* SC 87, fo. 31; SC 210, fo. 61; SC 228, fo. 60.

95. See *A Selection of Scottish Forfeited Estates Papers, 1715, 1745,* ed. A. H. Millar (Scottish History Society, 1909).

96. A. J. Youngson, *After the Forty-Five: the Economic Impact on the Scottish Highlands* (1973), p. 27, quoting Act 25 Geo. II c. 41.

97. See *Caldwell Papers,* ii, pp. 138-9, J. Stuart Mackenzie to Mure, 1 March 1768.

98. See A. M. Smith, 'The Administration of the Forfeited Annexed Estates, 1752-1784', in *The Scottish Tradition: Essays in Honour of Ronald Gordon Cant,* ed. G. W. S. Barrow (1974), pp. 198-210; A. M. Smith, 'The Forfeited Annexed Estates, 1752-1784' (University of St. Andrews Ph.D., 1975); *Reports on the Annexed Estates, 1755-1769,* ed. V. Wills (1973). John Shaw was kind enough to direct me to the work of Dr. Smith and Mrs. Wills.

99. R. Mitchison, 'Government and the Highlands, 1707-1745', in *Scotland in the Age of Improvement,* pp. 39-42.

100. A. E. Whetstone, 'Scottish County Government in the Eighteenth and Nineteenth Centuries' (University of Minnesota Ph.D., 1973), pp. 61, 68; Jewell, 'Legislation Relating to Scotland', pp. 148-64. I am very grateful to R. B. Sher for informing me of Dr. Whetstone's thesis.

101. NLS, Saltoun, SB 365, folder 2, 'Memorandum', 1761.

102. Riley, *English Ministers,* p. 169; H. W. Meikle, *Scotland and the French Revolution,* p. 28.

103. W. Ferguson, 'Electoral Law', pp. 19-20, 47, 48; Whetstone, 'County Government', p. 45.

104. NLS, Saltoun, SC 217, fo. 223, Milton to J. Stuart Mackenzie (draft, Nov. 1761).

105. *Ibid.,* SC 194, fo. 144, Milton to Argyll (draft), 'March 1757'; BL, Newcastle, Add. MSS. 32883, fos. 342-3, Argyll to Newcastle, 7 Sept. 1758.

106. SRO, Arniston, RH4/15/5, Earl of Morton to Lord President Arniston, 11 Nov. 1765.

107. Whetstone, 'County Government', p. 65.

108. *Calendar of Home Office Papers, 1773-1775,* no. 971, Lord Justice Clerk Glenlee (Thomas Miller) to Lord Suffolk, 7 May 1775. Glenlee himself, however, was not above a bit of politics; see Loudoun Papers, 1774, bundle 5, Glenlee to Loudoun, 8 May 1775.

109. Whetstone, 'County Government', pp. 68-69; W. Ferguson, 'Electoral Law', p. 21.

110. G. S. Pryde, *Central and Local Government in Scotland Since 1707* (London, Historical Association Pamphlet, 1960), p. 10; *A Source Book of Scottish History,* ed. W. C. Dickinson and G. Donaldson (second edition, 1961), iii, pp. 299-302.

111. W. Ferguson, *Scotland: 1689 to the Present* (1968), p. 158; T. Hamilton, 'Local Administration in Ayrshire, 1750-1800', *Collections of the Ayrshire Archaeological and Natural History Society,* v (1959), pp. 174-6.

112. Whetstone, 'County Government', pp. 146-191.

113. C. A. Malcolm, 'Introduction' to *The Minutes of the Justices of the Peace for Lanarkshire, 1707-1723,* ed. C. A. Malcolm (Scottish History Society, 1931), pp. ix-xxviii.

114. E. K. Carmichael, 'The Scottish Commission of the Peace, 1707-1760' (University of Glasgow Ph.D., 1977), pp. 211-14, 233-42, 294; NLS, Saltoun, SC 217, fos. 214-16.

115. Whetstone, 'County Government', pp. 114-132.

116. PRO, HO 102/2/120, T. Miller to Lord Sidney, 19 July 1784, cited in *ibid.*, p. 113.

117. For information on this complicated issue see W. Ferguson, 'Electoral Law', pp. 54-83; R. M. Sunter, 'Stirlingshire Politics', pp. 209-11.

118. T. Hamilton, 'Local Administration', pp. 174-6; W. Ferguson, 'Electoral Law', pp. 20, 165.

119. G. Pryde, *Central and Local Government*, p. 16; R. Mitchison, 'The Making of the Old Scottish Poor Law', *Past and Present*, no. 63 (May 1974), pp. 58-93.

120. Bute Papers, no. 376/1761, Earl of Marchmont to Lord Bute, 9 May 1761. For an example see NLS, Saltoun, SC 221, fos. 163-4, J. Stuart Mackenzie to Lord Milton, 9 Sept. 1762.

121. See the *Miscellany of the Scottish Burgh Records Society* (1881), Part III of which reprints the Sets, or constitutions, of all the Royal Burghs of Scotland.

122. D. Murray, *The Early Burgh Organisation of Scotland* (Glasgow, 1924), pp. 252-325; D. Robertson *et al, Edinburgh: 1329-1929* (1929), pp. 304-12.

123. Murray, *ibid.*, p. 228; Robertson, *ibid.*, p. 103.

124. T. Pagan, *The Convention of the Royal Burghs of Scotland* (Glasgow, 1926), p. 256; Ward, 'Land Tax', pp. 290-4.

125. W. Ferguson, 'Dingwall Burgh Politics and the Parliamentary Franchise in the Eighteenth Century', *SHR*, XXXVIII (1959), pp. 106-8.

126. For Ayr see W. L. Burn, 'The General Election of 1761 at Ayr', *English Historical Review*, LII (1937), pp. 103-9; for Aberdeen, see NLS, Saltoun, SC 89, fo. 121, J. Maule to the Magistrates of Aberdeen (copy), Dec. 1742.

Chapter 2: The Duke of Argyll and Scotland

1. This section is based generally on P. W. J. Riley, *The English Ministers and Scotland*; Riley, 'The Structure of Scottish Politics and the Union of 1707', in *The Union of 1707: Its Impact on Scotland*, ed. T. I. Rae, pp. 1-29; and J. M. Simpson, 'Who Steered the Gravy Train?', in *Scotland in the Age of Improvement*, ed. N. T. Phillipson and R. M. Mitchison, pp. 47-72. Richard Scott is engaged on a major study of Scottish politics in the Walpolean age which will supersede previous studies when it eventually appears.

2. Riley, *English Ministers*, pp. 22-23, 33.

3. *Ibid.*, p. 118.

4. T. Pagan (née Keith), *The Convention of the Royal Burghs of Scotland* (Glasgow, 1926), p. 256.

5. Riley, *English Ministers*, p. 230.

6. In this instance Dr. Riley's account may be supplemented by G. S. Holmes, 'The Hamilton Affair of 1711-12', *English Historical Review*, LXXVII (1962), pp. 257-82.

7. J. H. Plumb, *The Growth of Political Stability in England, 1675-1725* (paperback edition, Harmondsworth, Middlesex, 1973), p. 181.

8. Simpson, 'Who Steered the Gravy Train?', p. 58.

9. *Lady Louisa Stuart: Selections from her Manuscripts*, ed. J. Home (London, 1899), p. 15.

10. H. T. Dickinson and Ken Logue, 'The Porteous Riot: A Study of the Breakdown of Law and Order in Edinburgh, 1736-1737', in *The Journal of the Scottish Labour History Society*, No. 10 (June 1976), pp. 21-40.

11. John, Lord Hervey, *Some Materials Towards Memoirs of the Reign of King George II*, ed. R. Sedgwick (reprint of 1931 edition, New York, 1970), ii, p. 708.

12. Bute Papers, uncatalogued, second Duke of Argyll to J. Stuart Mackenzie, 9 Jan. 1741.

13. See W. J. M. Mackenzie, *Political Identity* (Manchester, 1978).

14. Hervey, *Memoirs*, iii, p. 296; NLS, Saltoun, SC 94, fo. 55, J. Maule to Milton, 19 May 1743.

15. H. Walpole, *Memoirs of the Reign of King George II*, second edition, ed. Lord Holland (London, 1846), i, p. 278; Hervey, *Memoirs*; *A Selection from the Papers of the Earls of Marchmont*, ed. Sir G. Rose (London, 1831); HMC, *Polwarth*, v.

16. *Scotland and Scotsmen*, i, p. 87.

17. *Printed Recollections Respecting the Family of the Fletchers of Salton*, p. 3.

18. I. Lindsay and M. Cosh, *Inveraray and the Dukes of Argyll* (1973), pp. 6, 8, 10; Bute Papers, uncatalogued, Ilay to J. Stuart Mackenzie, 29 Sept. 1738.

19. NLS, Saltoun, SC 87, fo. 176, Sir James Carnegie to Lord Milton, 9 Jan. 1742.

20. W. Ferguson, *Scotland*, p. 147.

21. NLS, Saltoun, SC 91, fo. 104, Argyll to Milton, 26 (Nov. 1743).

22. *Ibid.*, fo. 125, Argyll to Milton, 31 Dec. 1743.

23. Walpole, *Memoirs*, i, p. 276; W. Coxe, *Memoirs of the Administration of the right honourable Henry Pelham* (London, 1829), i, p. 262. Also see *Hardwicke Correspondence*, i, p. 421; J. W. Wilkes, *A Whig in Power: The Political Career of Henry Pelham* (Evanston, Illinois, 1964), p. 154.

24. R. M. Mitchison, 'Government and the Highlands', pp. 38-45; J. M. Simpson 'Who Steered the Gravy Train?', p. 59; Sir J. Fergusson, *Argyll in the Forty-Five* (London, 1951), pp. 33-34.

25. Sir J. Fergusson, *ibid.*, pp. 35-36; M. S. Bricke, 'Management and Administration', pp. 193-6.

26. W. Coxe, *Memoirs of Horatio, Lord Walpole* (London, third edition, 1820), ii, pp. 113-4, H. Fox to Sir C. Hanbury Williams, 19 Sept. 1745.

27. BL, Newcastle, Add. MSS. 32707, fo. 429, Cumberland to Newcastle, 17 July 1746, quoted in Jewell, 'Legislation Relating to Scotland', p. 56.

28. *History of Parliament: The House of Commons, 1715-1754*, ed. R. Sedgwick (London, 1970), i, pp. 159-60, H. Pelham to Newcastle, 24 July 1747.

29. NLS, Saltoun, SC 138, fo. 59, Argyll to Milton, 23 June 1747. Also see *ibid.*, fo. 53, Argyll to Milton 18 June 1747; R. M. Sunter, 'Stirlingshire Politics', p. 485. The new peers were the Duke of Gordon and the Earls of Rothes, Leven, Lauderdale and Aberdeen in place of the Earls of Stair (deceased), Breadalbane, Sutherland, Portmore, and Lord Somerville.

30. *More Culloden Papers*, ed. D. Warrand (Inverness, 1930), v, p. 182, Mitchell to Culloden, 22 May 1747. Compare this with the account in *ibid.*, pp. 184-5, N. Macleod to Culloden, 23 May 1747. For an excellent treatment of the debate and Argyll's role in it see Jewell, 'Legislation Relating to Scotland', pp. 169-207.

31. M. S. Bricke, 'Management and Administration', pp. 114, 157.

32. This passage is closely dependent on Jewell, 'Legislation Relating to Scotland', pp. 46-49; an interpretation which runs counter to J. B. Owen, *The Rise of the Pelhams* (London, 1957), pp. 318-19.

33. *History of Parliament*, ed. Sedgwick, i, p. 160.

34. HMC, *Polwarth*, v, p. 263-64, 18 Dec. 1747.

35. BL, Hardwicke, Add. MSS. 35423, fo. 160, Pelham to Hardwicke, 10 June 1753, quoted in Jewell, 'Legislation Relating to Scotland', p. 23.

36. For Bruce, see Jewell, 'Legislation Relating to Scotland', pp. 24-25. For an example of Dundas's activity, see SRO, Arniston, RH4/15/4, H. Pelham to Dundas, 16 May 1752.

37. Jewell, 'Legislation Relating to Scotland', pp. 19-20; Bricke, 'Management and Administration', pp. 131-2, 181-2.

38. BL, Hardwicke, Add. MSS. 35447, fo. 295, Argyll to Hardwicke, 7 Nov. 1752.

39. NLS, Saltoun, SC 221, fo. 183, Milton to J. Stuart Mackenzie (copy), 6 Dec. 1762.

40. Sir John Sinclair, *Observations on the Scottish Dialect* (London, 1782), p. 3. Perhaps Argyll's early education at Eton helped form his views on the subject.

41. [P. Bannerman] *A Sermon Preached at Salton, Upon Occasion of Death of the Honourable the Lord Milton* (1767), p. 50.

42. This paragraph is based on the account in Jewell, 'Legislation Relating to Scotland', pp. 210-36.

43. BL, Leeds, Egerton MSS. 3433, fos. 1-3, 'Abuses, or Neglects, in the general Management in Scotland, since the Rebellion. 1752' (copy); Walpole, *Memoirs*, i, pp. 256-64; Jewell, 'Legislation Relating to Scotland', pp. 237-40.

44. NLS, Saltoun, SC 174, fo. 131, Argyll to Milton, 6 April 1752. Also see Jewell, 'Legislation Relating to Scotland', pp. 240-5; Walpole, *Memoirs*, i, pp. 264-74.

45. BL, Newcastle, Add. MSS. 33050, fos. 183-4, Report of Pelham to the King; BL, Leeds, Egerton MSS. 3433, contains material forwarded to Secretary of State Holderness as part of the investigation; Jewell, 'Legislation Relating to Scotland', pp. 21-22, 246; Coxe, *Pelham*, ii, pp. 412-17, 420, 439-40.

46. NLS, Saltoun, SC 138, fo. 74, Argyll to Milton, 19 July 1747; *ibid.*, SC 174, fo. 129, Argyll to Milton, 26 March 1752. The description, 'elder statesman', is from R. Mitchison, *A History of Scotland* (London, 1970), p. 343.

47. Sir L. B. Namier, *England in the Age of the American Revolution* (second edition, London, 1961), pp. 68-69.

48. Hervey, *Memoirs*, iii, p. 734. Also see *Marchmont Papers*, ed. Rose, ii, p. 73.

49. Coxe, *Pelham*, ii, p. 414, Newcastle to Pelham, 29 April-12 May 1752. Also see pp. 412-13, Newcastle to Hardwicke, 21 March 1752.

50. BL, Newcastle, Add. MSS. 32922, fo. 15, Newcastle to Hardwicke, 17 April 1761. Also see Add. MSS. 32969, fos. 86-87, Newcastle to the Earl of Hopetoun, 18 Aug. 1765.

51. *Scotland and Scotsmen*, i, pp. 101, 113-14; BL, Hardwicke, Add. MSS. 35448, fos. 75-76, R. Craigie to Hardwicke, 12 March 1754.

52. BL, Newcastle, Add. MSS. 32854, fos. 15-16, H. Bland to Newcastle, 1 April 1755.

53. NLS, Saltoun, SC 184, fos. 193-4, Newcastle to Argyll, 2 June 1754; *History of Parliament: the House of Commons, 1754-1790*, ed. Sir L. B. Namier and J. Brooke (London, 1964), i, pp. 470, 471, 488, 496.

54. NLS, Saltoun, SC 178, fo. 23, W. Alston to Milton, 6 Oct. 1753; SC 182, fo. 149, Argyll to Milton, 21 March 1754; SC 182, fo. 163, Argyll to Milton, 13 April 1754.

55. NLS, Saltoun, SC 184, fo. 131, Grant of Delveys to Argyll, 9 April 1754; SC 184, fo. 283, J. Stuart Mackenzie to Milton, 24 April 1754; BL, Hardwicke, Add. MSS. 35448, fos. 110-11, H. Bland to Hardwicke, 6 July 1754; W. Ferguson, 'Electoral Law and Procedure', pp. 171-87. NLS, Saltoun, SC 182, fos. 20-21, J. Abercromby to Milton, 9 Sept. 1754; 'It has been said from what happened lately in some elections to the northward of this that the D. of A.ll is beat out of the north.'

56. *History of Parliament*, ed. Namier and Brooke, ii, pp. 187-8, 191; NLS, Saltoun, SC 17, fo. 46, A. Fletcher to Milton, 30 March 1754; SC 182, fo. 151, Argyll to Milton, 23 March 1754.

57. NLS, Saltoun, SC 182, fo. 155, Argyll to Milton, 29 March 1754.

58. SRO, Seafield, GD 248/562/55, Lord Dupplin to Lord Deskford, 19 June 1755. Also see *ibid.*, 19 Dec. 1754. I am very grateful to John Shaw for directing me to this source.

59. BL, Newcastle, Add. MSS. 32735, fos. 100-1, Hopetoun to Newcastle, 16 April 1754; fos. 145-6, Newcastle to Hopetoun (copy), 22 April 1754; fos. 182-3, Hopetoun to Newcastle, 26 April 1754; fos. 368-9, Newcastle to Hopetoun (copy), 3 June 1754; fos. 399-400, Hopetoun to Newcastle, 8 June 1754.

60. NLS, Yester, Accession 4862, Box 13, F 5, 5 Sept. 1754. For Hopetoun as Lord Commissioner, see NLS, Letterbook of Lord George Beauclerk, Accession 6477, p. 135, Beauclerk to General Ligonier, 25 April 1758.

61. Atholl Papers, Box 54, section 1, no. 219, J. Mackenzie of Delvine to Atholl, 19 Nov. 1770.

62. SRO, Seafield, GD 248/572/7, Newcastle to Deskford, 21 June 1754, 15 August 1754; 7 Sept. 1754.

63. NLS, Saltoun, SC 208, fo. 249, (Milton to Argyll, draft, Oct. 1754), misplaced amongst 1759 correspondence; BL, Newcastle, Add. MSS. 32736, fos. 107-8, E. Edlin to (J. West?), 27 July 1754; SRO, Seafield, GD 248/562/55, Lord Dupplin to Deskford, 28 Sept. 1754; 12 Nov. 1754.

64. NLS, Saltoun, SC 17, fo. 44, A. Fletcher to Milton, 28 March 1754.

65. BL, Newcastle, Add. MSS. 32922, fo. 40, Hardwicke to Newcastle, 18 April 1761.

66. HMC, *Polwarth*, v, p. 284, R. Dundas to Marchmont, 17 Aug. 1754; NLS, Yester, Accession 4862, Box 13, F 3, Dundas to Tweeddale, 18 Aug. 1754; BL, Newcastle, Add. MSS. 32736, fo. 523, Dundas to Newcastle, 14 Sept. 1754; SRO Arniston, RH4/15/4, Newcastle to Dundas, 19 Oct. 1754; *History of Parliament*, ed. Namier and Brooke, ii, p. 363; A. J. Youngson, 'Alexander Webster and his "Account of the Number of People in Scotland in the year 1755"', *Population Studies*, XV (Nov. 1961), p. 199.

67. NLS, Saltoun, SC 184, fo. 193, Newcastle to Argyll, 2 June 1754; NLS, Aerskine-Murray, MS. 5078, fo. 72, Newcastle to Tinwald, 2 June 1754; BL, Newcastle, Add. MSS. 32736, fos. 9-10, J. Erskine to Newcastle, 4 July 1754; BL, Hardwicke, Add. MSS. 35450, fo. 245, Breadalbane to Hardwicke, 19 May 1754.

68. See BL, Newcastle, Add. MSS. 32736, fos. 271-2, 451-2, 531-2; NLS, Saltoun, SC 185, fos. 10, 43; SC 182, fos. 7-21.

69. BL, Hardwicke, Add. MSS. 35448, fo. 210, Bland to Hardwicke, 26 Nov. 1754.

70. *Complete Peerage*, vii, pp. 322-3; *History of Parliament*, ed. Sedgwick, ii, p. 119; *History of Parliament*, ed. Namier and Brooke, ii, pp. 600-1.

71. SRO, Arniston, RH4/15/4, Dupplin to Dundas, 22 April (1755), misplaced with 1756 correspondence. Dupplin's letters to Deskford are in SRO, Seafield, GD 248/562/55; there are letters from Deskford to Dupplin in the Newcastle Papers, and a series of extracts of letters from Deskford and others to Dupplin in BL, Newcastle, Add. MSS. 33049, fos. 284-91; also Add. MSS. 32996, fos. 52-55.

72. See Newcastle's and Argyll's correspondence from the summer of 1754: NLS, Saltoun, SC 184, fos. 193-4; BL, Newcastle, Add. MSS. 32736, fos. 121-2, 151-2, 271-2, 448-50, 531-2; Add. MSS. 32737, fo. 340.

73. BL, Newcastle, Add. MSS. 32736, fos. 531-2, Argyll to Newcastle, 15 Sept. 1754; an answer to fo. 450, Newcastle to Argyll (copy), 7 Sept. 1754. Add. MSS. 32736, fos. 282-3, Bland to Newcastle, 17 Aug. 1754, is a good example of the information Newcastle was receiving from Bland.

74. SRO, Seafield, GD 248/562/55, A. Mitchell to Deskford, 6 Feb. 1755.

75. NLS, Saltoun, SC 182, fos. 177-8, Argyll to Milton, 30 Nov. (1754); fos. 185-6, Argyll to Milton, 20 Dec. (1754): 'MY TREATY WITH FOX seems to go on well.' In cipher.

76. L. Colley, 'The Mitchell Election Division, 24 March 1755', *Bulletin of the Institute of Historical Research*, XLIX (May 1976), pp. 80-107; NLS, Saltoun, SC 17, fos. 135, 137, 141, 145, 147, correspondence of Lord Milton and his son, Andrew Fletcher.

77. The Act of Settlement of 1701 secured life tenure for English judges save for cases of moral turpitude or treason. See Walpole, *Memoirs*, ii, pp. 4-10; NLS, Saltoun, SC 17, fo. 133, A. Fletcher to Milton, 20 Feb. 1755; BL, Hardwicke, Add. MSS. 35448, fos. 226-7, Lord President Glendoick to Hardwicke, 2 Jan. 1755.

78. SRO, Scott of Harden, GD 157/2251, no. 10, Marchmont to W. Scott, 3 March 1755. *History of Parliament*, ed. Namier and Brooke, ii, p. 362.

79. BL, Hardwicke, Add. MSS. 35415, fo. 110, Newcastle to Hardwicke, 18 Oct. 1755. Also see SRO, Seafield, GD 248/562/55, Dupplin to Deskford, 30 Oct. 1755; HMC, *Polwarth*, v, p. 296, A. Hume Campbell to Marchmont, 15 Oct. 1755.

80. Bute Papers, no. 46/1755, Elliot to Bute (Aug. 1755).

81. NLS, Saltoun, SC 186, fo. 82, Argyll to Milton, 25 March 1755.

82. NLS, Yester, Accession 4862, Box 13, F5, letters of Thomas Hay to Tweeddale, Aug.-Nov. 1754; *ibid.*, F 3, Argyll to Tweeddale, 10 June 1755; NLS Saltoun, SC 182, fo. 185, Argyll to Milton, 20 Dec. (1754). Deskford had applied for the place on the Board of Police which went to Tweeddale's brother (SRO, Seafield, GD 248/562/55, Dupplin to Deskford, 19 June 1755).

83. HMC, *Polwarth*, v, p. 303, Marchmont to A. Hume Campbell (draft), 19 Oct. 1755. Also see *ibid.*, p. 291; SRO, Scott of Harden, GD 157/2251, no. 3 and no. 11.

84. Bute Papers, no. 46/1755, G. Elliot to Bute (Aug. 1755). Also see no. 48/1755, Elliot to Bute, 31 Aug. (1755).

85. HMC, *Polwarth*, v, pp. 297-8, 299; NLS, Saltoun, SC 186, fo. 238, Marchmont to Milton, 20 Oct. 1755.

86. SRO, Seafield, GD 248/562/55, Dupplin to Deskford, 12 Nov. 1755; NLS, Saltoun, SB 330, folder 1, 'List of Commissioners and Trustees ...': originally Lord President Glendoick, Lord Edgefield, and Lord Auchinleck were proposed in addition to the Advocate; Lord Kames, Lord Cathcart (a peer), and Charles Hope Weir (M.P. for Linlithgowshire) were named.

87. BL, Newcastle, Add. MSS. 32857, fo. 67, Newcastle to R. Dundas (copy), 12 July 1755. Also see Add. MSS. 32856, fos. 173-4; NLS, Saltoun, SC 17, fos. 188, 192.

88. SRO, Seafield, GD 248/562/55, Dupplin to Deskford, 30 July 1755. Also see *ibid.*, 29 July 1755; SRO, Arniston, RH4/15/4, Dupplin to R. Dundas, 30 July 1755.

89. SRO, Craigievar, RH4/70/1, bundle 10, R. Dundas to A. Mitchell, 1 Nov. 1755; BL, Newcastle, Add. MSS. 32858, fos. 279-80, Deskford to Newcastle, 24 Aug. 1755.

90. Bute Papers, no. 88/1756, Argyll to Bute, 9 Oct. (1755), misplaced with 1756 correspondence; BL, Ilchester, Add. MSS. 51429, fo. 9, Argyll to H. Fox, 2 Oct. (1755); BL, Newcastle, Add. MSS. 32859, fos. 396-7, Argyll to Newcastle, 5 Oct. 1755, and fo. 425, 7 Oct. 1755. Also see Add. MSS. 32859, fos. 237-9; Add. MSS. 32860, fos. 78-79, 89; Add. MSS. 35448, fo. 292.

91. SRO, Arniston, RH4/15/4, all correspondence for Dec. 1755/Jan. 1756; Dupplin to Dundas, 25 June 1756; NLS, Saltoun, SC 18, fo. 80, A. Fletcher to Milton, 15 May 1756, in cipher.

92. NLS, Saltoun, SC 186, fo. 96, Argyll to Milton, 20 Nov. 1755; SRO, Arniston, RH4/15/4, Deskford to Dundas, 23 Dec. (1755, misplaced amongst 1756 letters).

93. See NLS, Saltoun, SC 186, fo. 96, Argyll to Milton, 20 Nov. 1755, for the comment on Newcastle; and HMC, *Polwarth*, v, p. 320, A. Hume Campbell to Marchmont, 12 July 1756, giving an account of an encounter with Argyll.

94. BL, Hardwicke, Add. MSS. 35415, fos. 110-11, Newcastle to Hardwicke, 18 Oct. 1755, Newcastle's emphasis.

95. Bute Papers, no. 95/1756, Argyll to Bute, 2 Nov. 1756. See J. L. McKelvey, *George III and Lord Bute* (Durham, North Carolina, 1973), pp. 33-47; BL, Newcastle, Add. MSS. 32867, fos. 46-47, W. Murray to Newcastle, 25 Aug. 1756; fo. 143, Hardwicke to Newcastle, 29 Aug. 1756.

96. BL, Ilchester, Add. MSS. 51430, fo. 23, Argyll to Fox, 3 Nov. (1756).

97. Bute Papers, no. 187/1757, Sir H. Erskine to Bute (Nov. 1756?). For details of Fox's dispute with Pitt see *History of Parliament*, ed. Namier and Brooke, ii, p. 599.

98. NLS, Aerskine-Murray, MS. 5079, fo. 102, Holderness to Lord Tinwald, 9 Dec. 1756.

99. *Ibid.*, fo. 111, J. St. Clair to Tinwald, 22 Jan. 1757; Torwoodlee Papers, Box 9, bundle 5, Marchmont to J. Pringle, 8 Feb. 1757.

100. NLS, Saltoun, SC 19, fo. 71, A. Fletcher to Milton, 12 March 1757. Also see E. M. Lloyd, 'The Raising of the Highland Regiments in 1757', *English Historical Review*, XVII (July 1902), pp. 466-9.

101. L. Sutherland, 'The City of London and the Devonshire-Pitt Administration, 1756-7', *Proceedings of the British Academy*, XLVI (1960), pp. 147-93; Walpole, *Memoirs*, ii, p. 275. NLS, Saltoun, SC 18, fo. 136; SC 19, fo. 47; SC 19, fo. 58; SC 194, fo. 164; BL, Ilchester, Add. MSS. 51430, fo. 23; BL, Newcastle, Add. MSS. 32873, fo. 151; SRO, Board of Customs Minutes, CE 1/9/1A, fo. 116.

102. NLS, Saltoun, SC 194, fo. 147, Argyll to Milton, 9 April 1757.

103. BL, Ilchester, Add. MSS. 51430, fo. 81, Argyll to Fox, 3 April 1757; fo. 83, Argyll to Fox, 6 April 1757.

104. *Letters to Henry Fox, Lord Holland*, ed. Earl of Ilchester (London, 1915), pp. 102-4, H. Fox to the Earl of Ilchester, 4 March 1757.

105. Bute Papers, no. 173/1757, J. Grenville to Bute, n.d. (spring 1757).

106. NLS, Saltoun, SC 194, fo. 162, Argyll to Milton, 11 June 1757.

107. Duncan Duff, *Scotland's War Losses* (Glasgow, the Scottish Secretariat, 1947), p. 12.

108. For the implementation of the Press Act see NLS, Letterbook of Lord George Beauclerk, Accession 6417, pp. 9-283, which provides further evidence for Duff's work cited above. I am very grateful to Dr. Paul Kelly of the NLS for directing me to this valuable source. For naval impressment see *Parliamentary History*, XV, pp. 547-53, 570-1.

109. NLS, Saltoun, SC 18, fos. 105, 108, A. Fletcher to Lord Milton, 15 July and 20 July 1756, both in cipher. SC 209, fo. 150, Milton to Argyll (draft), Feb. 1760.

110. *Scotland and Scotsmen*, ii, pp. 504-5.

111. John, Lord Campbell, *The Lives of the Chief Justices of England* (London, 1849), ii, p. 452. M. S. Bricke, 'Management and Administration', p. 243 n 102, only traces the myth to the *DNB* but agrees in finding no evidence for this assertion: both Ferguson, *Scotland: 1689 to the Present*, p. 147; and Simpson, 'Who Steered the Gravy Train?', p. 62, have accepted the story.

112. BL, Newcastle, Add. MSS. 32998, fo. 411, memorandum 9 March 1760; there is a similar comment in Add. MSS. 32895, fo. 80, Newcastle to Hardwicke (copy), 31 Aug. 1759.

113. Atholl Papers, Box 47, section 12, no. 145, Sir R. Menzies to J. Murray of Strowan, 13 Nov. 1760.

114. SRO, Scott of Harden, GD 157/2251, no. 44, Marchmont to W. Scott, 27 Dec. 1757; BL, Newcastle, Add. MSS. 32911, fos. 94-104, Newcastle to Hardwicke (copy), 6 Sept. 1760.

115. Ferguson, *Scotland*, p. 147.

116. BL, Newcastle, Add. MSS. 32999, fo. 15, 'Memorandum with the Duke of Argyll, the whole list of members gone through with his Grace', 27 June 1760; SRO, Arniston, RH4/15/4, 'Note of the Elections in Scotland', April 1760, in the new Lord President Arniston's hand; there is a copy in BL, Newcastle, Add. MSS. 33049, fos. 306-21.

Chapter 3. The Duke of Argyll and the Duke of Newcastle

1. NLS, Saltoun, SC 184, fos. 193-4, Newcastle to Argyll, 2 June 1754.

2. BL, Newcastle, Add. MSS. 32737, fos. 483-4, Bland to Newcastle, 24 Dec. 1754. This is very reminiscent of the language used by Duncan Forbes after the dismissal of the Duke of Roxburghe in 1725 (Riley, *English Ministers*, p. 285).

3. BL, Newcastle, Add. MSS. 32736, fos. 282-3, Bland to Newcastle, 17 Aug. 1754. Also see BL, Hardwicke, Add. MSS. 35448, fo. 120, Bland to Hardwicke, 27 July 1754; fos. 220-1, Bland to Hardwicke, 24 Dec. 1754.

4. BL, Hardwicke, Add. MSS. 35448, fos. 75-76, R. Craigie to Hardwicke, 12 March 1754; NLS, Yester, Accession 4862, Box 13, F 3, Dundas to Tweeddale, 18 Aug. 1754.

5. BL, Hardwicke, Add. MSS. 35448, fo. 120, Bland to Hardwicke, 27 July 1754; BL, Newcastle, Add. MSS. 32736, fos. 121-2, Newcastle to Argyll (copy), 31 July 1754; NLS, Saltoun, SC 182, fos. 173-4, Argyll to Milton, 31 July (1754).

6. SRO, Seafield, GD 248/572/7, Newcastle to Deskford, 19 Oct. 1754. Also see BL, Newcastle, Add. MSS. 32736, fos. 125-6, Newcastle to Queensberry (copy), 31 July 1754; BL, Hardwicke, Add. MSS. 35448, fo. 124, Hopetoun to Hardwicke, 27 July 1754; fo. 128, Findlater to Hardwicke, 3 Aug. 1754; fo. 148, Findlater to Hardwicke, 29 Aug. 1754.

7. NLS, Yester, Accession 4862, Box 13, F 5, Tweeddale to Granville (draft, Nov. ? 1754); T. Hay to Tweeddale, 9 Nov. (1754); T. Hay to Tweeddale (10 ? Nov. 1754). BL, Hardwicke, Add. MSS. 35448, fos. 184-5, copy in NLS, Aerskine-Murray, MS. 5078, fo. 112.

8. NLS, Yester, Accession 4862, Box 13, F 5, T. Hay to Tweeddale, 9 Nov. (1754). Also see BL, Leeds, Egerton MSS. 3434, fos. 112-78; BL, Hardwicke, Add. MSS. 35414, fos. 210-11, Newcastle to Hardwicke, 28 Oct. 1754; NLS, Aerskine-Murray, MS. 5078, fo. 110, Lord Justice Clerk's report on Hay, 5 Nov. 1754.

9. BL, Newcastle, Add. MSS. 32736, fo. 579, Findlater to Newcastle, 29 Aug. 1754.

10. Ross had been James Stuart Mackenzie's most important supporter during his attempt to be returned for the county of Ross in the 1754 general election. Mackenzie was Argyll's nephew, and recommended Ross to Lord Milton for the Banff Sheriffdom as soon as he heard it was vacant (NLS, Saltoun, SC 184, fo. 293, J. Stuart Mackenzie to Milton, 10 Sept. 1754; BL, Hardwicke, Add. MSS. 35448, fo. 196, Findlater to Hardwicke, 2 Nov. 1754).

11. SRO, Seafield, GD 248/562/55, Dupplin to Deskford, 12 Nov. 1754; GD 248/572/5, Findlater to Deskford, 2 Nov. 1754 and 4 Nov. 1754; BL, Newcastle, Add. MSS. 32861, fo. 255, Findlater to Newcastle, 9 Dec. 1755.

12. For Haldane, see *History of Parliament*, ed. Sedgwick, ii, pp. 95-96; BL, Newcastle, Add. MSS. 32737, fo. 340, Argyll to Newcastle, 10 Nov. 1754; Add. MSS. 32736, fo. 436, Hardwicke to Newcastle, 7 Sept. 1754. For Home see NLS, Saltoun, SC 17, fo. 130, A. Fletcher to Milton, 8 Feb. 1755.

13. BL, Newcastle, Add. MSS. 32996, fo. 52v, 'Minute from Ld Deskford's letters', 4 Feb. (1755); NLS, Saltoun, SC 186, fo. 80, Argyll to Milton, 4 March 1755; SC 178, fo. 23, W. Alston to Milton, 6 Oct. 1753. See the descriptions in *Scotland and Scotsmen*, i, pp. 323-27, 343-50.

14. BL, Hardwicke, Add. MSS. 35448, fo. 273, A. MacDowal to Hardwicke, 5 July 1755; fos. 280-1, R. Dundas to Hardwicke, 16 Sept. 1755. For an assessment of MacDowal's performance on the bench see *Scotland and Scotsmen*, i, pp. 127-31.

15. BL, Hardwicke, Add. MSS. 35448, fos. 150-1, Morton to Hardwicke, 2 Sept. 1754, the original recommendation renewed in 1755.

16. HMC, *Polwarth*, v, pp. 286-7, 288, 302; BL, Newcastle, Add. MSS. 32857, fo. 131, R. Dundas to Newcastle, 16 July 1755; fo. 425, Dundas to Newcastle, 29 July 1755.

17. *History of Parliament*, ed. Sedgwick, ii, p. 312; BL, Newcastle, Add. MSS. 32859, fo. 204, Newcastle to the Earl of Carlisle (copy), 25 Sept. 1755; fos. 237-9, Newcastle to Argyll (copy), 27 Sept. 1755; HMC, *Polwarth*, v, p. 295; NLS, Saltoun, SC 186, fo. 98, Argyll to Milton, 2 Dec. 1755.

18. BL, Newcastle, Add. MSS. 32859, fo. 425, Argyll to Newcastle, 7 Oct. 1755; Grant was the son of Lord Elchies, a prominent Scottish judge who had died in 1754. For the other recommendations see fo. 421, Bland to Newcastle, 7 Oct. 1755; BL, Hardwicke, Add. MSS. 35448, fo. 294, Glendoick to Hardwicke, 8 Oct. 1755; fo. 296, Findlater to Hardwicke, 11 Oct. 1755; fos. 267-8, Dundas to Hardwicke, 19 June 1755.

19. BL, Newcastle, Add. MSS. 32854, fo. 93, G. Elliot to Newcastle, 10 April 1755; BL, Hardwicke, Add. MSS. 35448, fos. 259-60, R. Dundas to Hardwicke, 4 June 1755; SRO, Arniston, RH4/15/4, Newcastle to Dundas, 12 July 1755; Lord Dupplin to Dundas, 29 July 1755 and 30 July 1755; Bute Papers, no. 48/1755, Elliot to Bute, 31 Aug. (1755); NLS, Minto, MS. 11014, fo. 3, Newcastle to Elliot, 26 Sept. 1755.

Argyll also attempted to secure the Sheriffdom of Berwickshire for a friend of the Earl of Home's, but was prevented from fulfilling this by frantic protests from Alexander Hume Campbell (the county M.P.) and the Earl of Marchmont.

20. BL, Hardwicke, Add. MSS. 35449, fo. 46, Hopetoun to Hardwicke, 11 Aug. 1756; fo. 50, Findlater to Hardwicke, 16 Aug. 1756.

21. SRO, Arniston, RH4/15/4, Findlater to Dundas, 12 Nov. 1756; BL, Newcastle, Add. MSS. 33056, fo. 373, 'memd Earl of Findlater'; NLS, Saltoun, SC 193, fos. 57-58, D. Ross to Milton, 15 Oct. 1756; SC 18, fo. 148, A. Fletcher to Milton, 23 Dec. 1756; SC 19, fo. 31, Fletcher to Milton, 15 Jan. 1757; SC 216, fo. 41, Milton to G. Elliot (draft), 21 May 1761.

22. For George Brown see NLS, SC 18, fo. 142, Fletcher to Milton, 7 Dec. 1756; fo. 142, Fletcher to Milton, 9 Dec. 1756; SC 227, fo. 176, Milton to J. Stuart Mackenzie, 27 Dec. 1764. Campbell of Stonefield was the son of the Sheriff-depute of Argyll and a brother-in-law of Lord Bute.

23. William L. Clements Library, Townshend Papers, J. Dalrymple to C. Townshend, 5 Oct. 1759.

24. BL, Hardwicke, Add. MSS. 35449, fo. 150, Dundas to Hardwicke, 23 Jan. 1759: Dundas wrote that a retreat to the bench would be better for Pringle's health but adds, significantly, that he had other reasons for wishing Pringle success which he would tell Hardwicke when he arrived in London.

25. BL, Newcastle, Add. MSS. 32855, fo. 108, Dundas to Newcastle, 22 May 1755; SRO, Arniston, RH4/15/5, T. Miller to Dundas, 11 March 1760.

26. NLS, Saltoun, SC 213, fo. 135, C. Townshend to Milton, 19 March 1760. Also see SC 207, fo. 157, Miller to Milton, 23 Jan. 1758 (misdate for 1759); SC 204, fo. 160, Milton to Argyll (copy), 23 Jan. 1759; SC 209, fo. 160, Argyll to Milton, April 1760.

27. SRO, Arniston, RH4/15/5, F. Garden to Dundas, 20 March 1760; NLS, Saltoun, SC 22, fo. 74, A. Fletcher to Milton, 5 April 1760; SC 212, fo. 199, Miller to Milton, 12 April 1760; SC 212, fos. 68, 70, Garden to Milton, March and 6 April 1760.

28. SRO, Arniston, RH4/15/4, Hardwicke to Dundas, 6 Sept. 1759; and Argyll to Dundas, 15 Dec. 1759.

29. *Ibid.*, Hardwicke to Dundas, 28 June 1755; and RH4/15/5, Hardwicke to Dundas, 16 March 1762; *Scotland and Scotsmen*, i, pp. 110-17, 335-8.

30. *Scotland and Scotsmen*, i, pp. 128-31.

31. BL, Newcastle, Add. MSS. 32736, fos. 451-2, Newcastle to Deskford (copy), 7 Sept. 1754; SRO, Seafield, GD 248/562/55, Dupplin to Deskford, 19 June 1755; 29 July 1755; 30 Oct. 1755.

32. SRO, Seafield, GD 248/562/55, Dupplin to Deskford, 28 Sept. 1754.

33. NLS, Aerskine-Murray, MS. 5078, fo. 80, G. Vaughan to Lord Tinwald, 30 July 1754. Also see fos. 66-68, N. Hardinge to the Commissioners of the Excise in Scotland (1 June 1754).

34. NLS, Aerskine-Murray, MS. 5078, fo. 72, Newcastle to Lord Justice Clerk Tinwald, 2 June 1754; BL, Newcastle, Add. MSS. 32736, fos. 9-10, J. Erskine to Newcastle, 4 July 1754; fos. 271-2, Newcastle to Argyll (copy), 17 Aug. 1754.

35. Bute Papers, No. 46/1755, G. Elliot to Bute (Aug. 1755); SRO, Seafield, GD 248/572/7, Newcastle to Deskford, 21 June 1754; BL, Newcastle, Add. MSS. 32736, fos. 153-4, Deskford to Newcastle, 4 Aug. 1754.

36. NLS, Saltoun, SC 183, fos. 4-5, Colin Campbell to Milton, 19 Oct. 1754; BL, Newcastle, Add. MSS. 32736, fos. 107-8, E. Edlin to (J. West?), 27 July 1754.

37. SRO, Seafield, GD 248/562/55, Dupplin to Deskford, 12 Nov. 1755.

38. For Morris, *ibid.*, A. Mitchell to Deskford, 15 Feb. 1755; BL, Newcastle, Add. MSS. 33049, fo. 284, Deskford to Dupplin (copy), 23 Oct. 1754. For Cardonnel see A. Carlyle, *Anecdotes and Characters*, pp. 11-13, 133, 154, 200, 208, 215; E. Hughes, *Studies in Administration and Finance, 1558-1825* (Manchester, 1934), p. 278. For LeGrand see J. Russell, 'Bonnington: Its Lands and Mansions', in *The Book of the Old Edinburgh Club*, XIX (1933), pp. 162-4; NLS, Saltoun, SC 190, fo. 178, C. Campbell to Milton, 5 Oct. 1756.

39. B. F. Jewell, 'Legislation Relating to Scotland', p. 32; SRO, Seafield, GD 248/572/7, Newcastle to Deskford, 7 Sept. 1754, copy in Add. MSS. 32736, fo. 452; GD 248/562/55, Dupplin to Deskford, 28 Sept. 1754.

40. BL, Newcastle, Add. MSS. 32737, fos. 507-8, Bland to Newcastle, 28 Dec. 1754.

41. Add. MSS. 32858, fos. 279-80, Deskford to Newcastle, 24 Aug. 1755.

42. Add. MSS. 32900, fos. 191-4, Deskford to (Dupplin), 19 Dec. 1754, misplaced with 1759 correspondence.

43. *Ibid.*

44. J. M. Price, 'New Time Series for Scotland's and Britain's Trade with the Thirteen Colonies and States, 1740 to 1791', *William and Mary Quarterly*, XXXII (April 1975), pp. 310-11; BL, Newcastle, Add. MSS. 33049, fo. 287, Deskford to (Dupplin, copy), 30 Nov. 1754; Add. MSS. 32737, fos. 405-6, Deskford to Newcastle, 3 Dec. 1754; fo. 536, Deskford to (Dupplin), 30 Dec. 1754; Add. MSS. 32852, fo. 51, Deskford to Newcastle, 2 Jan. 1755; SRO, Seafield, GD 248/562/55, Dupplin to Deskford, 12 Dec. 1754.

45. BL, Newcastle, Add. MSS. 33049, fo. 287, Deskford to (Dupplin, copy), 30 Nov. 1754; Add. MSS. 32737, fos. 423-4, Deskford to Dupplin, 10 Dec. 1754; SRO, Seafield, GD 248/562/55, Dupplin to Deskford, 19 Dec. 1754; 19 June 1755; NLS, Saltoun, SC 220, fos. 155-60, 'The Humble Petition of James Grosett son & heir of the late Walter Grosett'; 'The Grosett Manuscript', ed. D. N. Mackay, *Transactions of the Gaelic Society of Inverness*, XXVIII (1912-19), pp. 173-99.

46. NLS, Saltoun, SC 186, fo. 85, Campbell to Milton, April 1755; SRO, Seafield, GD 248/562/55, Dupplin to Deskford, 19 June 1755; SRO, Board of Customs Minutes, CE1/9/1A, fos. 24, 47.

47. BL, Newcastle, Add. MSS. 32854, fos. 15-16, Bland to Newcastle, 1 April 1755; Add. MSS. 32859, fos. 396-7, Argyll to Newcastle, 5 Oct. 1755; NLS, Saltoun, SC 186, fo. 74, Argyll to Milton, 4 Feb. 1755; fo. 182, C. Campbell to Milton, 12 Feb. 1755; fo. 184, Campbell to Milton, 13 Feb. 1755; SC 189, fos. 228-9 (Milton to Argyll, draft), n.d., misplaced with anonymous correspondence; SC 190, fos. 116v-17, Milton to Argyll (draft), n.d; NLS, Aerskine-Murray, MS. 5078, fo. 198, D. MacVicar to Lord Justice Clerk, 1 Dec. 1755; SRO, Seafield, GD 248/562/55, Dupplin to Deskford, 19 June 1755; SRO, Board of Customs Minutes, CE 1/9/1A, fo. 24; BL, Leeds, Egerton MSS. 3434, fo. 188, D. Scrymgeour to the Earl of Holderness, 6 Jan. 1756.

48. SRO, Seafield, GD 248/562/55, Dupplin to Deskford, 19 June 1755; 30 July 1755. NLS, Saltoun, SC 186, fo. 96, Argyll to Milton, 20 Nov. 1755.

49. NLS, Saltoun, SC 17, fo. 209, A. Fletcher to Milton, 20 Nov. 1755. Also see SC 18, fo. 97, A. Fletcher to Milton, 24 June 1756; SC 193, fo. 240 (Milton to A. Fletcher, draft), 17 June 1756, misplaced amongst anonymous correspondence; Atholl Papers, Box 47, section 8, no. 5, Deskford to Atholl, 8 Jan. 1756: 'promotion in the Customs in Scotland are now so much under the direction of his Grace the Duke of Argyle.'

50. NLS, Yester, Accession 4862, Box 13, F 3, Argyll to Tweeddale, 3 Jan. 1756 and Tweeddale to Argyll (draft), n.d; SRO, Arniston, RH4/15/4, G. Dundas to R. Dundas, 3 Feb. 1756 and Deskford to Dundas, 11 March 1756; NLS, Saltoun, SC 18, fos. 11, 25, 28, A. Fletcher to Milton, Jan.-Feb. 1756; BL, Newcastle, Add. MSS. 32861, fo. 417, Deskford to Newcastle, 23 Dec. 1755; Add. MSS. 32864, fo. 448, Deskford to Newcastle, 1 May 1756; Add. MSS. 32883, fo. 341, Argyll to Newcastle, 7 Sept. 1758.

51. BL, Newcastle, Add. MSS. 32883, fo. 84, Argyll to Newcastle, 24 Aug. 1758; fo. 195, Newcastle to Argyll (copy), 31 Aug. 1758; NLS, Saltoun, SC 194, fo. 133, Argyll to Milton, 19 Feb. (1758), misplaced with 1757 correspondence; SC 204, fo. 24, W. Alston to Milton, 16 Feb. 1759; SC 212, fo. 171, J. Maule to Milton, 10 May 1760; Bute/Loudoun Papers, 1760, bundle 7, Allan Whitefoord to the Earl of Loudoun, 4 July 1760 and 28 July 1760.

52. BL, Hardwicke, Add. MSS. 35448, fos. 150-1, Morton to Hardwicke, 2 Sept. 1754.

53. E. Hughes, *Studies in Administration and Finance*, p. 311 n1266.

54. Atholl Papers, Box 47, section 13, no. 159, J. Drummond to J. Murray of Strowan, 2 May 1761: 'Commissioner Dauber is a particular acquaintance of Lord Deskford's.'

55. George Burgess, nephew of Lord Somerville; NLS, Saltoun, SC 109, fos. 135-45, G. Burgess to Milton, 26 April-17 July 1758; SC 109, fo. 178, Argyll to Milton, 20 June 1758; SC 203, fo. 151, Lord

Somerville to Milton, July 1758.

56. NLS, Saltoun, SC 204, fo. 180, Argyll to Milton, 9 May 1759; *Oswald Memorials*, pp. 292-4, J. Dalrymple to J. Oswald, 4 July 1760; NLS, Caldwell, MS. 4942, fo. 140, Chief Baron Ord to W. Mure, 23 Dec. 1762.

57. NLS, Saltoun, SC 224, fo. 200, Milton to J. Stuart Mackenzie, 19 Dec. 1763; *History of Parliament*, ed. Sedgwick, i, pp. 561-2; BL, Newcastle, Add. MSS. 32919, fos. 295-6, R. Dauber to (H.V. Jones?), 26 Feb. 1761.

58. NLS, Saltoun, SC 199, fo. 174, Argyll to Milton, May 1758.

59. BL, Newcastle, Add. MSS. 32880, fo. 403, Dauber to Newcastle, 10 June 1758; Add. MSS. 32893, fos. 297-9, Dauber to (J. West), 26 July 1759; Add. MSS. 32919, fos. 295-6, Dauber to (H. V. Jones?), 26 Feb. 1761; Add. MSS. 32930, fos. 264-5, Dauber to Newcastle, 1 Nov. 1761. Dauber died in 1770, still a commissioner in Edinburgh.

60. NLS, Letterbook of John Maule, MS. 10781, pp. 89-90, 97-9, 100-1, letters of Maule to J. West, Feb.-Nov. 1754; NLS, Aerskine-Murray, MS. 5078, fo. 95, Newcastle to Lord Justice Clerk Tinwald, 13 Aug. 1754; BL, Hardwicke, Add. MSS. 35448, fos. 114-15, Idle to Hardwicke, 13 July 1754; fo. 301, Edlin to Hardwicke, 14 Oct. 1755.

61. BL, Hardwicke, Add. MSS. 35448, fos. 92-3; E. Edlin to Hardwicke, 29 April 1754; fos. 251-2, J. Idle to Hardwicke, 21 May 1755; BL, Newcastle, Add. MSS. 32860, fo. 46, C. Morris to Newcastle, 14 Oct. 1755; NLS, Saltoun, SC 186, fo. 91, Argyll to Milton, 4 June 1755. Corbyn Morris, Secretary of the Scottish Board of Customs, was the candidate they had in mind at first.

62. *History of Parliament*, ed. Sedgwick, ii, p. 312; BL, Newcastle, Add. MSS. 32859, fo. 204, Newcastle to the Earl of Carlisle (copy), 25 Sept. 1755; fos. 237-9, Newcastle to Argyll (copy), 27 Sept. 1755; HMC, *Polwarth*, v, p. 295, Hume Campbell to Marchmont, 15 Oct. 1755. An instance of Ord's connection with Milton is in SC 214, fo. 22, W. Alston to Milton, 23 March 1761.

63. Atholl Papers, Box 47, section 8, no. 112, A. Stuart to Atholl, 13 July 1756.

64. SRO, Seafield, GD 248/562/55, J. West to Deskford, 9 Aug. 1755; SRO, Arniston, RH4/15/4, R. Dundas to Lord Prestongrange (draft), 23 Oct. 1754; BL, Newcastle, Add. MSS. 32737, fos. 195-6, R. Dundas to Newcastle, 26 Oct. 1754; W. R. Ward, 'The Land Tax in Scotland, 1707-98', *Bulletin of the John Rylands Library*, XXXVII (1954-55), p. 298; NLS, Saltoun, SC 21, fos. 68, 87-88, for distribution of patronage.

65. NLS, Saltoun, SB 264, folder 2, memorandum by Lord Milton.

66. 'All I can do,' Argyll continued, 'is to play every card with prudence and decency and leave all accidents and correspondences to fate' (NLS, Saltoun, SC 186, fo. 78, Argyll to Milton, Feb. 1755).

67. A. J. Durie, 'Linen-spinning in the North of Scotland, 1746-1773', *Northern Scotland*, II (1974-75), pp. 13-36; Durie, 'The Markets for Scottish Linen, 1730-1775', *SHR*, LII (April 1973), pp. 30-49; NLS, Saltoun, SC 185, fo. 198, W. Tod to Milton, 19 Jan. 1754.

68. Durie, 'Linen-spinning in the North of Scotland', pp. 24-25; 'The Markets for Scottish Linen', pp. 38, 43. Durie, *The Scottish Linen Industry in the Eighteenth Century* (1979), p. 147.

69. NLS, Saltoun, SC 184, fos. 193-4, Newcastle to Argyll, 2 June 1754.

70. Durie, 'Linen-spinning', p. 26; Durie 'Markets', p. 45; Durie, *The Scottish Linen Industry in the Eighteenth Century*, pp. 132-3, 151.

71. M. Postlethwayt, *The Universal Dictionary of Trade and Commerce*, ii (London, 1755), p.674. The information for the article on Scotland was provided by Francis Grant, brother of William Grant (Lord Prestongrange).

72. BL, Newcastle, Add. MSS. 32737, fos. 359-60, G. Drummond to Newcastle, 18 Nov. 1754; NLS, Saltoun, SC 183, fo. 266, Drummond to Milton, 14 Nov. 1754.

73. SRO, Seafield, GD 248/562/55, A. Mitchell to Lord Deskford, 6 Feb. 1755; NLS, Saltoun, SC 17, fo. 127, A. Fletcher to Milton, 30 Jan. 1755.

74. BL, Newcastle, Add. MSS. 33049, fo. 287, Deskford to Dupplin (copy), 30 Nov. 1754: 'I have not taken any share in promoting this application because I apprehend that at present it is rather like to give a little trouble to the ministry than be successful.'

75. SRO, Seafield, GD 248/562/55, A. Mitchell to Deskford, 6 Feb. 1755.

76. *Ibid.*, Dupplin to Deskford, 19 June 1755; BL, Newcastle, Add. MSS. 32996, fo. 144, minute of meeting, Newcastle House, 18 June 1755; Add. MSS. 32856, fo. 231, G. Drummond to Newcastle, 26

June 1755; Add. MSS. 32857, fos. 69-70, Newcastle to Drummond (copy), 12 July 1755; Drummond to Newcastle, 17 July 1755.

77. BL, Newcastle, Add. MSS. 32859, fos. 396-7, Argyll to Newcastle, 5 Oct. 1755. Also see fos. 237-9, Newcastle to Argyll (copy), 27 Sept. 1755; fos. 240-1, Newcastle to R. Dundas (copy), 27 Sept. 1755; Add. MSS. 32858, fos. 279-80, Lord Deskford to Newcastle, 24 Aug. 1755.

78. BL, Newcastle, Add. MSS. 32859, fo. 446, G. Drummond to Newcastle, 9 Oct. 1755.

79. NLS, Saltoun, SC 187, fo. 224, G. Drummond to Milton, 20 Dec. 1755, reporting his first interview with Newcastle after arriving in London.

80. Durie, 'Linen-spinning in the North of Scotland', p. 25; NLS, Saltoun, SC 18, fo. 16, A. Fletcher to Milton, 29 Jan. 1756.

81. This paragraph is based on the accounts in NLS, Saltoun, SC 18, fos. 40, 46, 50, A. Fletcher to Milton, March 1756; SC 193, fo. 140, W. Tod to Milton, 16 March 1756; Atholl Papers, Box 47, section 8, no. 46, H. Harrison to Atholl, 18 March 1756. There are some speeches recorded in *Parliamentary History*, XV, pp. 665-95; and I have referred to the following biographies in the *History of Parliament*, ed. Namier and Brooke: W. Baker, W. Beckford, A. Hume, R. Nugent, T. Potter, G. Amyand; all of whom were mentioned in Fletcher's letters.

82. Durie, 'Linen-spinning', p. 26; Durie, *The Scottish Linen Industry*, pp. 146-147; SRO, Seafield, GD 248/562/55, A. Mitchell to Deskford, 6 Feb. 1755; NLS, Saltoun, SC 18, fo. 23, A. Fletcher to Milton, 12 Feb. 1756; fo. 48, 13 March 1756.

83. Durie, *The Scottish Linen Industry*, p. 147; NLS, Saltoun, SC 187, fo. 219, G. Drummond to Milton (Oct. 1755).

84. NLS, Saltoun, SC 188, fo. 32, D. Flint to Milton, 18 Oct. 1755.

85. NLS, Saltoun, SC 187, fo. 214, G. Drummond to Milton, 9 Oct. 1755, also mentions two Edinburgh merchants named Spence and Biggar who might go to London 'to publish their wild notions in opposition to our measures — in which they would certainly have the Advocate's countenance'. See SC 187, fos. 219, 222, two letters from Drummond to Milton from October 1755; SC 189, fo. 178, W. Tod to Milton, 4 Dec. 1755.

86. NLS, Saltoun, SC 189, fo. 178, W. Tod to Milton, 4 Dec. 1755.

87. SC 189, fo. 18, W. Tod to Milton, 20 Dec. 1755; SC 193, fos. 119-20, Tod to Milton, 14 Jan. 1756.

88. *Ibid.*, fos. 119-20, 132, W. Tod to Milton, 14 Jan. and 17 Feb. 1756.

89. See Postlethwayt, *Universal Dict. of Trade*, ii, pp. 674-5.

90. NLS, Saltoun, SC 17, fo. 118, 14 Jan. 1755, in cipher.

91. NLS, Saltoun, SC 18, fo. 5, A. Fletcher to Milton, 3 Jan. 1756; SC 193, fos. 113-4, W. Tod to Milton, 1 Jan. 1756.

92. NLS, Saltoun, SC 18, fos. 11, 48, 50, A. Fletcher to Milton, Jan.-March 1756; SC 193, fos. 119-20, 128, 141, W. Tod to Milton, Jan.-March 1756.

93. BL, Newcastle, Add. MSS. 32863, fo. 344, Newcastle to Argyll (copy), 18 March 1756, and fo. 366, n.d. (March 1756).

94. Durie, 'Linen-spinning in the North of Scotland', p. 27; *The Scottish Linen Industry in the Eighteenth Century*, p. 155.

95. The Treasury used the phrase 'Commission for the Forfeited Annexed Estates' in the commission issued in 1755, but this is hardly descriptive, as the estates in question were, literally, annexed forfeited estates. The commission was referred to by most contemporaries as that of the 'Annexed Estates', so I have followed their usage in making reference to it.

96. NLS, Letterbook of John Maule, MS. 10781, p. 17, J. West to J. Maule, 5 July 1749.

97. SRO, Arniston, RH4/15/4, Earl of Findlater to R. Dundas, 8 Nov. 1754.

98. Letterbook of J. Maule, p. 100, Maule to West, 25 Nov. 1754.

99. BL, Hardwicke, Add. MSS. 35448, fos. 130-1, W. Grant to Hardwicke, 15 Aug. 1754. Also see fos. 53-54, Bland to Newcastle (copy), 20 Dec. 1753; SRO, Seafield, GD 248/572/8, Hardwicke to Findlater, 21 Aug. 1753; NLS, Aerskine-Murray, MS. 5078, fo. 80, G. Vaughan to Lord Tinwald, 30 July 1754.

100. BL, Hardwicke, Add. MSS. 35448, fos. 51-52, Bland to Hardwicke, 25 Dec. 1753; *Scotland and Scotsmen*, ii, pp. 511, 516. For the tacksmen in general, see E. Cregeen, 'The Tacksmen and their

Successors', *Scottish Studies*, XIII (1969), pp. 93-144.

101. SRO, Seafield, GD 248/562/55, Dupplin to Deskford, 12 Nov. 1754.

102. *Ibid.*, 19 June 1755: 'If there should be any attempt to make that Commission subservient to highland power or highland views, every step taken for that purpose must be directly opposite to the intention of the Legislature, to the whole spirit of the Act, and the plan so strongly delineated therein.'

103. BL, Hardwicke, Add. MSS. 35448, fos. 57-58, Bland to Hardwicke, 22 Feb. 1754; BL, Newcastle, Add. MSS. 32995, fos. 282-4, 'Commissioners for Executing the Annexation Act', 10 July 1754.

104. NLS, Saltoun, SC 186, fo. 91, 4 June 1755; SRO, Craigievar, RH4/70/1, bundle 5, Deskford to A. Mitchell, 10 June 1755. Also see NLS, Saltoun, SC 182, fo. 183, Argyll to Milton, 19 Dec. 1754; BL, Newcastle, Add. MSS. 33049, fos. 284v-85, Deskford to Dupplin (copy), 21 Nov. 1754.

105. NLS, Saltoun, SC 174, fos. 143-4, (Milton to Argyll, draft), Dec. 1752.

106. BL, Newcastle, Add. MSS. 32737, fos. 423-4, Deskford to (Dupplin), 10 Dec. 1754. Also see Add. MSS. 33049, fos. 284v-85, Deskford to Dupplin (copy), 21 Nov. 1754; NLS, Saltoun, SC 17, fo. 85, A. Fletcher to Milton, 31 Dec. 1754.

107. BL, Hardwicke, Add. MSS. 35448, fos. 178-9, Bland to Hardwicke, 17 Oct. 1754; fos. 200-1, Lord Prestongrange to Hardwicke, 16 Nov. 1754; HMC, *Polwarth*, v. pp. 284-5, Marchmont to C. Morris (draft), 17 Oct. 1754.

108. BL, Hardwicke, Add. MSS. 35448, fos. 178-9; BL, Newcastle, Add. MSS. 33049, fos. 284v-85.

109. SRO, Seafield, GD 248/562/55, Dupplin to Deskford, 19 June and 12 Nov. 1755; SRO, Arniston, RH4/15/4, Hardwicke to Dundas, 20 May 1755; BL, Newcastle, Add. MSS. 32852, fos. 331-2, S. Brooksbank to Newcastle, 1 Feb. 1755. For Brooksbank, senior, see *History of Parliament*, ed. Sedgwick, i, p. 495; there is some information about Brooksbank, younger, in W. R. Ward, 'Some Eighteenth Century Civil Servants', *English Historical Review*, LXX (1955), p. 41.

110. BL, Newcastle, Add. MSS. 32859, fo. 81, E. Edlin to Newcastle, 18 Sept. 1755; Add. MSS. 32900, fo. 408, S. Brooksbank to Newcastle, 28 Dec. 1759; BL, Hardwicke, Add. MSS. 35448, fos. 259-60, R. Dundas to Hardwicke, 4 June 1755.

111. BL, Newcastle, Add. MSS. 32856, fos. 169-72, Hopetoun to Newcastle, 24 June 1755; fos. 173-4, R. Dundas to Newcastle, 24 June 1755; SRO, Arniston, RH4/15/4, Hardwicke to Dundas, 12 July 1755.

112. BL, Newcastle, Add. MSS. 32859, fo. 81, E. Edlin to Newcastle, 18 Sept. 1755.

113. BL, Newcastle, Add. MSS. 32856, fos. 490-1, Newcastle to Hopetoun (copy), 8 July 1755; Add. MSS. 32864, fo. 440, 'Memorandum from Mr. Brooksbank', 30 April 1756; Add. MSS. 32883, fo. 341, Argyll to Newcastle, 7 Sept. 1758.

114. NLS, Saltoun, SC 185, fo. 105, G. Ross to Milton (Oct. 1754). There is a short biography of Ross in *History of Parliament*, ed. Namier and Brooke, iii, pp. 378-9.

115. BL, Hardwicke, Add. MSS. 35448, fos. 178-9, Bland to Hardwicke, 17 Oct. 1754. Also see BL, Newcastle, Add. MSS. 32855, fo. 88, Hardwicke to Newcastle, 19 May 1755; Add. MSS. 32857, fos. 427-8, S. Brooksbank to Newcastle, 29 July 1755; NLS, Saltoun, SC 17, fo. 188, A. Fletcher to Milton, 3 July 1755; SRO, Seafield, GD 248/562/55, Dupplin to Deskford, 19 June 1755; and J. West to Deskford, 9 Aug. 1755.

116. SRO, Arniston, RH4/15/4, Hardwicke to Dundas, 19 Nov. 1754; BL, Hardwicke, Add. MSS. 35448, fos. 271-2, Dundas to Hardwicke, 24 June 1755; BL, Newcastle, Add. MSS. 32857, fos. 427-8, S. Brooksbank to Newcastle, 29 July 1755; NLS, Saltoun, SC 186, fo. 91, Argyll to Milton, 4 June 1755.

117. SRO, Minutes of Commission of Annexed Estates, E 721/1, p. 12; BL, Newcastle, Add. MSS. 32857, fos. 427-8, S. Brooksbank to Newcastle, 29 July 1755; SRO, Seafield, GD 248/572/5, Findlater to Deskford, 25 June 1755.

118. BL, Newcastle, Add. MSS. 32861, fos. 110-1, S. Brooksbank to Newcastle, 27 Nov. 1755.

119. A. M. Smith, 'The Administration of the Forfeited Annexed Estates, 1752-1784', in *The Scottish Tradition: Essays in Honour of Ronald Gordon Cant*, ed. G. W. S. Barrow (1974), pp. 201-2.

120. BL, Hardwicke, Add. MSS. 35448, fo. 305, (S. Brooksbank) to Hardwicke, 9 Oct. 1755; SRO, Arniston, RH4/15/4, D. Moncrieff to Dundas, 25 Dec. 1755; NLS, Saltoun, SC 199, fo. 109, S.

Brooksbank to Milton, 27 May 1758.

121. *Caldwell Papers*, i, pp. 129-30, Deskford to W. Mure, 2 Aug. 1761.

122. NLS, Aerskine-Murray, MS. 5079, fo. 106, Argyll to Tinwald (Dec. 1756?).

123. NLS. Saltoun, SC 216, fo. 45, Milton to G. Elliot (draft), May 1761.

124. SRO, Arniston, RH4/15/4, Deskford to Dundas, 22 Feb. 1756.

125. NLS, Saltoun, SC 18, fos. 32, 38, A. Fletcher to Milton, 24 Feb. and 2 March 1756, both in cipher.

126. BL, Hardwicke, Add. MSS. 35449, fos. 2-3, E. Edlin to Hardwicke, 18 Jan. 1756.

127. NLS. Saltoun, SB 336, folder 2, 'Account of the Annexed Estates'.

128. BL, Hardwicke, Add. MSS. 35448, fo. 164, 'Memorial to His Majesty's Advocate from William Alston Agent for forfeitures'; SRO, Arniston, RH4/15/4, Hardwicke to Dundas, 19 Nov. 1754, 21 Jan. and 20 July 1758; *History of Parliament*, ed. Namier and Brooke, ii, p. 363; NLS, Letterbook of John Maule, MS. 10781, pp. 116-20, J. Maule to Argyll, n.d. (1756?).

129. BL, Hardwicke, Add. MSS. 35449, fos. 74-75, E. Edlin to Hardwicke, 2 Jan. 1757.

130. NLS, Letterbook of John Maule, MS. 10781, p. 116, J. Maule to Argyll, n.d. (1756?).

131. NLS, Saltoun, SC 202; fo. 234, J. Maule to Milton, 8 April 1758; fo. 236, Maule to Milton, 13 April 1758; SRO, Commission of Annexed Estates Minutes, E 721/2, 12 Aug. 1757.

132. Act 32 GII c. 36; *Edinburgh Evening Courant*, 19 June 1759, contains notices placed in the press by the Barons of Exchequer regarding payment of the debts.

133. Act 31 GII c. 16 (1758); NLS, Saltoun, SC 199, fos. 159-60, Argyll to Milton, 11 Feb. (1758); fo. 163, Milton to Argyll, Feb. 1758; NLS, Letterbook of John Maule, MS. 10781, p. 100, J. Maule to J. West, 25 Nov. 1754.

134. NLS, Saltoun, SB 336, folder 2, 'Account of the Annexed Estates', 1761.

135. William L. Clements Library, Townshend Papers, Lord Elibank to C. Townshend, 7 Jan. 1760.

Chapter 4. The Duke of Argyll and Lord Bute

1. James, Earl Waldegrave, *Memoirs from 1754 to 1758* (London, 1821), p. 38.

2. NLS, Saltoun, SC 138, fo. 51, Argyll to Milton, 9 June 1747.

3. SC 206, fo. 189, John Home to Milton, 10 May 1759. When Bute applied for an office for James Erskine, a relation by marriage, he communicated directly with Newcastle (Bute Papers, no. 173/1758, Newcastle to Bute, 24 Nov. 1758).

4. J. L. McKelvey, *George III and Lord Bute*, p. 137.

5. Bute Papers, nos. 82 & 149/1757, Eglinton to Bute, n.d. and 8 Dec. 1757.

6. *Ibid.*, no. 108a/1759, Mure to Bute, 8 July 1759; *Boswell's London Journal*, ed. F. A. Pottle (London, 1950), entry for 14 March 1763, p. 217; *Complete Peerage*, v, p. 24n; *Oswald Memorials*, pp. 185-6, Eglinton to Oswald, 25 Jan. 1763.

7. South Glamorgan Libraries (Cardiff), Bute Papers, 134/1, Eglinton to Bute, 26 Jan. 1760.

8. Bute Papers, no. 83/1759, P. Craufurd to Bute, 30 May 1759; no. 88a/1759, W. Mure to Bute, 4 June 1759. The letter cited in *History of Parliament*, ed. Namier and Brooke, ii, p. 273, as evidence of Mure suggesting the idea to Bute, is incorrectly printed in *Caldwell Papers*, i, p. 119, as 14 Jan. 1759. It is actually dated 14 June 1759 (NLS, Caldwell, MS. 4941, fo. 294).

9. Bute Papers, no. 127/1759, W. Mure to Bute (10 Aug. 1759).

10. *Ibid.*, nos. 144 & 161/1759, Mure to Bute, 22 Aug. and 28 Sept. 1759.

11. William L. Clements Library, Townshend Papers, Elibank to Townshend, 21 Dec. 1759 (quoted in Sir L. Namier and J. Brooke, *Charles Townshend*, p. 59); J. Dalrymple to Townshend, 26 Jan. (1760, mistakenly dated 1759); W. Robertson to Townshend, 23 Feb. 1760. Contrary to Carlyle's *Anecdotes and Characters*, p. 197, Townshend arrived in Edinburgh in late June 1759 (*Edinburgh Evening Courant*, 21 June 1759).

12. Carlyle, *Anecdotes and Characters*, pp. 197-8. Also see NLS, Saltoun, SC 208, fos. 131, 134-5, Townshend to Milton, 6 and 23 Sept. 1759; William L. Clements Library, Townshend Papers, A. Carlyle to Townshend (2-14? Nov. 1759); J. Dalrymple to Townshend, 5 Oct., 16 Oct., and 12 Nov. 1759.

13. Townshend Papers, Elibank to Townshend, 7 Jan. 1760.

14. *Ibid.*, A. Carlyle to Townshend, 1 Nov. 1759.

15. *Edinburgh Evening Courant*, 18 Aug. 1759; Townshend Papers, Carlyle to Townshend, 11 Sept. 1759; Lord Milton to Townshend, 11 Sept. 1759.

16. Townshend Papers, 4 Oct. 1759.

17. NLS, Saltoun, SC 21, fos. 110-15, A. Fletcher to Milton, 26 June, 14 July, and 2 Aug. 1759.

18. *Caldwell Papers*, i, p. 120, Bute to Mure, 30 Aug. 1759 (corrected from NLS, Caldwell, MS. 4941, fo. 296); BL, Newcastle, Add. MSS. 32903, fo. 96, Hardwicke to Newcastle, 5 March 1760.

19. NLS, Saltoun, SC 205, fo. 26, Loudon to Argyll, 8 Sept. 1759; *Caldwell Papers*, i, pp. 121-2, Sir H. Erskine to Mure, 5 Sept. 1759; Bute/Loudoun Papers, 1759, bundle 4, Charles Dalrymple of Orangefield to Loudoun, 11 Sept. 1759; Bute Papers, no. 161/1759, W. Mure to Bute, 28 Sept. 1759.

20. *Caldwell Papers*, i, p. 120, Bute to Mure, 30 Aug. 1759; NLS, Saltoun, SC 205, fo. 175, P. Craufurd to Milton, 10 Sept. 1759.

21. Bute Papers, nos. 161 & 168/1759, Mure to Bute, 28 Sept. and 16 Oct. 1759; no. 162/1759, P. Craufurd to Bute, Oct. 1759; Townshend Papers, Carlyle to Townshend, 16 Oct. 1759.

22. Townshend Papers, J. Dalrymple to Townshend, 12 Nov. 1759.

23. *Caldwell Papers*, i, pp. 123-4, Bute to Mure, 20 Nov. 1759.

24. Townshend Papers, J. Dalrymple to Townshend, 12 Nov. 1759.

25. Bute/Loudoun Papers, 1759, bundle 4, C. Dalrymple to Loudoun, 11 Sept. 1759. The queries indicate words of doubtful legibility.

26. Bute Papers, no. 154/1759, Craufurd to Bute, 10 Oct. 1759; South Glamorgan Libraries (Cardiff), Bute Papers, 44/1, W. Cunningham to (W. Mure?), 9 April 1760.

27. Bute Papers, no. 172/1759, Eglinton to Bute, 18 Oct. 1759; BL, Leeds, Egerton MSS. 3434, fos. 246-7, Auchinleck to Holderness, 12 Oct. 1759.

28. *Ibid.*, no. 174/1759, Charles Hamilton (Provost of Irvine) to Bute, 23 Oct. 1759; Egerton MSS. 3434, fo. 250, Argyll to Holderness, 23 Oct. 1759.

29. Bute/Loudoun Papers, 1759, bundle 7, W. Ferguson to Loudoun, 18 Dec. 1759. NLS, Saltoun, SC 206, fos. 22-25, W. Ferguson to Sir A. Fergusson and Sir A. Fergusson to Argyll, both copies of letters written in Nov. 1759; these letters were written for Argyll to show to ministers in London (SC 204, fo. 185*v*, Milton to Argyll (draft), 21 Nov. 1759).

30. See NLS, Letterbook of Lord George Beauclerk, Accession 6417, pp. 26-27, 35-37, 108-9, 160, 164.

31. For example see [A. Fletcher, Lord Milton] *Queries Addressed to the Serious Consideration of the Public* (Edinburgh, 1760). There are copies in NLS, Saltoun, SB 368; and in BL, Newcastle, Add. MSS. 33049, fos. 322-3.

32. BL, Newcastle, Add. MSS. 32895, fos. 7-9, Newcastle to Argyll (copy), 29 Aug. 1759; fo. 80, Newcastle to Hardwicke (copy), 31 Aug. 1759; fos. 134-6, Argyll to Newcastle, 2 Sept. 1759.

33. BL, Leeds, Egerton MSS. 3434, fo. 277, Argyll to Holderness, 18 Jan. 1760; fos. 280-1, Holderness to Lord Auchinleck (copy), Jan. 1760.

34. BL, Newcastle, Add. MSS. 32902, fo. 484, Mansfield to Newcastle, 28 Feb. 1760. Also see fos. 453-6, Newcastle to Hardwicke (copy), 28 Feb. 1760; and Add. MSS. 32998, fos. 404-11, 'An Exact Account of Every Thing That has passed with the Duke of Newcastle upon the Affair of the Government of Dunbarton Castle', 9 March 1760.

35. NLS, Letterbook of Lord George Beauclerk, Accession 6417, pp. 253-68.

36. William L. Clements Library, Townshend Papers, Lord Elibank to Townshend, 21 Dec. 1759; *Scots Magazine*, XXI (Nov.-Dec. 1759), pp. 628-9.

37. BL, Leeds, Egerton MSS. 3434, fos. 258-76; NLS, Saltoun, SB 368, folder 1, 'Heads of an Intended Bill for Establishing a Militia in Scotland'; SC 22, fos. 28, 30, 32, A. Fletcher to Milton, Jan. 1760; SC 209, fo. 138, Argyll to Milton, 19 Jan. 1760.

38. Townshend Papers, A. Carlyle to Townshend (2-14? Nov. 1759).

39. NLS, Saltoun, SC 210, fo. 119, Sir J. Carnegie to Milton, 17 Jan. 1760; Townshend Papers, G. Brown to Townshend, Dec. 1759.

40. NLS, Saltoun, SC 213, fo. 132*v*, Milton to C. Townshend, 13 March 1760.

41. NLS, Minto, MS. 11001, fos. 57-58, G. Elliot to Lord Minto, 5 April (1760). Also see NLS, Saltoun, SC 22, fo. 60, A. Fletcher to Milton, 6 March 1760: 'No Symptoms appear of adjusting

matters about PAT: CRAUFURD who says he will give it up provided BUTE will allow him.' In cipher.

42. The comment is from BL, Hardwicke, Add. MSS. 35419, fos. 236-9, Newcastle to Hardwicke, 21 July 1760. Also see *History of Parliament*, ed. Namier and Brooke, ii, p. 439; BL, Newcastle, Add. MSS. 32911, fo. 101, Newcastle to Hardwicke (copy), 6 Sept. 1759; NLS, Saltoun, SC 21, fos. 125, 136, 140, A. Fletcher to Milton, Oct.-Dec. 1759; and SC 22, fo. 85, 30 Aug. 1760.

43. BL, Newcastle, Add. MSS. 32911, fos. 101-2.

44. Bute Papers, no. 83/1760, J. Stuart Mackenzie to Bute, 12 Nov. 1760; NLS, Saltoun, SC 209, fo. 143, Argyll to Milton, 9 Feb. (1760); SC 211, fos. 9-15, G. Elliot to Milton, 3 Oct. and 13 Dec. 1760; SC 22, fo. 49, Fletcher to Milton, 23 Feb. 1760, in cipher.

45. McKelvey, *George III and Lord Bute*, pp. 133-6. A reading of the relevant entries in the *History of Parliament* provides enough information to refute McKelvey's point.

46. Huntington Library, Loudoun Papers, LO 7552, Argyll to Loudoun, 1 Nov. 1760.

47. BL, Newcastle, Add. MSS. 32916, fos. 79-80, 150, Hardwicke to Newcastle, (14 Dec.) and 17 Dec. 1760.

48. Bute Papers, no. 194/1760, Elliot to Bute (16 Dec. 1760, incorrectly dated 19 Dec. in pencil). NLS, Saltoun, SC 22, fo. 96, Fletcher to Milton, (17) Dec. 1760.

49. NLS, Saltoun, SC 209, fo. 195, Argyll to Milton, 26 Dec. 1760; Torwoodlee Papers, Box 1, bundle 4, Marchmont to James Pringle, 20 Dec. 1760.

50. BL, Newcastle, Add. MSS. 32917, fo. 90, Newcastle to Hardwicke (copy), 3 January 1761.

51. SRO, Seafield, GD 248/562/55, Dupplin to Deskford, 17 Feb. 1761; Atholl Papers, Box 47, section 13, no. 46, A. Drummond to Atholl, 19 Feb. 1761.

52. Bute Papers, uncatalogued, Bute to J. Stuart Mackenzie, 17 April 1761; NLS, Saltoun, SC 217, fo. 25, J. Home to Milton, 10 Feb. 1761; SC 23, fo. 23, Fletcher to Milton, 11 Feb. 1761.

53. BL, Newcastle, Add. MSS. 32917, fos. 90-91, Newcastle to Hardwicke (copy), 3 Jan. 1761; and fo. 203, 9 Jan. 1761; Bute Papers, no. 253/1760, W. Mure to Bute (Jan. 1761, misplaced with 1760 letters).

54. BL, Newcastle, Add. MSS. 32919, fo. 100, Patrick Boyle (Lord Shualton of the Court of Session) to (the Duke of Queensberry?), 18 Feb. 1761; Bute Papers, no. 195/1761 and 197/1761, Sir H. Erskine to Bute, March 1761; NLS, Saltoun, SC 23, fo. 31, Fletcher to Milton, 3 March 1761.

55. Bute Papers, no. 194/1761, Argyll to Sir H. Erskine, March (1761); NLS, Saltoun, SC 23, fos. 23-4, A. Fletcher to Milton, 11 Feb. 1761; *Caldwell Papers*, i, pp. 150-1, (Sir Henry Bellenden) to W. Mure, 26 March 1761, incorrectly printed, but referred to correctly in *History of Parliament*, ed. Namier and Brooke, ii, p. 183n. The letter is NLS, Caldwell, MS. 4942, fos. 132-3.

56. NLS, Saltoun, SC 214, fo. 45*v*, (W. Mure) to Milton, 26 (March 1761), misplaced with the letters of William Alston; fo. 132, Milton to Argyll (draft), 19 March 1761.

57. W. L. Burn, 'The General Election of 1761 at Ayr', *English Historical Review*, LII (1937), pp. 103-9; NLS, Saltoun, SC 215, fo. 46, Loudoun to Milton, 28 March 1761; Huntington Library, Loudoun Papers, LO 10616 and LO 10707, copies of letters from Loudoun to Argyll, 28 March and 13 April 1761.

58. NLS, Newhailes, bundle 480, Sir A. Fergusson to Sir David Dalrymple, 30 March 1761.

59. South Glamorgan Libraries (Cardiff), Bute Papers, 2/205/1-3, Sir A. Fergusson to Bute, 28 March 1761. I owe this reference to the kindness of R. B. Sher.

60. SRO, Seafield, GD 248/562/55, Dupplin to Deskford, 17 Feb. 1761; NLS, Saltoun, SC 23, fo. 33, A. Fletcher to Milton, 5 March 1761.

61. NLS, Saltoun, SC 214, fo. 120*v*-1, G. Burgess to Milton, 21 Feb. 1761. For Thompson, the new secretary, see BL, Newcastle, Add. MSS. 32855, fo. 108, R. Dundas to Newcastle, 22 May 1755. Dauber's letter is mentioned in Add. MSS. 32919, fo. 295, R. Dauber to (H. V. Jones?), 26 Feb. 1761.

62. NLS, Saltoun, SC 214, fo. 113, G. Brown of Coalstoun to Milton, 1 April 1761; fos. 134-5, 141, Argyll to Milton, 20 and 25 March 1761; SC 210, fos. 204-17, SC 215, fos. 177, 178, Sir Robert Dalyell to Milton, 1760 and 1761. BL, Newcastle, Add. MSS. 32916, fos. 179-80, Hope Weir to Newcastle, 18 Dec. 1760.

63. Atholl Papers, Box 47, section 13, no. 65, Argyll to Atholl, 5 March 1761, and no. 75, Atholl to Argyll (draft), 12 March 1761.

64. BL, Newcastle, Add. MSS. 32999, fos. 15-17, 'Memorandum with the Duke of Argyll'; *History of Parliament*, ed. Namier and Brooke, ii, p. 565.

65. Atholl Papers, Box 47, section 13, no. 1, A. Drummond to Atholl, 3 Jan. 1761; no. 46, Drummond to Atholl, 19 Feb. 1761; no. 58, Breadalbane to Atholl, 5 March 1761; no. 66, Drummond to Atholl, 7 March 1761.

66. Bute Papers, nos. 11 and 25/1761, P. Campbell to Bute, 18 and 21 Feb. 1761; no. 197/1761, Sir H. Erskine to Bute, March 1761. (Cardiff) Bute Papers, 2/166/3, Erskine to Bute, 14 March 1761.

67. NLS, Saltoun, SC 214, fo. 127, Argyll to Milton, 7 Feb. 1761.

68. BL, Newcastle, Add. MSS. 32922, fo. 5, Newcastle to Hardwicke (copy), 16 April 1761.

69. *Ibid*; and fos. 3-4, Hardwicke to Newcastle, 16 April 1761.

70. BL, Newcastle, Add. MSS. 32922, fos. 15-22, Newcastle to Hardwicke (copy), 17 April 1761. Also see fo. 40, Hardwicke to Newcastle, 18 April 1761.

71. Add. MSS. 32922, fos. 3-6, 13-22, 65, 168-9; HMC, *Polwarth*, v, pp. 352-3, Newcastle to Marchmont, 24 April 1761.

72. Bute Papers, uncatalogued, Bute to Stuart Mackenzie, 17 April 1761.

73. Bute Papers, no. 300/1761, John Home to Bute, 22 April 1761: '[Adam] Ferguson who was present when it came told me that the old man after reading it by himself attempted to read it aloud to his family, and at the second sentence burst tears. The genius of your country dictated every line of it.' I owe this reference to the kindness of R. B. Sher.

74. South Glamorgan Libraries (Cardiff), Bute Papers, 10/18/1, Milton to Bute, 12 Feb. 1763; NLS, Saltoun, SC 227, fos. 98-99, Milton to Stuart Mackenzie (copy), 25 Feb. 1764; J. Cater, 'The Making of Principal Robertson in 1762', *SHR*, XLIX (1970), p. 68. Thus Carlyle's remark — 'Milton Declin'd Being longer employ'd' — is false (*Anecdotes and Characters*, p. 210n).

75. BL, Hardwicke, Add. MSS. 35450, fo. 309, Breadalbane to Hardwicke, 16 May 1761: 'I was asked to be of the number, but having no black clothes (for all were in deep mourning with weepers), I was glad of that pretense to excuse myself from a ceremony very useless and I think improper.'

76. *Edinburgh Evening Courant*, 16 May 1761; *Scots Magazine*, XX (May 1761), p. 278.

77. BL, Hardwicke, Add. MSS. 35449, fo. 312, Earl of Morton to Hardwicke, 18 May 1761.

78. Add. MSS. 35450, fo. 312, Breadalbane to Hardwicke, 19 June 1761.

79. NLS, Saltoun, SC 216, fos. 4 and 55, G. Elliot to Milton, 21 April and 11 June 1761.

80. NLS, Minto, MS. 11015, fo. 82, J. Swinton to G. Elliot, 6 Dec. 1760.

81. NLS, Saltoun, SC 216, fos. 39-40, 48-51, G. Elliot to Milton, 19 May and 5 June 1761. BL, Hardwicke, Add. MSS. 35449, fo. 296, R. Ord to Hardwicke, 28 March 1761; BL, Newcastle, Add. MSS. 32922, fos. 3-4, Hardwicke to Newcastle, 16 April 1761: 'Lord Milton is said to have been the great Jobber in it, & I own I cannot help wishing that he could be left out.'

82. Bute Papers, no. 513/1761, G. Elliot to Bute (24-30 June 1761); NLS, Saltoun, SC 216, fos. 39-40, 67, 88-89, G. Elliot to Milton, May-June 1761.

Chapter 5. James Stuart Mackenzie and the Government of Scotland

1. The best biography is by Lady Haden Guest in *History of Parliament*, ed. Namier and Brooke, iii, pp. 503-7.

2. Sir L. Namier, *England in the Age of the American Revolution* (second edition, London, 1961), pp. 157-61; J. Brewer, 'The Misfortunes of Lord Bute: A Case-Study in Eighteenth-Century Political Argument and Public Opinion', *The Historical Journal*, XVI (1973), pp. 3-43.

3. *Lady Louisa Stuart*, pp. 51-57; Thomas Carlyle, *History of Frederick II* (London, 1873), v, pp. 258-61 (I owe this reference to Mr. David Gavine); *History of Parliament*, ed. Sedgwick, ii, pp. 454-5.

4. Louis Dutens, *Memoirs of a Traveller Now in Retirement*, i, p. 101. See W.L. Matheson, *The Awakening of Scotland: 1747-1797* (Glasgow, 1910), pp. 53-54; *History of Parliament*, ed. Namier and Brooke, iii, pp. 505-7; J. Simpson, 'Who Steered the Gravy Train?', p. 64.

5. *Lady Louisa Stuart*, pp. 51-52.

6. The quotations, in the order in which they are given in the text, are from: NLS, Saltoun, SC 218, fo. 148, Milton to Bute (draft), 28 Aug. 1761; *Lady Louisa Stuart*, p. 51; NLS, Saltoun, SC 184, fos. 288-9, Mackenzie to Milton, 10 May 1754; SC 217, fo. 167, Mackenzie to Milton, 17 Sept. 1761.

7. *Lady Louisa Stuart*, pp. 51-52.

8. Carlyle, *Anecdotes and Characters*, p. 151.

9. The quotations are taken from NLS, Caldwell, MS. 4942, fos. 42 and 48, Mackenzie to Mure, 19 Nov. and 15 Dec. 1761; and *Caldwell Papers*, i, p. 240, Mackenzie to Mure, 24 Feb. 1764. I owe this point to the kindness of R.B. Sher.

10. Bute Papers, Letterbook of J. Stuart Mackenzie, p. 108, Mackenzie to Lord Rollo, 6 May 1765. Also see Atholl Papers, Box 49, section 6, no. 31, J. Murray to Atholl, 11 March 1767; *Caldwell Papers*, i, p. 260, Mackenzie to Mure, 4 Aug. 1764.

11. NLS, Caldwell, MS. 4942, fo. 56, Erroll to Mure, 26 Dec. 1761.

12. *Caldwell Papers*, i, p. 192, J. Coutts to Mure, 9 Sept. 1763.

13. NLS, Saltoun, SC 224, fo. 182, Milton to Mackenzie (copy), 22 Oct. 1763.

14. NLS, Saltoun, SC 217, fos. 166-7, Mackenzie to Milton, 17 Sept. 1761; fo. 173, Milton to Mackenzie (draft), 24 Sept. 1761. Elliot had made much the same complaint: see SC 216, fos. 99-103, Elliot to Milton, 21 Aug. 1761; Bute Papers, no. 609/1761, Elliot to Bute, 30 Aug. 1761.

15. NLS, Saltoun, SC 217, fos. 173-6, Milton to Mackenzie (draft), 24-28 Sept. 1761; Bute Papers, Letterbook of J. Stuart Mackenzie, pp. 5, 8, 10, 14; NLS, Caldwell, MS. 4942, fos. 7-8, 38-39, 44.

16. *Caldwell Papers*, ii, p. 12, Mackenzie to Mure, 16 Feb. 1765.

17. *Caldwell Papers*, ii, pp. 8-11, Mackenzie to Mure, 5 Feb. 1765; Bute Papers, uncatalogued, list of the counties of Scotland with the numbers of parishes, ministers, inhabitants and fighting men for each county; and 'Extent of the Several Counties of Scotland with the Number of Inhabitants'.

18. Bute Papers, no. 609/1761, G. Elliot to Bute, 30 Aug. 1761; no. 532/1762, Mackenzie to C. Jenkinson, 15 Oct. (1762).

19. NLS, Minto, MS. 11001, fos. 61-63, Elliot to Sir G. Elliot (Lord Minto of the Court of Session), (early 1762).

20. NLS, Saltoun, SC 221, fo. 141, Mackenzie to Milton, 22 May 1762.

21. SC 216, fos. 92-93, Elliot to Milton, 21 Aug. 1761.

22. NLS, SC 222, fos. 132-3; SC 225, fo. 80; SC 227, fos. 98-99, 162; SC 220, fo. 188; SC 228, fo. 93.

23. NLS, Saltoun, SC 217, fo. 214, Mackenzie to Milton, 23 Nov. 1761; fo. 229, Mackenzie to Milton, 15 Dec. 1761. The commissions finally passed the Seals in the summer of 1762.

24. *Ibid.*, SC 218, fo. 261, 'Scrols of letters sent to Members of Parliament 1761'; SC 219, fo. 154, Sir J. Carnegie to Milton, 20 Oct. 1762.

25. BL, Hardwicke, Add. MSS. 35450, fo. 309, Breadalbane to Hardwicke, 16 May 1761.

26. Carlyle, *Anecdotes and Characters*, p. 235, although the details of his account are garbled. Also see J. Cater, 'The Making of Principal Robertson', p. 67.

27. BL, Newcastle, Add. MSS. 32963, fos. 34-35, Sir A. Gilmour to Newcastle, 25 Oct. 1764.

28. Campbell of Shawfield was angry because Bute had given the Crown's feu-duties from the island of Islay, where Shawfield had an estate, to Lord Frederick Campbell (*Letters to Henry Fox, Lord Holland*, pp. 219-21, Lord Digby to Holland, 31 May 1765; Walpole, *Memoirs of the Reign of King George III*, i, p. 178). The reasons for the opposition of the others are noted in their biographies in *History of Parliament*, ed. Namier and Brooke.

29. *A Letter from a Citizen in Town to his Friend* (1762); NLS, Saltoun, SC 221, fos. 110, 121, drafts of Milton's letters to Mackenzie of 21 Jan. and 4 Feb. 1762; [Robert Dick] *The True State of the Case* (7 March 1763), p. 2.

30. *Atholl Chronicles*, iv, pp. 8-9, J. Murray of Strowan to A. Drummond of Megginch (copy), 27 Jan. 1764, corrected from Atholl Papers, Box 49, section 3, no. 56.

31. BL, Newcastle, Add. MSS. 32963, fos. 34-35, Sir A. Gilmour to Newcastle, 25 Oct. 1764.

32. *Caldwell Papers*, i, p. 176, Bute to Mure, 9 April 1763.

33. Quotations, in order, are from: *Letters from George III to Lord Bute*, ed. Sedgwick (London, 1939), no. 294, 4 April 1763; Bute Papers, uncatalogued, Grenville to J. Stuart Mackenzie, 29 April 1763.

34. NLS, Saltoun, SC 224, fos. 121-2, Mackenzie to Milton, 21 April 1763.

35. *Additional Grenville Papers*, ed. J. Tomlinson (Manchester, 1962), pp. 149-51, Grenville to C. Jenkinson, 4 July 1764.

36. SRO, Arniston, RH4/15/5, Queensberry to Arniston, 24 March 1764.

37. SRO, Board of Customs Minutes, CE 1/11, 3 Sept. 1764; *Jenkinson Papers*, ed. N. Jucker (London, 1949), pp. 315, 317, 330, 337-8.

38. Atholl Papers, Box 49, section 1, no. 296, Adam Drummond of Megginch to J. Murray of Strowan, 15 Oct. 1762 (misdate for 1763).

39. *History of Parliament*, ed. Namier and Brooke, i, p. 497; Bedford Papers, HMC 8, Vol. XLVII, fo. 214, Garlies to Grenville, 19 and 23 Dec. 1763.

40. *Ibid.*, fo. 218, Bedford to Grenville (copy), 25 Dec. 1763.

41. *Ibid.*, Vol. XLVIII, fo. 22, Garlies to Bedford, 16 Jan. 1764.

42. *Grenville Papers*, ii, pp. 485-6, Grenville diary, 20 (Jan. 1764).

43. NLS, Saltoun, SC 226, fo. 272, A. Gray to Milton, 13 April 1764. For Bruce's role in Stirlingshire see Sunter, 'Stirlingshire Politics', p. 218.

44. *Letters from George III to Lord Bute*, no. 334, 19 April 1764. Ferguson, along with Alexander Lockhart, had gone to Carlisle after the 1745 rebellion to defend Jacobite prisoners at their trials, and (again with Lockhart) had defended former Lord Provost Archibald Stewart against a charge of treason in 1747. There is an account of this episode in *Scotland and Scotsmen*, i, p. 154, although Ramsay's account is garbled in ascribing ministerial status to Sir Lawrence Dundas. Also see NLS, Saltoun, SC 227, fos. 142-3, Mackenzie to Milton, 5 May 1764.

45. Bute Papers, no. 43/1764, Mackenzie to Bute, 28 May 1764. Ferguson of Pitfour was given a Justiciary gown at the same time.

46. John Erskine of Balgownie, a friend of Milton's relation John Wedderburn of St. Germain (NLS, Saltoun, SC 227, fo. 155; SC 228, fo. 131).

47. *The Correspondence of John, Fourth Duke of Bedford*, ed. Lord J. Russell (London, 1842-46), ii, pp. 346-7, Newcastle to Bedford, 21 July 1758.

48. *Additional Grenville Papers*, pp. 138-9, 144.

49. *Ibid.*, pp. 153-4, Grenville to Mackenzie, 6 July 1764.

50. *Grenville Papers*, ii, pp. 388-90, Mackenzie to Grenville, 15 July 1764.

51. Bute Papers, no. 64/1764, Mackenzie to Bute, 15 July 1764. Most of this letter is printed in *History of Parliament*, ed. Namier and Brooke, iii, p. 505.

52. *Additional Grenville Papers*, pp. 169-70, Fife to Grenville, 2 Aug. 1764. Also see pp. 161-4, 166-7.

53. *Caldwell Papers*, i, pp. 275-6, Mackenzie to Mure, 27 Nov. 1764. Also see *Jenkinson Papers*, pp. 397-8; *Additional Grenville Papers*, pp. 184, 187-8.

54. Bute Papers, no. 68/1764, Mackenzie to Bute, 18 July 1764; and no. 74/1764, 20 Aug. 1764.

55. Bute Papers, no. 81/1764, Mackenzie to Bute, 5 Sept. 1764; SRO, Scott of Harden, GD 157/2250, no. 9, G. Elliot to W. Scott, 4 May 1764.

56. Bute Papers, no. 81/1764. Also see NLS, Saltoun, SC 227, fos. 174-5, Mackenzie to Milton, 27 Nov. 1764.

57. NLS, Saltoun, SC 229, fos. 85-86, Mackenzie to Milton, 15 Jan. 1765. Lord Milton's remark is in SC 227, fo. 176, Milton to Mackenzie (draft), 27 Dec. 1764.

58. *Caldwell Papers*, i, pp. 280-3, Mackenzie to Mure, 31 Dec. 1764.

59. *Ibid.*, ii, p. 7, Mackenzie to Mure, 17 Jan. 1765.

60. SRO, Scott of Harden, GD 157/2250, no. 12, Elliot to W. Scott, 22 March 1765.

61. D. Jarrett, 'The Regency Crisis of 1765', *English Historical Review*, LXXXV (1970), pp. 282-315.

62. *Grenville Papers*, iii, pp. 181, 184, Grenville diary, 21-22 May 1765.

63. Walpole, *Memoirs of the Reign of King George III*, ii, p. 175.

64. NLS, Saltoun, SB 364, folder 2, 'Memorandum'.

65. *Grenville Papers*, iii, pp. 187-8, Grenville diary.

Chapter 6. English Ministers and Scotch Politicians

1. *Scots Magazine*, XIV (Aug. 1752), p. 371.

2. *Edinburgh Evening Courant*, 13 Feb. 1762.

3. NLS, Delvine, MS. 1405, fos. 49-50, Atholl to J. Mackenzie of Delvine, 25 Feb. 1766.

4. *Ibid.*, MS. 1406, fos. 117-8, Atholl to Mackenzie, 10 Dec. 1770.

5. Newcastle failed to persuade Dupplin (now Earl of Kinnoull), Lord President Arniston or the Earl of Hopetoun to serve as Scottish minister. See BL, Newcastle, Add. MSS. 32968, fo. 367; Add. MSS. 32969, fos. 82, 86-87, 279-82; Add. MSS. 32970, fos. 371-2, 375-6. Also see the better known letter in *Arniston Memoirs*, pp. 178-9, Arniston to Lord G. Beauclerk, 9 Nov. 1765.

6. See *Intimate Society Letters of the Eighteenth Century*, ed. J. Campbell, Duke of Argyll (London, 1910), i, p. 168, the Earl of Suffolk to the Duchess of Argyll, 20 Aug. 1773; H. Furber, *Henry Dundas* (London, 1931), p. 6, quoting letters now in the William L. Clements Library. There were previous commitments for the appointments of David Ross and Alexander Lockhart to the Court of Session in 1775, both dating from James Stuart Mackenzie's involvement in Scottish affairs (see Bute/Loudoun Papers, 1774, bundle 5, Hon. Alex. Gordon to Loudoun, 26 April 1774; BL, Hardwicke, Add. MSS. 35451, fo. 226, Earl of Breadalbane to the Earl of Hardwicke, 2 Feb. 1776; Atholl Papers, Box 49, section 5, no. 231, J. Mackenzie of Delvine to the Duke of Atholl, 29 Dec. 1766).

7. SRO, Seafield, GD 248/572/4, Stuart Mackenzie to the Earl of Findlater, 2 Nov. 1767.

8. *Ibid.*, Queensberry to (Findlater), 28 May 1767.

9. *Scotland and Scotsmen*, i, p. 154. Ramsay wrote his memoirs at the beginning of the nineteenth century, and in this instance ascribed the reputation Sir Lawrence enjoyed after 1768 to an earlier period; see Chapter V, p. 113.

10. *Calendar of Home Office Papers, 1766-69*, no. 1306, Lord Garlies to (Lord Weymouth?), 4 Oct. 1769.

11. *History of Parliament*, ed. Namier and Brooke, ii, p. 359. Lady Haden Guest's biography of Sir Lawrence in the *History of Parliament* is an excellent summary of his career.

12. *Scotland and Scotsmen*, ii, p. 247.

13. J. Lindsay, *The Canals of Scotland* (Newton Abbot, 1968), pp. 18-20; BL, Grenville, Add. MSS. 57826, fo. 109, G. Chalmers to Grenville, 14 March 1767; W. Cowan, *The Maps of Edinburgh, 1544-1929* (second edition, 1932), p. 45, Sir J. Pringle to G. Laurie, 23 Dec. 1767.

14. Bute/Loudoun Papers, 1768, bundle 3, J. Thomson to Loudoun, 17 Dec. 1768; Atholl Papers, Box 54, section 2, no. 22, J. Mackenzie of Delvine to the Duke of Atholl, 5 Feb. 1771.

15. R. M. Sunter, 'Stirlingshire Politics', pp. 222-4. Dundas's friendship with Sandwich was especially valuable after the latter moved to the Admiralty in 1772.

16. Zetland Papers, ZNK X 1/2, no. 199, T. Dundas of Fingask to Sir L. Dundas, 22 Dec. 1773.

17. *Caldwell Papers*, ii, pp. 230-1, Duke of Argyll to Mure, 24 Feb. 1774, J. Craufurd to Mure, 7 April 1774; Atholl Papers, Box 54, section 5, no. 63, Col. J. Murray to Atholl, 21 April 1774; no. 78, Murray to Atholl, 14 May 1774.

18. Zetland Papers, ZNK X 1/2, no. 191, R. Rigby to Sir L. Dundas, 3 Dec. 1773; no. 194, Rigby to Dundas, 11 Dec. 1773; no. 195, W. Norton to Dundas, 17 Dec. 1773; no. 200, Norton to Dundas, 23 Dec. 1773; Atholl Papers, Box 54, section 5, no. 63, Col. J. Murray to Atholl, 21 April 1774; *History of Parliament*, ed. Namier and Brooke, ii, p. 180; *Caledonian Mercury* and *Edinburgh Evening Courant* for October 1774.

19. S. G. Checkland, *Scottish Banking: A History, 1695-1973* (Glasgow and London, 1975), pp. 158-9.

20. Zetland Papers, ZNK X 1/2, no. 296, T. Dundas of Castlecary to Sir L. Dundas, 4 Oct. 1777.

21. *Boswell: the Ominous Years, 1774-1776*, ed. C. Ryskamp and F.A. Pottle (London, 1963), p. 130. Ryskamp and Pottle mistakenly identify the person who recounted this news to Boswell as David Ross the manager of the Edinburgh Theatre Royal; in fact it was the David Ross who was shortly to become a Lord of Session as Lord Ankerville.

22. Dr. Ian Adams of the Department of Geography at the University of Edinburgh has been exploring Dundas's actions to prevent emigration in 1775. Zetland Papers, ZNK X 1/2, no. 222, T. Dundas of Castlecary to Sir L. Dundas, 5 Oct. 1775, gives an account of the meeting of Stirlingshire J.P.s to discuss Dundas's instructions. Also see C. Matheson, *The Life of Henry Dundas* (London, 1933), pp. 38-39.

23. W. Ferguson, 'Electoral Law and Procedure', pp. 92-94; SRO, Buccleuch, GD 224/30/10, H. Dundas to Buccleuch, 16 March 1776; *To the D. of B[uccleuch]* (Oct. 1777).

24. *Correspondence of King George III*, ed. Sir J. Fortescue, iv, p. 41, George III to Lord North, 24

Feb. 1778.

25. 'Horatio', *A Dream* (20 Sept. 1777), pp. 2-3. The embargo on shipping refers to Dundas's ban on emigration; and the great seal was the Signet Seal, which he then held jointly with Andrew Stuart. 'Additional tolls' refers to road legislation.

26. *The History of the Rise, Opposition to, and Establishment of the Edinburgh Regiment* (24 Jan. 1778). 'A certain banker' was probably William Ramsay of Barnton, who had been instrumental in Dundas's takeover of the Royal Bank of Scotland in 1776 (Checkland, *Scottish Banking*, p. 158).

27. *History of Parliament*, ed. Namier and Brooke, ii, p. 355.

28. G. W. T. Omond, *The Lord Advocates of Scotland* (1883), ii, pp. 96-97.

29. I. D. L. Clark, 'Moderation and the moderate party in the Church of Scotland, 1752-1805' (University of Cambridge Ph.D., 1963), p. 115 and appendix c.

30. SRO, Arniston, RH4/15/5, H. Dundas to Arniston, 28 Jan. 1781.

31. *Ibid.*, 28 March and 18 April 1782; *Arniston Memoirs*, p. 214; J. Cannon, *The Fox-North Coalition* (Cambridge, 1969), pp. 47, 49.

32. Boswell, *A Letter to the People of Scotland* (1785), p. 11. Also see A. Fergusson, *The Honourable Henry Erskine* (Edinburgh and London, 1882), pp. 241-54.

33. Cannon, *The Fox-North Coalition*, p. 215. This contradicts Furber, *Henry Dundas*, p. 27.

Conclusion

1. H. J. Hanham, 'The Development of the Scottish Office', in *Government and Nationalism in Scotland*, pp. 65-69.

2. Quoted in Simpson, 'Who Steered the Gravy Train?', p. 49. Originally printed in *More Culloden Papers*, ed. D. Warrand (Inverness, 1923-30), ii, p. 322. The passage is from a letter from Forbes to John Scrope, 31 Aug. 1725.

3. The row over the role of the Controller of BBC Scotland in 1978, for example, seems to me to involve the same principles. See *The Scotsman* and *The Guardian* for 22 December 1978.

Bibliography

MANUSCRIPT SOURCES
The following are not surveys of manuscript collections but descriptions of the material within them which I have found useful in the preparation of this study.

National Library of Scotland

Saltoun Papers, Accession 2933

This is a major collection of manuscripts which is just beginning to be explored by scholars. It has been put on deposit at the National Library by the present Fletcher of Saltoun, where it has been sorted, calendared, and catalogued by correspondent. The bulk of the papers are those of Andrew Fletcher, Lord Milton, S.C.J., and are especially voluminous for the period 1727-1764.

Boxed material
classified by subject, unfoliated (with the exception of SB 362), and only roughly sorted into folders.

SB 229 (Manufactures): SB 329 (Board of Trustees): SB 330 (Board of Trustees): SB 336 (Forfeited & Annexed Estates): SB 342 (Papers Relating to the Signet): SB 357 (Edinburgh City; Stamp Duties): SB 361 (Post Office): SB 362 (Court of Session; Ciphers) A small number of letters from the Duke of Argyll to Lord Milton, from the year 1750, were also found in this box: SB 363 (Parliamentary Elections) Principally material on the county of Haddington: SB 364 (Chancery; Police Courts; Public Occurrences): SB 365 (Scots Revenue) All of the material in this box predates 1739: SB 366 (Colleges & Tails) i.e. Entails: SB 368 (Excise & Army) Includes material on the militia: SB 370 (Customs)

Family Correspondence
Includes the correspondence of Lord Milton with his son Andrew Fletcher, Member of Parliament and personal secretary to the Duke of Argyll.

SC 17 (1754-55): SC 18 (1756): SC 19 (1757): SC 20 (1758): SC 21 (1759): SC 22 (1760):SC 23 (1761-62): SC 24 (1763-65)

General Correspondence
Including Lord Milton's correspondence with the Duke of Argyll and James Stuart Mackenzie.

SC 87-90 (1742): SC 91-95 (1743): SC 104 (1745 correspondence with the Duke of Argyll): SC114 (1746 correspondence with the Duke of Argyll): SC 138 (1747 correspondence with the Duke of Argyll): SC 174 (1752 correspondence with the Duke of Argyll): SC 182-85 (1754): SC 186-89 (1755): SC 190-93 (1756): SC 194-98 (1757): SC 199-203 (1758): SC 204-208 (1759): SC 209-213 (1760): SC 214-218 (1761): SC 219-22 (1762): SC 223-25 (1763): SC 226-28 (1764): SC 229 (1765)

A Note on Ciphers
Lord Milton's correspondence with his son, the Duke of Argyll and John Maule is often partially written in cipher, particularly in the period 1742-56. There are several cipher keys in SB 362, in addition to papers relating to the Court of Session; with their help it has been possible to decipher the correspondence consulted. The relevant items include SB 362, fo. 5, which is a small paper showing twenty-six symbols resembling today's shorthand with corresponding letters of the alphabet. The cipher is complemented by the use of dots in conjunction with the symbols to signify vowels following a consonant. Richard Scott of Edinburgh has also deciphered this system. Milton and his friends used a number code as well as the cipher referred to above, the keys to which can be found in SB 362. The key

for the code in use until December 1755 (see SC 17, fo. 216) is SB 362, fos. 26-27; that in use afterwards is SB 362, fos. 18-19. Words given in cipher have been given in upper case letters in passages quoted in the text.

Yester Papers, Accession 4862

Box 13, F 3 contains some correspondence of the Marquess of Tweeddale for 1754-56.
Box 13, F 5 contains a large amount of correspondence concerning the appointment of Thomas Hay to the Court of Session in 1754.
Box 19, F 3 correspondence of Tweeddale's brother, Lord George Hay, on the affairs of the Board of Police.

These papers are complemented by correspondence in an earlier accession of Yester Papers, MS. 7074.

Manuscript Letterbook of Lord George Beauclerk, Commander-in-Chief of the Forces in Scotland, 1756-1760, Accession 6417
   Beauclerk was Commander-in-Chief in Scotland until 1766, but this letterbook contains copies of letters for the period 1756-1760 only.

Mackenzie of Delvine Papers
   John Mackenzie of Delvine was an Edinburgh Writer to the Signet who, among other things, served the Dukes of Atholl as their legal agent.

MS. 1403: correspondence with the second Duke of Atholl.
MSS. 1404-1406: correspondence with John Murray of Strowan, later third Duke of Atholl.

Mure of Caldwell Papers
   Includes the papers of William Mure of Caldwell, Member of Parliament, 1741-1761; Baron of Exchequer, 1761-1774. Many of these manuscripts have been published in an 1854 volume of the Maitland Club edited by Mure's grandson, *Selections from the Family Papers Preserved at Caldwell*. Some of the papers printed in 1854 are not present in the collection, others in the collection have not been printed, and others, particularly the letters of James Stuart Mackenzie for 1761-1763, have not been correctly printed.

MSS. 4941-42: MS. 4942 contains many of James Stuart Mackenzie's letters not published in the Maitland Club volume, or published under the wrong date. For example, the letter published under the date of 16 Feb. 1762 (*Caldwell Papers*, i, pp. 145-6; MS. 4942, fos. 74-75) leaves out three passages and includes two others from a letter of 10 April 1762 (MS. 4942, fos. 90-91). The other correspondence in the printed volumes is more accurately reproduced, as are the letters after 1763, most of which can be found in MSS. 4943-44.

Aerskine-Murray Papers
   Papers of Charles Erskine, Lord Justice Clerk Tinwald. After the purchase of his family's ancestral estate in Clackmannan, he changed his judicial title to Lord Alva.

MSS. 5078-5081: general correspondence for the years 1754-61.

Manuscript Letterbook of John Maule, MS. 10781
   copies of letters written while Maule was a Baron of Exchequer, 1748-1761.

Minto Papers

MSS. 11001, 11003, 11009, 110014-15 correspondence of Sir Gilbert Elliot (Lord Minto, S.C.J.) and Gilbert Elliot, Member of Parliament, 1754-74.
MS. 11032 'An Account of the Political Crisis of May-June 1765' by Gilbert Elliot, M.P.

Scottish Record Office
Abercairny Papers

GD 24/1/552 letters of Lord Deskford to Henry Home (later Lord Kames, S.C.J.), written in the 1730s.

Scott of Harden Papers
  includes the papers of Walter Scott, M.P. for the county of Roxburgh, 1747-65.

GD 157/2250 correspondence with Gilbert Elliot
GD 157/2251 correspondence with the Earl of Marchmont
GD 157/2256 correspondence with George Brown of Elliston

Buccleuch Papers

GD 224/30/2 correspondence regarding the Linlithgow district of burghs election of 1774.
GD 224/30/3 correspondence of the third Duke of Buccleuch with Henry Dundas, 1787.
GD 224/30/10 letter of Henry Dundas to Buccleuch on the militia issue, 16 March 1776.

Seafield Papers
  This collection has not yet been sorted and catalogued. It contains the papers of the Ogilvy family (the fifth and sixth Earls of Findlater) and of the Grant family (who possessed a considerable interest in the county of Moray in the eighteenth century).

GD 248/562/55 includes a series of lengthy letters from Lord Dupplin to Lord Deskford, 1754-55; some additional correspondence with Dupplin, 1756-61; correspondence with Andrew Mitchell, 1754-56; and letters from John West, 1755.
GD 248/565/83 assorted correspondence, 1752-56, including letters from Henry Pelham.
GD 248/572/4 Findlater correspondence, 1766-68.
GD 248/572/5 assorted correspondence, including letters from Corbyn Morris and Sir Andrew Mitchell.
GD 248/572/7 letters from the Duke of Newcastle.
GD 248/572/8 letters from the Earl of Hardwicke.
GD 248/679/2 includes a letter of Henry Dundas, 1772.
GD 248/839 correspondence, 1766-67.

State Papers, Scotland
  photostat copies of documents in the Public Record Office in S.P. 54.

RH2/4/379-80 papers from the Secretary of State for the Northern Department's office, 1754-61.
RH2/4/381-82 papers from the Secretary of State's office, 1761-1764; calendared and partially published in the *Calendar of Home Office Papers of the Reign of George III*.

Sheriff Court Records

SC 67/59/4 Minute book of the freeholders headcourt of Stirlingshire, 1775-77.

Exchequer Records (Scotland)

E 721/1-5 minutes of the Commission of Annexed Estates, 1755- 3 March 1761.

Customs and Excise Records (Scotland)

CE 1/9-11 minutes of the Scottish Board of Customs, 1755-65.

Arniston Papers
  microfilm, at West Register House, of letterbooks kept at Arniston House, Midlothian, containing the general correspondence of the Dundas of Arniston family.

RH 4/15/4-5 correspondence, 1752-82, obviously incomplete, but containing items of great interest; includes material published in the *Arniston Memoirs*.

Craigievar Papers

Papers of Sir Andrew Mitchell now in the British Library, Add. MSS. 58283-367. RH 4/70/1 includes useful correspondence with Lord Deskford, 1752-55.

British Library

Newcastle Papers

Limitations of time and resources required that a collection of such size, kept at such a distance from Edinburgh, should be consulted selectively. Using the printed index to correspondents, Newcastle's correspondence with the following persons was consulted in its entirety:

William Alexander, General Humphrey Bland, Stamp Brooksbank, Archibald Campbell, third Duke of Argyll, John Campbell, third Earl of Breadalbane, Sir Hew Dalrymple, Richard Dauber, Charles Douglas, third Duke of Queensberry, George Drummond, Robert Dundas, Edward Edlin, Gilbert Elliot, Andrew Fletcher, Lord Milton, S.C.J., Sir Alexander Gilmour, John Hay, fourth Marquess of Tweeddale, Thomas Hay, Lord Dupplin, later ninth Earl of Kinnoull, John Hope, second Earl of Hopetoun, Charles Hope Weir, Alexander Hume Campbell, Hugh Hume Campbell, third Earl of Marchmont, George Mackay, James Maitland, seventh Earl of Lauderdale, Corbyn Morris, James Ogilvy, fifth Earl of Findlater, James Ogilvy, Lord Deskford, later sixth Earl of Findlater, Joseph Tudor

The following volumes of correspondence and papers have been examined in their entirety:

Add. MSS. 32870-77 (1757)
Add. MSS. 32896-936 (20 Sept. 1759 — 9 April 1762)
Add. MSS. 32968-74 (16 July 1765 — 20 April 1766)
Add. MS. 32992 (undated correspondence)
Add. MSS. 32995-6, 32998-9 (memoranda)
Add. MSS. 33034-5 (papers on proceedings in Parliament)
Add. MS. 33049 (political and other papers connected with Scotland)

Hardwicke Papers

Add. MSS. 35447-9 Scottish correspondence, 1753-62.
Add. MS. 35450 correspondence with the third Earl of Breadalbane.
Add. MS. 35451 correspondence of the second Earl of Hardwicke with the third Earl of Breadalbane.
Add. MSS. 35414-5, 35419 correspondence with the Duke of Newcastle.

Bute Papers (fragment)

Add. MS. 36796 register of correspondence of the third Earl of Bute, 1739-62.

Liverpool Papers

Includes material printed in *The Jenkinson Papers*. Correspondents whose letters were particularly useful are noted in parentheses.

Add. MS. 38197 (John Maule and William Mure)
Add. MS. 38202 (George Middleton)
Add. MS. 38203 (J. Stuart Mackenzie and D. Moncrieff)
Add. MS. 38204 (George Burgess)
Add. MS. 38304 (draft letters by Jenkinson to Stuart Mackenzie and Moncrieff)
Add. MSS. 38339, 38374, 38469 (miscellaneous material)

Ilchester Papers

Papers of Henry Fox, later Lord Holland. These papers have not yet been finally arranged. Some have been printed in *Letters to Henry Fox, Lord Holland*, ed. Earl of Ilchester (London, 1915).

Add. MSS. 51429-30 general correspondence, including letters of the third Duke of Argyll.
Add. MS. 51433 includes a letter of J. Stuart Mackenzie to Lord Holland, 3 June 1765, explaining his forced resignation from office.

Grenville Papers

Formerly in the possession of John Murray, publishers. Includes items printed in *The Grenville Papers* and *Additional Grenville Papers*.

Add. MS. 57809 correspondence with Charles Jenkinson.
Add. MS. 57185 correspondence with Lord Fife.
Add. MS. 57817A correspondence with Thomas Whately.
Add. MSS. 57821-27 general correspondence, 1761-1770; the letters of George Chalmers were particularly useful.

Leeds Papers

Includes the papers of Lord Holderness, Secretary of State for the Northern Department from 1754-61.

Egerton MSS. 3433-34 papers relating to Scotland from the Secretary of State's office; voluminous material on the investigation of Scottish affairs in 1752 and some interesting material on the militia agitation of 1759.

Edinburgh University Library

Laing Papers

II. 489. Scottish Court of Exchequer Papers, 1752-1770.
III. 364. Memoir of the family of Saltoun by Elizabeth Halkett, grand-daughter of Lord Milton.

North Yorkshire County Record Office, Northallerton

Zetland Papers

Includes the papers of Sir Lawrence Dundas and Sir Thomas Dundas of Castlecary.

ZNK X 1/2 general correspondence of Sir Lawrence Dundas; few items, but these few of great interest.
ZNK X 1/3 election papers.
ZNK X 2/7 correspondence of Sir Alexander Gilmour and Sir Thomas Dundas of Castlecary.

Sheffield City Library

Wentworth Woodhouse Muniments

After consulting the survey by the National Register of Archives, xerox material was kindly supplied by the librarian, but there was disappointingly little material listed in the survey which even remotely referred to Scotland.

Bury St. Edmunds and West Suffolk Record Office

Grafton Papers

The same procedure was followed as with the Wentworth Woodhouse Muniments, with similar results.

Cardiff Central Library

Bute Papers

The librarian very kindly responded to a request to forward xerox copies of letters by Lord Bute, William Mure, the third Duke of Argyll, James Stuart Mackenzie, Sir Harry Erskine, Gilbert Elliot, Sir Adam Fergusson, Lord Milton, and the Earl of Eglinton.

Huntington Library, San Marino, California

Loudoun Papers

Microfilm copies supplied by the librarian of letters by Lord Bute, the third Duke of Argyll, Sir

Adam Fergusson, the Duke of Grafton, Lord North, the Earl of Eglinton, and draft letters by the Earl of Loudoun. See T.I. Rae, 'The Loudoun Papers In The Huntington Library', *SHR*, XLIX (1970), pp. 227-31.

Mount Stuart, Isle of Bute

Bute Papers

Carefully preserved and catalogued, surveyed in great detail by the National Register of Archives (Scotland) in survey no. 631.

Correspondence of the third Earl of Bute, 1755-1774; most of the correspondence is from the years 1754-64.

Manuscript volume: 'Letters and Papers Relating to the Estate and Family of Bute', 1754-1788.

Papers of James Stuart Mackenzie

Surviving fragments of his personal papers found at Cardiff Castle, but including very little correspondence. The collection mostly consists of assorted papers from his period of responsibility for Scottish affairs, including a leather-bound book of recommendations for offices made to Mackenzie from 1761-1765.

Manuscript Letterbook of James Stuart Mackenzie, 1761 — 13 May 1765

Includes copies of most of his letters for this period, although checks with his letters in the Caldwell and Saltoun Papers reveal discrepancies; some letters recorded here are not present in the appropriate collection, where it survives, and letters present in the Caldwell or Saltoun Papers are not recorded here. Many of the letters have only been summarised.

Loudoun Papers, Mount Stuart

Also surveyed by the National Register of Archives (Scotland) in survey no. 631. The collection is sorted by year but not by date or correspondent. It was purchased by a former Marquess of Bute when the Loudoun Papers were auctioned. I found the NRA(S) survey of great assistance in consulting these manuscripts.

Green Deed Box, 1759-1763

1759, bundles 4 and 7; 1760, bundles 2, 4, 7 and 8; 1761, bundles 2-5

Green Deed Box, 1764-1767

1765, bundles 5 and 6; 1767, bundles 3 and 4

Green Deed Box, 1768-1771

1768, bundles 1-4, and 6; 1770, bundles 1-3, and 7; 1771, bundles 2-4

Green Deed Box, 1772-1775

1772, bundle 3; 1773, bundle 3; 1774, bundles 1, 3-5; 1775, bundles 2 and 3; 1776, bundles 4 and 5; 1777, bundle 3; 1781, bundle 2

Bundle, letters of the Earl of Bute and James Stuart Mackenzie to the Earl of Loudoun withdrawn from the Loudoun Papers.

Blair Atholl Castle, Perthshire

Atholl Papers

Some of these papers have been published in *Chronicles of the Atholl and Tullibardine Families*. There is an excellent typescript survey of the papers at West Register House in Edinburgh, given the National Register of Archives (Scotland) designation no. 234. It was made at the University of Aberdeen in the 1950s and contains a brief summary of each letter in this large collection, as well as typescript copies of a significant number of them. The following boxes of correspondence were examined at Blair Atholl:

Boxes 47, 49, 50, 54, and 65.

N

William L. Clements Library, Ann Arbor, Michigan

Townshend Papers

These papers were consulted while they were on deposit at the Scottish Record Office, but have since been moved to Michigan. They form a small but important collection consisting of Charles Townshend's correspondence with the Scottish friends he made during his visit to Scotland in the summer of 1759, most of it dating from 1759 and 1760. Some have been partially quoted, with some errors, in Sir L. Namier and J. Brooke, *Charles Townshend* (London, 1964).

Bedford Estate Office, London

Bedford Papers

Surveyed by the Historic Manuscripts Commission in their eighth report. I have consulted Bedford's correspondence with his Scottish connections.

Signet Library, Edinburgh

MS. 106:54, 'An Account of the Officers of the Customs & Salt Duty at the Out Ports in Scotland, their Salaries, the supposed Value of each Office; their Character, & by whose Interest they held their Employments, as they stood on the Establishment at the 5th of January 1755'.

It is not known how this manuscript came to be deposited in the Signet Library, or who the author was, but it is interesting to note that the date of the account coincides with Lord Deskford's period of activity at the Board of Customs.

Torwoodlee House, By Galashiels

Torwoodlee Papers, in the possession of Mrs. D.L. Pringle.

Includes the papers of James Pringle of Bowland, one of the principal clerks of the Court of Session and an associate of the Earl of Marchmont. His correspondence with Marchmont and Alexander Hume Campbell has been consulted, with the help of survey 482 of the National Register of Archives (Scotland).

Thirlestane Castle, Lauder

Lauderdale Papers, in the possession of Capt. the Hon. G.E. Maitland-Carew.

These papers were consulted with the help of survey 832 of the National Register of Archives (Scotland).

Items from the Newhailes Papers and the Buccleuch Papers at Drumlanrig (Queensberry Papers) were also examined at West Register House with the aid of the National Register of Archives (Scotland).

PRINTED SOURCES

PAMPHLET LITERATURE (by year of publication)

E[dinburg]h's Instructions to their Member. London, 1734, 7pp. (NLS).

[Francis Hutcheson] *Considerations on Patronages. Addressed to the Gentlemen of Scotland*. London, 1735, 24pp. (Edinburgh University Library).

[Andrew Crosbie] *An Address to the Inhabitants and Landholders of the Town of Dumfries*. Dumfries?, 1759, 24pp. (Ewart Public Library, Dumfries).

'Civicus' [Lord Milton], *Queries Addressed to the Serious Consideration of the Public*. 26 April 1760, 1p. (BL, Saltoun Papers NLS).

[Adam Ferguson] *The History of the Proceedings in the Case of Margaret, Commonly called Peg, only lawful Sister to JOHN BULL, Esq*. London, 1761 (NLS).

Andrew Henderson, *Considerations on the Question Relating to the Scots Militia*. Second edition, Westminster, 1761, 46pp. (BL).

[John Maclaurin] *Conviction to Those Who Are Capable of Conviction: That it is the True Interest of the*

City of Edinburgh, that Mr. F[orreste]r be chosen to Represent the Community in the Ensuing Parliament; and, That the Thanks of the Community Ought to be Given, in the most public Manner, to the Peer Who Recommended Him. 1761, 14pp. (NLS). A satire.

A Letter From a Citizen in Town to his Friend. (Feb. 1762), 4pp. (NLS).

A New Year's Gift to the Inhabitants of the City of Glasgow, QUERIES Proposed concerning the Powers, and Management of the Town Council of the city of Glasgow, for some years past. With some Remarks upon the Model agreed to, in the calling of a Minister to any vacancy that shall happen in the City, with the Voice of the Christian People. (Glasgow 1762), (Mitchell Library, Glasgow).

An Historical Account of the Debates which happened in the years, 1755, 1761, and 1762, about the MODEL, or FORM of calling ministers to the city of Glasgow. In a LETTER from J.C. a Citizen, to W.M. a Country Gentleman. Published for the information of the inhabitants and all concerned. Glasgow, 20 March 1762, 26pp. with 10pp. appendix (Mitchell Library).

A Continuation of the Historical Account of the Debates Which Happened in the Years 1755, 1761, and 1762, Concerning the Model, or Form, For calling Ministers to the City of Glasgow. In a Second Letter From J— C—, a Citizen, to W— M—, a Country Gentleman. Glasgow, June 1762, 28pp. (Mitchell Library).

Henry the Corby's Nest: or the CRY of LIBERTY, CIVIL and SACRED, to the Inhabitants of the Good Town of Edinburgh of whatever Rank, Station, or Occupation. (Sept. 1763), 1p. (Edinburgh Room, Edinburgh Public Library).

A Letter From a Member of Parliament in London to His Friends in Edinburgh, Relating to the Present Critical State of Affairs, and the Dangerous Antipathy that seems daily to increase between the PEOPLE OF ENGLAND AND SCOTLAND. 1763, 33pp. (Signet Library). There was a London edition as well.

[Andrew Henderson] *A Letter to the Author of the North Briton: in which the Low Scurrilities and Glaring Falsehoods of that Paper are detected; Their Tendency toward Sedition and Rebellion Exposed: and the Whole illustrated with many curious Anecdotes, among which a Striking Character of Lord Bute and of Archibald, late Duke of Argyle.* London, 1763, 52pp. (Edinburgh University Library).

Letter to John Wilkes, Esq; Member of Parliament, by a Briton. 1763, 4pp. (BL).

A LETTER: from Scots Sawney the Barber to Mr. Wilkes an English Parliamenter. 25 June 1763, 4pp. (BL).

The Citizen, Number I. 1764, 16pp. (Edinburgh Room).

The Edinburgh Paradise Regain'd, or The City Set at Liberty, to propagate and improve her Trade and Commerce. 1764, 28pp. (Edinburgh University Library).

[Tobias Smollett] *A North Briton Extraordinary.* Second edition, London, 1765, 23pp. (Edinburgh University Library and NLS).

A Mirror for the Multitude; or Wilkes no Patriot. London, 1768?, 52pp. (Edinburgh University Library). Written by a Scot.

[P. Bannerman] *A Sermon Preached at Salton, Upon Occasion of the Death of the Honourable the Lord Milton.* 1767, 60pp. (NLS).

[Andrew Crosbie] *Thoughts of a Layman Concerning Patronage and Presentations.* 1769, 52pp. (Edinburgh University Library).

A North Briton Extraordinary: written by a Scotsman Now a Volunteer in the Corsican Service. London, 1769, 85pp. (Edinburgh University Library and NLS).

'Regulus', *The Town Council: a Poem.* London, 1774, 20pp. (NLS). A polemic against the town council of Edinburgh.

AN EXAMINATION: of the Principles and Conduct of the Town-Council of Edinburgh, from the commencement of Mr. Laurie's administration to the present time; with Remarks on the Set, or Constitution of the City. By a Burgess and Guild-Brother. 1776, 53pp. (Edinburgh Room and BL).

'Horatio', *A Dream.* 20 Sept. 1777, 3pp. (BL).

'John Hancock, Preses', *The Manifesto of the Edinburgh Congress.* 19 Aug. 1777, 10pp. (Edinburgh Room). A burlesque of the Incorporations of Trades in Edinburgh.

'A Freeman', *A Rhapsody.* 9 Sept. 1777, 10pp. (NLS).

The Caldron Clouted or, An Answer to Auld Reekie's Garland. 9 Sept. 1777, 1p. (NLS).

'Aristides', *An Address to the Citizens of Edinburgh.* 23 Sept. 1777, 4pp. (Edinburgh Room).

An ADDRESS To The Freemen of the several Incorporations of Edinburgh. (1777) 1p. (BL).

Common Sense: A Letter to the Fourteen Incorporations of Edinburgh. 9 Sept. 1777, 7pp. (BL).
To the D[uke] of B[uccleuch]. (Oct. 1777) 12pp. (BL and NLS).
[Hugo Arnot] *A Letter to the Lord Advocate of Scotland.* 18 Nov. 1777, 16pp. (NLS).
The History of the Rise, Opposition to, and Establishment of the Edinburgh Regiment. 24 Jan. 1778, 18pp. (NLS).
To the Inhabitants of Edinburgh. 1780, 4pp. (Edinburgh Room).
'Cato', *To The Citizens of Edinburgh.* 26 Sept. 1780, 8pp. (Edinburgh Room).
'Horatio', *A Letter to the Town-Council and Citizens of Edinburgh.* 9 Sept. 1780, 8pp. (Edinburgh University Library).
'Common Sense', *To The Gentlemen-Electors of the City of Edinburgh.* 16 Sept. 1780, 7pp. (Edinburgh University Library).
Supplement to Falsehoods Detected. 1780, 7pp. (Edinburgh University Library).
'Priuli', *Reflections on the Different Modes of Proceeding by which Sir Lawrence Dundas, Bart. and William Miller, Esq, Advocate; Were Returned as Members of Parliament for the City of Edinburgh.* 22 Sept. 1780, 10pp. (Edinburgh Room).
James Boswell, *A Letter to the People of Scotland on the Present State of the Nation.* 1783, 43pp. (NLS).
James Boswell, *A Letter to the People of Scotland, on the Alarming Attempt to infringe the Articles of the Union, and introduce a Most Pernicious Innovation, by diminishing the number of the Lords of Session.* London, 1785, 70pp. (NLS).
William Creech, *Letters Addressed to Sir John Sinclair, Bart. Respecting the Mode of Living, Arts, Commerce, Literature, Manners, &c. of Edinburgh in 1763, And Since that Period, Illustrating the Statistical Progress of the Capital of Scotland.* 1793, 52pp. (Edinburgh University Library).
[Lord Buchan] *Printed Recollections Respecting the Family of the Fletchers of Salton.* 1803, 8pp. (NLS).

PERIODICALS

The three most important Scottish journals of the period have been examined at points where I hoped they could offer a significant amount of evidence. I have tried to indicate what has and has not been examined. Information on the development of the Scottish press in this period is available in M.E. Craig, *The Scottish Periodical Press, 1750-1789* (1931).
Scots Magazine
Used throughout the period 1745-1782 but most carefully for the following years: 1752, 1759, 1760-64, 1767-70, 1774.
The Caledonian Mercury
The Edinburgh Evening Courant
Both of these journals were consulted for the following periods: 1754, 1759, 1760-65, 1767-71, 1773-74.

MEMOIRS AND CORRESPONDENCE (after J. Brewer, *Party Ideology and Popular Politics at the Accession of George III*).

ALBEMARLE

The Albemarle Papers; Being the Correspondence of William Anne, Second Earl of Albemarle, ed. C.S. Terry (Aberdeen, New Spalding Club, 1911), Vol. II.
ARGYLL
Intimate Society Letters of the Eighteenth Century, ed. J. Campbell, ninth duke of Argyll (London, 1910), two volumes.
ATHOLL
Chronicles of the Atholl and Tullibardine Families, ed. J. Stewart Murray, seventh duke of Atholl (1908), five volumes.
BEDFORD
The Correspondence of John, Fourth Duke of Bedford, ed. Lord John Russell (London, 1842-46), three volumes.

BOSWELL

Boswell's London Journal, 1762-1763, ed. F.A. Pottle (London, 1950).

Boswell in Search of a Wife, 1766-1769, ed. F. Brady and F.A. Pottle (London, 1957).

Boswell for the Defence, 1769-1774, ed. W.K. Wimsatt, Jr. and F.A. Pottle (London, 1960).

Boswell: the Ominous Years, 1774-1776, ed. C. Ryskamp and F.A. Pottle (London, 1963).

CARLYLE

Autobiography of Dr. Alexander Carlyle of Inveresk, ed. J. Hill Burton (second edition, 1910).

A. Carlyle, *Anecdotes and Characters of the Times,* ed. J. Kinsley, (London, 1973).

This is a new edition of the autobiography using the title Carlyle himself gave his manuscript. Although Carlyle is quite often wrong in dating his memoirs, hardly surprising when one considers when they were written (1800-1805), his account has been extremely useful when used in conjunction with contemporary material.

CHATHAM

Correspondence of William Pitt, Earl of Chatham, ed. W.S. Taylor and J.H. Pringle (London, 1838-40), four volumes.

'Letters from William Pitt to Lord Bute', ed. R. Sedgwick in *Essays Presented to Sir Lewis Namier,* ed. R. Pares and A.J.P. Taylor (London, 1956).

CHESTERFIELD

Lord Chesterfield's Characters (London, 1927).

COCKBURN

Henry Cockburn, *Memorials of His Times* (second edition, 1909).

DEMPSTER

Letters of George Dempster to Sir Adam Fergusson, 1756-1813; with some account of his life, ed. Sir J. Fergusson (London, 1934).

DODINGTON

The Political Journal of George Bubb Dodington, ed. J. Carswell and L.A. Dralle (Oxford, 1965).

DUNDAS

The Arniston Memoirs: Three Centuries of a Scottish House, 1571-1838, ed. G.W.T. Omond (1887).

DUTENS

[Louis Dutens] *Memoirs of a Traveller Now in Retirement, written by himself* (London, 1806), five volumes.

EGMONT

'Leicester House Politics 1750-60, from the Papers of John, Second Earl of Egmont', ed. A.N. Newman in *Camden Miscellany Vol. XXIII* (London, Camden Society, fourth series, 1969), pp. 85-228.

FIFE

Lord Fife and His Factor: Being the Correspondence of James Second Lord Fife, 1729-1809, ed. A. & H. Taylor (London, 1925).

FORBES OF CULLODEN

Culloden Papers, ed. H. Duff (London, 1815).

More Culloden Papers, ed. D. Warrand (Inverness, 1923-30), Vols. III-V.

FOX

The Life and Letters of Lady Sarah Lennox . . . Also a short Political Sketch of the Years 1760 to 1763 by Henry Fox, first Lord Holland, ed. the Countess of Ilchester and Lord Stavordale (London, 1902).

Letters to Henry Fox, Lord Holland, ed. G. Strangeways, Earl of Ilchester (London, Roxburghe Club, 1915).

GEORGE III

The Correspondence of King George the Third, ed. Sir J. Fortescue (London, 1927-28), Vols. I-III.

Sir L. Namier, *Additions and Correction to Sir J. Fortescue's edition of the Correspondence of George III, vol. I* (Manchester, 1937).

Letters from George III to Lord Bute, 1756-1766, ed. R. Sedgwick (London, 1939).

GRAFTON

Autobiography and Political Correspondence of Augustus Henry, Third Duke of Grafton, K.G., ed. Sir W.R. Anson (London, 1898).

GRANT OF GRANT
The Chiefs of Grant, ed. W. Fraser (1883), Vol. III.
GRENVILLE
The Grenville Papers: being the correspondence of R. Grenville, Earl Temple, and the Rt. Hon. G. Grenville, their friends and contemporaries, ed. W.J. Smith (London, 1852-53), four volumes.
Additional Grenville Papers, 1763-1765, ed. J.R.G. Tomlinson (Manchester, 1962).
HARDWICKE
The Life and Correspondence of Philip Yorke, Earl of Hardwicke, Lord High Chancellor of Great Britain (Cambridge, 1913), three volumes.
HERVEY
John, Lord Hervey, *Some Materials Towards Memoirs of the Reign of King George II,* ed. R. Sedgwick (London, 1931).
HUME
The Letters of David Hume, ed. J.Y.T. Greig (Oxford, 1932), two volumes.
New Letters of David Hume. ed. R. Kilibansky and E.C. Mossner (Oxford, 1954).
JENKINSON
The Jenkinson Papers, 1760-1766, ed. N.S. Jucker (London, 1949).
MARCHMONT
A Selection from the Papers of the Earls of Marchmont, ed. Sir G. Rose (London, 1831), three volumes.
Historical Manuscripts Commission, *Report on the Manuscripts of the Right Honourable Lord Polwarth,* ed. H. Paton (1961), Vol. V.
MURE OF CALDWELL
Selections From the Family Papers Preserved at Caldwell, Part II, ed. W. Mure (Glasgow, the Maitland Club, 1854), two volumes.
NEWCASTLE
A Narrative of the Changes in the Ministry, 1765-1767, ed. M. Bateson (London, Camden Society, New Series, LIX, 1898). Letters of the Duke of Newcastle to John White, M.P.
OSWALD
Memorials of the Public Life and Character of the Right Hon. James Oswald of Dunniker, ed. J. Oswald (1825). Contains most of Oswald's correspondence that survived a fire at Dunniker after his death.
RAMSAY OF OCHTERTYRE
Scotland and Scotsmen in the Eighteenth Century From the Manuscripts of John Ramsay, Esq. of Ochtertyre, ed. A. Allardyce (1888), two volumes.
The problems and advantages of using Ramsay's memoirs are the same as those involved in using Carlyle's *Anecdotes.* Ramsay's recollections were written about 1775, with additions up to his death in 1812. The chronology and exact dates of events or observations are sometimes wrong, but these recollections are still very valuable when used in conjunction with contemporary material.
ROBINSON
Parliamentary Papers of John Robinson 1774-1784, ed. W.T. Laprade (London, Camden Society, third series, XXXIII, 1922).
SOMERVILLE
T. Somerville, *My Own Life and Times, 1741-1814* (1861).
STUART
Lady Louisa Stuart: Selections from her Manuscripts, ed. J. Home (1899).
STUART MACKENZIE
Ancient Deeds and Other Writs in the Mackenzie-Wharncliffe Charter-chest, ed. J.W. Barty (1906).
SUFFOLK
Letters to and from Henrietta, Countess of Suffolk and her second husband, the Hon. George Berkeley, ed. J.W. Croker (London, 1824).
WALDEGRAVE
Memoirs from 1754 to 1758 by James Earl Waldegrave K.G. (London, 1821).
WALPOLE
H. Walpole, *Memoirs of the Last Ten Years of the Reign of George the Second* (London, 1822), two

volumes.

H. Walpole, *Memoirs of the Reign of King George the Second*, ed. Lord Holland (London, 1846), three volumes.

H. Walpole, *Memoirs of the Reign of King George the Third*, ed. Sir D. Le Marchant (London, 1845), four volumes.

OTHER PRINTED CONTEMPORARY SOURCES

Arnot, H., *The History of Edinburgh, From the Earliest Accounts to the Year 1780* (third edition, 1816).
Calendar of Home Office Papers of the Reign of George III (1760-1775), ed. J. Redington and R.A. Roberts (London, 1878-99), four volumes.
Clerk, Sir J. and J. Scrope, *Historical View of the Forms and Powers of the Court of Exchequer in Scotland* (1820). Written between 1707 and 1724.
Extracts from the Records of the Convention of the Royal Burghs of Scotland, 1738-1759, ed. T. Hunter (1915).
Extracts from the Records of the Convention of the Royal Burghs of Scotland, 1759-1779, ed. T. Hunter (1918).
Henderson, A., *The Life of William Augustus, Duke of Cumberland* (London, 1766).
Historical Manuscripts Commission, *Fifth Report* (1876).
Historical Manuscripts Commission, *Report on the Laing Manuscripts Preserved in the University of Edinburgh*, ed. H. Paton (1925), Vol. II.
Home, J., *The History of the Rebellion in the Year 1745* (London, 1802).
Kincaid, A., *The History of Edinburgh From the Earliest Accounts to the Present Time* (1787).
'Memorial Concerning the State of the Records of Scotland, 1762', ed. E. Hughes, in *SHR*, XXVIII (1949), pp. 146-54.
Old Ross-shire and Scotland: as seen in the Tain and Balnagown Documents, ed. W. MacGill (Inverness, 1909).
Postlethwayt, M., *The Universal Dictionary of Trade and Commerce* (London, 1753-55). The entry on Scotland was written from information provided by Francis Grant, deputy Inspector General of the Annexed Estates.
Reports on the Annexed Estates, 1755-1769, From the Records of the Forfeited Estates Preserved in the Scottish Record Office, ed. V. Wills (1973).
Scottish Population Statistics, including Webster's Analysis of Population 1755, ed. J.G. Kyd (Scottish History Society, 1952).
A Selection of Scottish Forfeited Estates Papers, 1715; 1745, ed. A.H. Millar (Scottish History Society, 1909).
Smollett, T., *The Expedition of Humphry Clinker*, ed. A. Ross (paperback edition, London, 1967).
States of the Annual Progress of the Linen Manufacture, 1727-1754; From the Records of the Board of Trustees for Manufactures . . . in Scotland Preserved in the Scottish Record Office, ed. R.H. Campbell (1964).
The Statutes at Large (London, 1764-71), Vols. VII-X.
The Trial of James Stewart (the Appin Murder), ed. D.N. Mackay (second edition, 1931). Original documents connected with the trial.
View of the Political State of Scotland in the Last Century, ed. Sir C.A. Adam (1887). Written for the use of William Adam by Laurence Hill, an Edinburgh Writer to the Signet; see D.G. Henry, 'The Political State of Scotland in the Last Century', *SHR*, XLVI (1967), pp. 87-89.

SECONDARY SOURCES

WORKS OF REFERENCE

Brunton, G. and D. Haig, *An Historical Account of the Senators of the College of Justice* (London, 1832).
Campbell, J., Lord Campbell, *The Lives of the Lord Chancellors and Keepers of the Great Seal of*

England, From the Earliest Times Till the Reign of King George IV (London, 1847), Vols. V and VI.
Campbell, J., Lord Campbell, *The Lives of the Chief Justices of England* (London, 1849), two volumes.
The Complete Peerage of England, Scotland, Ireland, Great Britain and the United Kingdom, ed. V. Gibbs and others (London, 1910-59), thirteen volumes.
The Dictionary of National Biography.
The History of Parliament: the House of Commons, 1715-1754, ed. R. Sedgwick (London, 1971), two volumes. Most of the Scottish material is by Lady Haden Guest and John Simpson.
The History of Parliament: the House of Commons, 1754-1790, ed. Sir L. Namier and J. Brooke (London, 1964), three volumes. Most of the Scottish material is by Lady Haden Guest.
Omond, G.W.T., *The Lord Advocates of Scotland* (1883), two volumes.
The Parliamentary History of England from the Norman Conquest to the year 1803, ed. W. Cobbett (London, 1806-20), Vols. XIV-XVI.
Sainty, J.C., *Treasury Officials: 1660-1870* (London, 1972).
Sainty, J.C., *Officials of the Secretaries of State* (London, 1973).
Sainty, J.C., *Officials of the Boards of Trade: 1660-1870* (London, 1974).
Sainty, J.C., *Admiralty Officials: 1660-1870* (London, 1975).
The Scots Peerage; Founded on Wood's Edition of Sir Robert Douglas's Peerage of Scotland, ed. Sir J. Balfour Paul (1904-11), eight volumes.

UNPUBLISHED SECONDARY SOURCES

Brewer, J., 'Political Argument and Propaganda in England, 1760-1770' (University of Cambridge Ph.D., 1973).
Bricke, M.S., 'Management and Administration of Scotland, 1707-1765' (University of Kansas Ph.D., 1972). Dr. Bricke places too much emphasis on offices rather than personalities and politics.
Carmichael, E.K., 'The Scottish Commission of the Peace, 1707-1760' (University of Glasgow Ph.D., 1977).
Clark, I.D.L., 'Moderation and the Moderate Party in the Church of Scotland, 1752-1805' (University of Cambridge Ph.D., 1963).
Durie, A.J., 'The Scottish Linen Industry, 1707-1775, With Particular Reference to the Early History of the British Linen Company' (University of Edinburgh Ph.D., 1973).
Fagerstrom, D.I., 'The American Revolutionary Movement in Scottish Opinion, 1763 to 1783' (University of Edinburgh Ph.D., 1951).
Ferguson, W., 'Electoral Law and Procedure in Eighteenth and Early Nineteenth Century Scotland' (University of Glasgow Ph.D., 1957). The summaries of electoral law until 1832 in chapters I and II are very important.
Foley, A.L., P. Hayton and P.J. Maddock, 'The Forth-Clyde Canal from its Conception to its Completion, 1762-1794' (University of Edinburgh Junior Honours History thesis, 1971), in the Edinburgh University Library.
Hamer, M.T., 'From the Grafton Administration to the Ministry of North, 1768-1772' (University of Cambridge Ph.D., 1970).
Jewell, B.F., 'The Legislation Relating to Scotland After the Forty-Five' (University of North Carolina Ph.D., 1975). This research should be published.
McElroy, D.D., 'A Century of Scottish Clubs, 1700-1800' (typescript, 1969), in the NLS.
Phillipson, N.T., 'The Scottish Whigs and the Reform of the Court of Session, 1785-1830' (University of Cambridge Ph.D., 1967).
Smith, A.M., 'The Forfeited Annexed Estates, 1752-1784' (University of St. Andrews Ph.D., 1975). Particularly concerned with the role of the Commission of Annexed Estates in developing the transportation network of the highlands.
Sunter, R.M., 'Stirlingshire Politics, 1707-1832' (University of Edinburgh Ph.D., 1971).
Whetstone, A.E., 'Scottish County Government in the Eighteenth and Nineteenth Centuries' (University of Minnesota Ph.D., 1973).

ARTICLES AND ESSAYS

Adam Smith, J., 'Some Eighteenth Century Ideas of Scotland', in *Scotland in the Age of Improvement*, ed. N.T. Phillipson and R.M. Mitchison (1970), pp. 118-23.

Baird, W., 'George Drummond: An Eighteenth Century Lord Provost', *Book of the Old Edinburgh Club*, IV (1911), pp. 1-54.

Brady, F., 'So Fast to Ruin: The Ayr Bank Crash', *Collections of the Ayrshire Archaeological and Natural History Society*, XI (1973), pp. 27-44.

Brewer, J., 'The Faces of Lord Bute: A Visual Contribution to Anglo-American Political Ideology', *Perspectives in American History*, VI (1972), pp. 95-116.

Brewer, J., 'The Misfortunes of Lord Bute: A Case-Study in Eighteenth-Century Political Argument and Public Opinion', *The Historical Journal*, XVI (1973), pp. 3-43.

Brewer, J., 'The Earl of Bute', in *The Prime Ministers*, ed. H. Van Thal (London, 1974), pp. 103-13.

Brewer, J., 'Rockingham, Burke and Whig Political Argument', *The Historical Journal*, XVIII (1975), pp. 188-201.

Burn, W.L., 'The General Election of 1761 at Ayr', *English Historical Review*, LII (1937), pp. 103-9.

Campbell, R.H., 'An Economic History of Scotland in the Eighteenth Century', *Scottish Journal of Political Economy*, XI (1964), pp. 17-24.

Campbell, R.H., 'The Industrial Revolution: A Revision Article', *SHR*, XLVI (1967), pp. 37-55.

Campbell, R.H., 'The Union and Economic Growth', in *The Union of 1707: Its Impact on Scotland*, ed. T.I. Rae (Glasgow, 1974), pp. 58-74.

Campbell, R.H., 'The Scottish Improvers and the Course of Agrarian Change in the Eighteenth Century', in *Comparative Aspects of Scottish and Irish Economic and Social History, 1600-1900*, ed. L.M. Cullen and T.C. Smout (1977), pp. 204-15.

Cater, J., 'The Making of Principal Robertson in 1762', *SHR*, XLIX (1970), pp. 60-84.

Christie, I., 'The Cabinet during the Grenville Administration, 1763-1765', *English Historical Review*, LXXIII (1958), pp. 86-92.

Clark, I.D.L., 'From Protest to Reaction: The Moderate Regime in the Church of Scotland, 1752-1805', in *Scotland in the Age of Improvement*, pp. 200-24.

Clive, J., and B. Bailyn, 'England's Cultural Provinces: Scotland and America', *William and Mary Quarterly*, third series, XI, (1954), pp. 200-13.

Colley, L., 'The Mitchell Election Division, 24 March 1755', *Bulletin of the Institute of Historical Research*, XLIX (1976), pp. 80-107.

Cregeen E., 'The Tacksmen and their Successors', *Scottish Studies*, XIII (1969), pp. 93-144.

Cregeen, E., 'The Changing Role of the House of Argyll in the Scottish Highlands', in *Scotland in the Age of Improvement*, pp. 5-23.

Davie, G.E., 'Hume, Reid, and the Passion for Ideas', in *Edinburgh in the Age of Reason; a commemoration* (1967), pp. 23-39.

Devine, T.M., 'The American War of Independence and Scottish Economic History', in *Scotland, Europe and the American Revolution*, ed. O. Dudley Edwards and G. Shepperson (1976), pp. 61-65.

Devine, T.M., 'Colonial Commerce and the Scottish Economy, c. 1730-1815', in *Comparative Aspects of Scottish and Irish Economic and Social History*, pp. 177-90.

Dickinson, H.T., 'The Duke of Newcastle', in *The Prime Ministers*, pp. 75-91.

Dickinson, H.T. and Ken Logue, 'The Porteous Riot: A Study of the Breakdown of Law and Order in Edinburgh, 1736-1737', *Journal of the Scottish Labour History Society*, no. 10 (June 1976), pp. 21-40.

Duff, D., *Scotland's War Losses* (Glasgow, the Scottish Secretariat, 1947), 64pp.

Durie, A.J., 'The Markets for Scottish Linen, 1730-1775', *SHR*, LII (1973), pp. 30-49.

Durie, A.J., 'Linen-spinning in the North of Scotland, 1746-1773', *Northern Scotland*, II (1974-75), pp. 13-36.

Emerson, R.L., 'The Social Composition of Enlightened Scotland: the Select Society of Edinburgh, 1754-1764', *Studies on Voltaire and the Eighteenth Century*, no. 114 (1973), pp. 291-329.

Fabel, R., 'The Patriotic Briton: Tobias Smollett and English Politics, 1756-1771', *Eighteenth Century Studies*, VIII (1974), pp. 100-14. Fabel completely ignores the national aspect of Smollett's thought and does not have a solid grasp of the politics of the period.

Fagerstrom, D.I., 'Scottish Opinion and the American Revolution', *William and Mary Quarterly*, third series, XI (1954), pp. 252-75.

Ferguson, W., 'Dingwall Burgh Politics and the Parliamentary Franchise in the Eighteenth Century', *SHR*, XXXVIII (1959), pp. 89-108.

Ferguson, W., 'The Making of the Treaty of Union of 1707', *SHR*, XLII (1964), pp. 89-110.

Fergusson, Sir J., '"Making Interest" in Scottish County Elections', *SHR*, XXVI (1947), pp. 119-33.

Forbes, D., 'Adam Ferguson and the Idea of Community', in *Edinburgh in the Age of Reason*, pp. 40-47.

Forbes Gray, W., 'Edinburgh in Lord Provost Drummond's Time', *Book of the Old Edinburgh Club*, XXVII (1949), pp. 1-24.

Gavine, D., 'James Stewart Mackenzie (1719-1800) and the Bute MSS', *Journal for the History of Astronomy*, V (1974), pp. 208-14.

Hamilton, H., 'Scotland's Balance of Payments Problem in 1762', *Economic History Review*, second series, IV (1952-53), pp. 344-57.

Hamilton, H., 'The Failure of the Ayr Bank, 1772', *Economic History Review*, second series, VIII (1956-57), pp. 405-17.

Hamilton, H., 'Economic Growth in Scotland, 1720-1770', *Scottish Journal of Political Economy*, VI (1959), pp. 85-98.

Hamilton, T., 'Local Administration in Ayrshire, 1750-1800', *Collections of the Ayrshire Archaeological and Natural History Society*, V (1959), pp. 174-80.

Hanham, H.J., *The Scottish Political Tradition* (1964). An inaugural lecture for the Chair of Politics at the University of Edinburgh.

Hayes, J., 'Scottish Officers in the British Army', *SHR*, XXXVII (1958), pp. 23-33.

Jarrett, D., 'The Regency Crisis of 1765', *English Historical Review*, LXXXV (1970), pp. 282-315.

Kemp, B., 'Frederick Prince of Wales', in *Silver Renaissance*, ed. A. Natan (London, 1961), pp. 38-56.

Leftwich, B.R., 'Selections from the Customs Records Preserved at Dumfries', *Transactions of the Dumfriesshire and Galloway Natural History and Antiquarian Society*, third series, XVII (1926).

Lloyd, E.M., 'The Raising of the Highland Regiments in 1757', *English Historical Review*, XVII (1902), pp. 466-9.

Lovat Fraser, J.A., *David Balfour's Duke of Argyll* (Inverness, 1928), 16pp. Reprint from the *Inverness Courier*.

Lythe, S.G.E., 'The Tayside Meal Mobs, 1772-3', *SHR*, XLVI (1967), pp. 26-36.

Malcolm, C.A., 'The Solicitòr-General for Scotland', *Juridical Review*, LIV (1942), pp. 67-69, 125-43.

McCahill, M.W., 'The Scottish Peerage and the House of Lords in the Late Eighteenth Century', *SHR*, LI (1972), pp. 172-96.

McKelvey, J., 'William Robertson and Lord Bute', *Studies in Scottish Literature*, VI (1969), pp. 238-47. Much inferior to the article by J. Cater.

Miller, F., 'Andrew Crosbie, Advocate', *Transactions of the Dumfriesshire and Galloway Natural History and Antiquarian Society*, V (1919). Also published as a pamphlet.

Mitchison, R.M., 'Movement of Scottish Corn Prices in the Seventeenth and Eighteenth Centuries', *The Economic History Review*, second series, XVIII (1965), pp. 278-83.

Mitchison, R.M., 'The Government and the Highlands, 1707-1745', in *Scotland in the Age of Improvement*, pp. 25-46.

Mitchison, R.M., 'The Making of the Old Scottish Poor Law', *Past and Present*, no. 63 (1974), pp. 58-93. Also see R.A. Cage, 'The Making of the Old Scottish Poor Law', and R.M. Mitchison, 'A Rejoinder', *Past and Present*, no. 69 (1975), pp. 113-21.

Murray, A., 'Administration and the Law', in *The Union of 1707: Its Impact on Scotland*, pp. 30-57.

Murray, A., 'The Lord Clerk Register', *SHR*, LIII (1974), pp. 124-56.

Nairn, T., 'Old Nationalism and New Nationalism', in *The Red Paper on Scotland*, ed. G. Brown (1975), pp. 22-57, reprinted in T. Nairn, *The Break-up of Britain* (London, 1977), pp. 126-95.

Oliver, J.W., 'Fergusson and *Ruddiman's Magazine*', in *Robert Fergusson, 1750-1774: Essays by Various Hands to Commemorate the Bicentenary of His Birth*, ed. Sidney Goodsir Smith (1952), pp. 84-98.

Phillipson, N.T., 'Nationalism and Ideology', in *Government and Nationalism in Scotland*, ed. J.N. Wolfe (1969), pp. 167-88.

Phillipson, N.T., 'Scottish Public Opinion and the Union in the Age of the Association', in *Scotland in the Age of Improvement,* pp. 125-47.

Phillipson, N.T., 'Lawyers, Landowners, and the Civic Leadership of Post-Union Scotland', *Juridical Review,* 1976, pp. 97-120.

Pocock, J.G.A., 'Machiavelli, Harrington, and English Political Ideologies in the Eighteenth Century', *William and Mary Quarterly,* third series, XXII (1965), pp. 549-83, reprinted in J. Pocock, *Politics, Language and Time* (London, 1972), pp. 104-47.

Prevost, W.A.J., 'The Solway Smugglers and the Customs Port at Dumfries', *Transactions of the Dumfriesshire and Galloway Natural History and Antiquarian Society,* LI (1975), pp. 59-67.

Price, J.M., 'New Time Series for Scotland's and Britain's Trade with the Thirteen Colonies and States, 1740 to 1791', *William and Mary Quarterly,* third series, XXXII (1975), pp. 307-25.

Pryde, G.S., *Central and Local Government in Scotland Since 1707* (London, 1960), 26pp. Historical Association Pamphlet no. 45.

Riley, P.W.J., 'The Structure of Scottish Politics and the Union of 1707', in *The Union of 1707: Its Impact on Scotland,* pp. 1-29.

Robertson, D., 'The Burgh Courts', in *Edinburgh: 1329-1929: Sexcentenary of the Bruce Charter* (1929), pp. 102-30.

Sedgwick, R., 'William Pitt and Lord Bute: An Intrigue of 1755-1758', *History Today,* VI (1956), pp. 647-54.

Simpson, J.M., 'Who Steered the Gravy Train?', in *Scotland in the Age of Improvement,* pp. 47-72.

Smith, A.M., 'The Administration of the Forfeited Annexed Estates, 1752-1784', in *The Scottish Tradition: Essays in Honour of Ronald Gordon Cant,* ed. G.W.S. Barrow (1974), pp. 198-210.

Smout, T.C., 'Scottish Landowners and Economic Growth, 1650-1850', *Scottish Journal of Political Economy,* XI (1964), pp. 218-34.

Smout, T.C., 'The Road to Union', in *Britain After the Glorious Revolution, 1689-1714,* ed. G. Holmes (London, 1969), pp. 180-91.

Smout, T.C., 'Famine and Famine-Relief in Scotland', in *Comparative Aspects of Scottish and Irish Economic and Social History,* pp. 21-31.

Sutherland, L.S., 'The City of London and the Devonshire-Pitt Administration, 1756-7', *Proceedings of the British Academy,* XLVI (1960), pp. 147-93.

Swinfen, D.B., 'The American Revolution in the Scottish Press', in *Scotland, Europe and the American Revolution,* pp. 66-74.

Thompson, E.P., 'The Moral Economy of the English Crowd in the Eighteenth Century', *Past and Present,* no. 50 (1971), pp. 76-136.

Walton, F.P., 'The Courts of the Officials and the Commissary Courts, 1512-1830', in *An Introductory Survey of the Sources and Literature of Scots Law* (the Stair Society, 1936), pp. 133-53.

Ward, W.R., 'The Land Tax in Scotland, 1707-1798', *Bulletin of the John Rylands Library,* XXXVII (1954-55), pp. 288-308. Also published as an offprint pamphlet.

Ward, W.R., 'Some Eighteenth Century Civil Servants: the English Revenue Commissioners, 1754-98', *English Historical Review,* LXX (1955), pp. 25-54.

Youngson, A.J., 'Alexander Webster and His "Account of the Number of People in Scotland in the year 1755" ', *Population Studies,* XV (1961), pp. 198-200.

BOOKS (a select list)

Atherton, H.M., *Political Prints in the Age of Hogarth* (London, 1974).

Ayling, S., *George the Third* (London, 1972).

Ayling, S., *The Elder Pitt: Earl of Chatham* (London, 1976).

Bailyn, B., *The Ideological Origins of the American Revolution* (Cambridge, Massachusetts, 1967).

Black, E.C., *The Association: British Extra-Parliamentary Political Organization, 1769-1793* (Cambridge, Massachusetts, 1963).

Brady, F., *Boswell's Political Career* (New Haven and London, 1965).

Brewer, J., *Party Ideology and Popular Politics at the Accession of George III* (Cambridge, 1976).

Brooke, J., *The Chatham Administration, 1766-1768* (London, 1956).

· Brooke, J., *King George III* (London, 1972).
⌐ Brown, P. Hume, *History of Scotland* (Cambridge, 1909), Vol. III.
· Browning, R., *The Duke of Newcastle* (New Haven and London, 1975).
  Burton, J. Hill, *The Lives of Simon, Lord Lovat, and Duncan Forbes of Culloden* (London, 1846).
· Campbell, R.H., *Scotland Since 1707* (Oxford, 1965).
  Cannon, J., *The Fox-North Coalition. Crisis of the Constitution, 1782-4* (Cambridge, 1969).
  Cannon, J., *Parliamentary Reform, 1640-1832* (Cambridge, 1973).
· Checkland, S.G., *Scottish Banking: A History, 1695-1973* (Glasgow and London, 1975).
  Christie, I., *The End of North's Ministry, 1780-1782* (London, 1958).
⌐ Christie, I., *Wilkes, Wyvill and Reform* (London, 1962).
  Clark, D.M., *The Rise of the British Treasury: Colonial Administration of the Eighteenth Century* (New Haven, 1960).
  Coxe, W., *Memoirs of the Life and Administration of Sir Robert Walpole, Earl of Orford* (London, 1798), Vol. III.
  Coxe, W., *Memoirs of the Administration of the right honourable Henry Pelham* (London, 1829).
· Craig, D., *Scottish Literature and the Scottish People, 1680-1830* (London, 1961).
· Daiches, D., *The Paradox of Scottish Culture: the eighteenth-century experience* (London, 1964). The Whidden lectures for 1964 at McMaster University.
ˋ Devine, T.M., *The Tobacco Lords: A Study of the Tobacco Merchants of Glasgow and their Trading Activities c. 1740-90* (1975).
  Dickinson, H.T., *Walpole and the Whig Supremacy* (London, 1973).
  Durie, A.J. *The Scottish Linen Industry in the Eighteenth Century* (1979).
  Drummond, A.L. and J. Bulloch, *The Scottish Church, 1688-1843* (1973).
  Elliot, G.F.S., *The Border Elliots and the Family of Minto* (1897). Privately printed.
· Ellis, K., *The Post Office in the Eighteenth Century: A Study in Administrative History* (London, 1958).
· Ferguson, W., *Scotland: 1689 to the Present* (1968).
  Ferguson, W., *Scotland's Relations with England: A Survey to 1707* (1977).
  Fergusson, A., *The Honourable Henry Erskine: Lord Advocate For Scotland* (1882).
  Fergusson, Sir J., *Lowland Lairds* (London, 1944).
  Fergusson, Sir J., *Argyll in the Forty-Five* (London, 1951). Concerns the county, not the Duke.
  Fergusson, Sir J., *The Sixteen Peers of Scotland* (Oxford, 1960). Only a sketch.
  Foord, A.S., *His Majesty's Opposition, 1714-1830* (London, 1964).
  Furber, H., *Henry Dundas, First Viscount Melville* (London, 1931).
  Graham, H.G., *The Social Life of Scotland in the Eighteenth Century* (fifth edition, London, 1969).
  Haldane, A.R.B., *Three Centuries of Scottish Posts: an Historical Survey to 1836* (1971).
· Hamilton, H., *An Economic History of Scotland in the Eighteenth Century* (Oxford, 1963).
  Hanham, H.J., *Scottish Nationalism* (London, 1969).
  Harvie, C., *Scotland and Nationalism* (London, 1977).
  Hechter, M., *Internal Colonialism: the Celtic Fringe in British National Development, 1536-1966* (London, 1975).
  Hoon, E.E., *The Organization of the English Customs System, 1696-1786* (reprint, Newton Abbot, 1968).
  Hughes, E., *Studies in Administration and Finance, 1558-1825, with Special Reference to the History of Salt Taxation in England* (Manchester, 1934).
  Hunter, J., *The Making of the Crofting Community* (1976).
  James, F.G., *Ireland in the Empire, 1688-1770* (Cambridge, Massachusetts, 1973).
  Langford, P., *The First Rockingham Administration, 1765-1766* (London, 1973).
· Lindsay, I.G. and M. Cosh, *Inveraray and the Dukes of Argyll* (1973). Very good on the personalities and friends of the second, third, fourth and fifth Dukes.
  Lindsay, J., *The Canals of Scotland* (Newton Abbot, 1968).
  Mackenzie, W.J.M., *Political Identity* (Harmondsworth, 1978).
⌐ Marshall, D., *Eighteenth Century England* (second edition, London, 1974). In my opinion the best of the general histories.
  Matheson, C., *The Life of Henry Dundas, First Viscount Melville* (London, 1933).

Mathieson, W. Law, *The Awakening of Scotland: 1747-1797* (Glasgow, 1910).

Maxwell, Sir H., *A History of Dumfries and Galloway* (1896).

McKelvey, J.L., *George III and Lord Bute: The Leicester House Years* (Durham, North Carolina, 1973). Competent but unimaginative.

Meikle, H.W., *Scotland and the French Revolution* (1912, reprinted, London, 1969). A splendid monograph.

Menary, G., *Duncan Forbes of Culloden* (London, 1936).

Namier, Sir L., *The Structure of Politics at the Accession of George III* (second edition, London, 1957).

Namier, Sir L., *England in the Age of the American Revolution* (second edition, London, 1963).

Namier, Sir L. and J. Brooke, *Charles Townshend* (London, 1964).

O'Gorman, F., *The Rise of Party in England, the Rockingham Whigs, 1760-82* (Manchester, 1975).

Owen, J.B., *The Rise of the Pelhams* (London, 1957).

Pagan, T., *The Convention of the Royal Burghs of Scotland* (Glasgow, 1926).

Pares, R., *King George III and the Politicians* (Oxford, 1953).

Perry, T.W., *Public Opinion, Propaganda and Politics in Eighteenth-Century England* (Cambridge, Massachusetts, 1962).

Plumb, J.H., *Sir Robert Walpole: The Making of a Statesman* (London, 1956).

Plumb, J.H., *Sir Robert Walpole: The King's Minister* (London, 1960).

Plumb, J.H., *The Growth of Political Stability in England, 1675-1725* (London, 1967).

Porritt, E. and A., *The Unreformed House of Commons: Parliamentary Representation Before 1832* (Cambridge, 1903), Vol. II.

Riley, P.W.J., *The English Ministers and Scotland, 1707-1727* (London, 1964). A very good piece of research and much the best study on Scottish administrative history.

Ross, I., *Lord Kames and the Scotland of his Day* (London, 1973). Flawed in its understanding of the politics of the day.

Rudé, G. *Wilkes and Liberty. A Social Study of 1763 to 1774* (Oxford, 1962).

Smout, T.C., *A History of the Scottish People, 1560-1830* (paperback edition, London, 1972).

Thomas, P.D.G., *Lord North* (London, 1976).

Thompson, E.P., *Whigs and Hunters: The Origin of the Black Act* (London, 1975).

Thomson, M.A., *The Secretaries of State, 1681-1782* (Oxford, 1932).

Turberville, A.S., *The House of Lords in the Eighteenth Century* (Oxford, 1927).

Walker, D., *The Scottish Legal System* (third edition, 1969).

Winstanley, D.A., *Lord Chatham and the Whig Opposition* (London, 1912).

Youngson, A.J., *The Making of Classical Edinburgh, 1750-1840* (1966).

Youngson, A.J., *After the Forty-Five: the Economic Impact on the Scottish Highlands* (1973).

Index

194